ROMAN LETTERS

ROMAN LETTERS

An Anthology

Edited and Translated by

NOELLE K. ZEINER-CARMICHAEL

WILEY Blackwell

This edition first published 2014

Registered Office
John Wiley & Sons Ltd, The Atrium, Southern Gate, Chichester, West Sussex, PO19 8SQ, UK

Editorial Offices
350 Main Street, Malden, MA 02148-5020, USA
9600 Garsington Road, Oxford, OX4 2DQ, UK
The Atrium, Southern Gate, Chichester, West Sussex, PO19 8SQ, UK

For details of our global editorial offices, for customer services, and for information about how to apply for permission to reuse the copyright material in this book please see our website at www.wiley.com/wiley-blackwell.

Library of Congress Cataloging-in-Publication Data

Roman letters : an anthology / edited and translated by Noelle K. Zeiner-Carmichael.
pages cm
Includes bibliographical references and index.
ISBN 978-1-4443-3950-5 (hardback) – ISBN 978-1-4443-3951-2 (paperback) –
ISBN 978-1-118-61739-7 (mobi) 1. Latin letters – History and criticism. 2. Greek letters – History and criticism. 3. Latin letters – Translations into English. 4. Greek letters – Translations into English. 5. Letter writing, Latin – History – To 1500. 6. Letter writing, Greek – History – To 1500. 7. Authors, Latin – Correspondence. 8. Authors, Greek – Correspondence. I. Zeiner-Carmichael, Noelle, 1974- editor of compilation.
PA6089.R65 2014
876′.0109 – dc23

2013018152

A catalogue record for this book is available from the British Library.

Cover image: Roman still life painting with writing implements. Naples, National Archaeological Museum. Photo © 2013 Scala, Florence / Fotografica Foglia, courtesy of the Ministero Beni e Att. Culturali. Tabula Claudiana (the Lyon Tablet), 48 AD. Musée de la Civilisation Gallo-Romaine, Lyon. Photo © 2013 DeAgostini Picture Library/Scala, Florence.
Cover design by Simon Levy

Set in 10.5/13pt Minion by Laserwords Private Limited, Chennai, India
Printed in Malaysia by Ho Printing (M) Sdn Bhd

1 2014

Dear Finn and Niamh,

Your little notes, your laughter, your hugs all bring me endless joy and comfort.
A book is a book, but you two are the greatest creations ever.

All my love,
Mama

1 February 2013

Contents

List of Figures

Preface

The goal of this anthology is to make classical epistolary texts more accessible and approachable to non-specialists and to contribute to the growing scholarly attention on Roman letters as *literature*. After years of teaching ancient Roman letters in translation to undergraduates at a public liberal arts institution, I had a realization of several recurrent pedagogical challenges. First, outdated and occasionally out of print translations made many letters physically, linguistically, and culturally inaccessible to students. Second, the absence of a concise single-volume text severely inhibited close reading and intertextual comparison in the classroom. Lastly, the rising cost of higher education has made the requirement of multiple volumes for one class increasingly burdensome for students. Expecting students to bring six or seven different volumes to each class in order to trace thematic and literary parallels among authors was simply impractical. These challenges inspired the development of a new type of text, purposely designed (1) to showcase the breadth and depth of the ancient epistolary genre as literature; (2) to provide modern translations that are relatable and meaningful to young, yet engaged readers; and (3) to highlight intertextual thematic parallels among the various types of letters – all within, and with the help of, one cohesive volume.

This book is the resulting anthology. It is primarily geared toward undergraduate and non-specialist readerships, and the collected texts survey a range of historical contexts, authors, and letter types. As with any anthology, the greatest challenge was finding the right balance between breadth and depth; so a few words about selection are appropriate. In order to emphasize the communicative role that letters play in interpersonal relationships, I included texts that comprise a full cycle of correspondence (an initial letter and its reply). To highlight the ways in which letters (and literature) were disseminated, there are examples of embedded letters – letters preserved in other genres – and copies of other people's letters. Many letters deal with the same topic but engage different recipients, a phenomenon that illustrates how a letter-writer consciously adjusts content and tone to fit the intended recipient. Additionally, this volume contains texts that vary significantly in style, tone, formality, and degree of literariness, even when they are written by the same author. Selections include well-known, "canonical" authors, such as Cicero and Pliny, but also less familiar papyrus finds, inscriptions, and texts not formally classified as letters (e.g., poems of Catullus and Propertius). Moreover, some texts were conscientiously chosen because of their self-referential nature: they comment on the letter genre and its function in the ancient world, or on the inherent logistical challenges of letter-writing within the geographical expanse of the Roman Empire.

With the exception of the final chapter (epistolary theorists), the volume covers a period running from the first century BCE to the second century CE. This range is neither ideal nor complete, but a more extensive chronological span would have either vastly expanded the length of this volume or substantially reduced the number of texts included for each author, thereby lessening the opportunities for a meaningfully close literary and thematic analysis. The temporal end-bracket of the second century CE is based on the political, literary, and cultural shifts that begin to occur in the Roman Empire of the third century. However, the prioritization of the classical period should in no way be taken to imply a value judgment as to its literary or historical primacy; it is rather a reflection of its role in establishing the conventions and themes for subsequent Roman letter-writers. The Roman epistolary genre obviously continued well past the second century, so these chronological limits do not suggest any abrupt break in epistolary continuity.

There is no accompanying commentary: such knowledge-driven interruptions detract from the reader's personal engagement with the text as a phenomenological experience. A short overview accompanies each new author or collection, along with a few suggestions for further reading. Whenever possible, explanatory notes have been incorporated in these introductions – or even in the translation itself. In addition, when necessary, individual letters are prefaced by introductions designed to clarify historical events or other essential details. All these elements are mere starting points, and instructors and readers are encouraged to explore additional primary and secondary sources for individual letters or topics.

For a book entitled *Roman Letters*, "Roman" is broadly defined. The letters selected were written within the geographical boundaries of the Roman Empire whether or not the author self-identifies as "Roman." Letters penned by such authors include prose and verse; Greek and Latin; primary, "unreprocessed" letters surviving as archaeological finds (such as on papyrus or in inscriptions); and others, which have been preserved as part of some larger epistle collection. Moreover, in an effort to bridge the gap that often occurs when reading Christian and non-Christian epistolary texts in isolation, this volume includes a few selections from the New Testament. Their juxtaposition should prove fruitful in the observation of similarities despite inherent differences in purpose and audience, and it should underscore the continuity and consistency of the epistolary tradition within the larger geographical expanses of the ancient Roman world. I have also included two selections demonstrating ancient epistolary theory, to provide a completely different perspective on the genre.

The maps offer general geographical orientation and help readers to visualize the expanse that many letters traveled. The concordance of texts is an efficient means of searching for specific letters by author. The general index helps readers navigate various themes throughout the volume; it is merely a starting point, since readers will enjoy following their own interests and observations in tracing the many overlaps, literary cross-references, and contradictions spanning the volume's content.

In preparing this anthology I composed more translations than I could possibly include, owing to strict page limits. The omissions are regrettable. Nonetheless, since the omitted texts constitute additional examples, useful for comparison and contrast, I've included (for now) about forty supplementary selections on the accompanying book website: www.wiley.com/go/romanletters. When appropriate I have indicated specific complementary letters, and readers are encouraged to browse the website for additional texts and related resources. Over time, I hope to expand the number of additional letters available on the website.

Acknowledgments

I am immensely grateful to work at a school that values the teacher–scholar model and where translation is considered legitimate scholarship. The College of Charleston and the Department of Classics have afforded me numerous teaching opportunities to develop my interests in epistolary literature, and my courses have contributed directly to the production of this book. Students in my Latin, Greek, and culture classes over the past few years have been a continuous source of inspiration, and their expertise in social media provided valuable insight into the intersections between the ancient world and the modern. I'd like to thank, in particular, Amy Decker, Jacklyn Eby, Marca Hoyle, Melissa Huber, Laura Lewis, Brad Marialke, Brianna McDonnell, and Kathleen Tuttle. I also owe sincere gratitude to Diamond Anderson, Conor Bender, Colleen Etman, David Hester, Scott Heyer, Jacqueline Kastberg, Charles Maravel, Kevin Mclean, Anthony Pugliese, John Raymond, Enis Sanchez, Ryan Simpson, Christina Stansell, and Ryan Wilkie. As first readers (in fact as test readers), they had feedback that was instrumental in making some particularly difficult editing decisions.

I am also grateful for institutional and collegial support. The School of Languages, Cultures, and World Affairs and its dean, David Cohen, generously funded various stages of the book's writing and production. My colleagues in the Department of Classics have been exceptionally flexible and patient. I'd like to thank my Chair, Tim Johnson, for his support, both administrative and personal. Very many thanks go to Darryl Phillips for his valuable feedback on early drafts and for our many fun conversations about translation and letter-writing. Darryl's enthusiasm and encouragement helped me take a mere idea and turn it into a full-fledged book project. He is the best sort of colleague to have.

A grant from the National Endowment for the Humanities funded my participation in the summer seminar "Communication, Empire, and the City of Rome," during which the guidance and leadership of Richard Talbert and Michael Maas helped me think about communication and networking in new ways. I am especially grateful to Richard Talbert, whose suggestion to include maps and images has enhanced the book's readability. The American Academy at Rome, which hosted the seminar, provided the perfect *locus amoenus* for completing the introduction and for catching up with my long-term mentor, Ellie Leach – who is responsible for revealing to me the wonders of Cicero's correspondence for the first time. The insightful feedback from the anonymous readers for Wiley-Blackwell significantly improved the final product. Likewise, my editors at Wiley-Blackwell, Haze Humbert and Ben Thatcher, have been a pleasure to work with and made the entire process enjoyable. Special thanks go to my copy-editor, Manuela Tecusan, for her expertise, sharp eye, and not least of all for her lively interest in this project.

Above all, the caring patience of family and friends has seen this project to the end. I am indebted to my parents for their continuous love and support and for teaching me the beauty of a handwritten note. Cara Delay, Sandy Slater, and Cassie Thomas have become much more than colleagues and friends: they are family. They have, each in her own way, provided invaluable moral and intellectual support. I am especially grateful to them for being such loving aunts and exemplary role models to my young children. The otherwise insurmountable task of writing a book while parenting would not have been possible without their selfless love and devotion.

Finally, this book would never have seen the light of day without the unwavering love and support of my life partner, Tim Carmichael, who made countless sacrifices as a scholar, as a dad, and as a husband so I could finish this book on time. I cannot thank him enough for his critical eye and meticulous editing, but most of all for being an ever-calming presence and an *exemplum* of strength and generosity for our little ones. It's your turn now.

A Note on Translation

Translations are like letters: they convey information, thoughts, and ideas across time and space; they speak to an intended "recipient," but often with a wider audience in mind. Like carefully crafted letters, translations consider aspects of clarity, style, and purpose. They represent original, creative productions that are utilitarian and entertaining and, like letters, they encourage active reader engagement.

Translation is an interpretive, subjective exercise. Just as an ancient letter never is a pure, literal representation of the writer's thoughts and emotions (see Chapter 1), fresh, modern translations of ancient texts eschew a literal, word-for-word (*verbum pro verbo*) transference of meaning, aiming instead at the transmission of ideas and thoughts – the reflected image of the ancient world. Translations offer a semiotic mechanism for bridging the gap between the ancient world and the modern, for connecting the ancient writer with the non-specialist reader.

More than ever, translations that are culturally relevant and meaningfully accessible are needed for maintaining the relevance of classics in a culture that continues to challenge the value of the ancient world (and of humanities more generally) and in an academic environment where, all too commonly, undergraduate institutes are becoming more professionalized. For this anthology I have composed translations precisely with the undergraduate student or non-specialist reader in mind. For the sake of an audience of this kind I have taken a middle road between literal and liberal, respecting fidelity to the original but not at the cost of comprehension and reader approachability. I have translated all verse into prose, and I have made every attempt to render the original Latin and Greek into voices that represent each author and work, while conveying the variations among individual letter-writers and their epistles. The extensive historical range and variety of content, context, and tone that the selections in this anthology comprise have presented considerable challenges for overall consistency and smoothness. I have freely incorporated modern colloquialisms and expressions, and occasional anachronisms occur: in these instances, however,

I have consciously prioritized reader approachability and comprehension over literal historical accuracy. In addition, I have exploited the potential of an all-prose format for expanding certain images and cultural references; and I did this in order to avoid the need for a commentary. Above all, my desire has been to capture what I take to be the true spirit, flavor, and sense of the originals. At the same time I have earnestly tried to preserve a careful balance between using modern language and maintaining a sense of distance from the ancient past. In this way I hope these translations successfully bridge the gap between the ancient Roman epistolary world and our contemporary electronic age.

List of Abbreviations

Cicero

Ad Brut. = *Epistulae ad Brutum*
Att. = *Epistulae ad Atticum*
Fam. = *Epistulae ad familiares*
Quint. = *Epistulae ad Quintum fratrem*

Fronto

Ad amicos = *Epistulae ad amicos*
Ad Caes. = *Epistula ad Marcum Caesarem*
Ad Ant. = *Epistulae ad Marcum Antoninum imperatorem*
Nep. am. = *De nepote amisso*

Horace

Epist. = *Epistulae*

Martial

Epigr. = *Epigrammata*

Ovid

Her. = *Heroides*
Pont. = *Epistulae ex Ponto*
Tr. = *Tristia*
P. Oxy. = *Oxyrhynchus Papyri*

Paul the Apostle

Philem. = *Epistula ad Philemonem*

Pliny the Younger

Ep. = *Epistulae*

Sallust

Cat = *Bellum Catilinae*

SEG = *Supplementum epigraphicum Graecum* (Leiden 1923→)

Sel. Pap. = A. S. Hunt and C. C. Edgar, 1932–4. *Selected Papyri*, vols 1–2 (Loeb Classical Library). London: Harvard University Press.

Seneca the Younger

Ep. = *Epistulae*

Statius

Silv. = *Silvae*

Suetonius

Aug. = *Divus Augustus* / *Life of Augustus*

Claud. = *Divus Claudius* / *Life of Claudius*

Tab. Vindol. = *Tabulae Vindolandenses* / *The Writing Tablets from Vindolanda*

Map 0.1 Italy. Source: Ancient World Mapping Center © 2012 (awmc.unc.edu). Used by permission

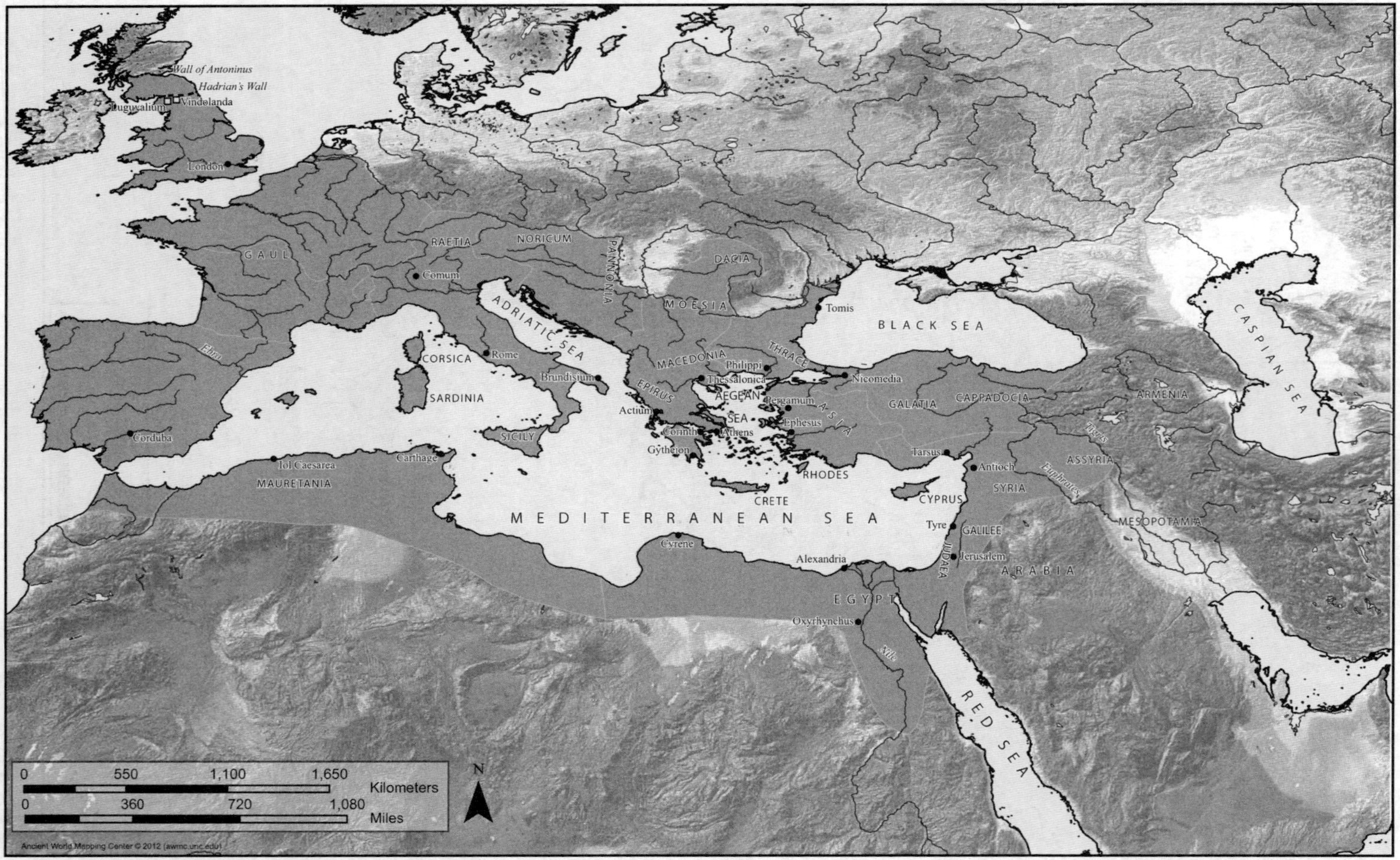

Map 0.2 The Roman Empire. Source: Ancient World Mapping Center © 2012 (awmc.unc.edu). Used by permission

CHAPTER ONE

Letters and Letter-Writing in Ancient Rome

The art of general letter-writing in the present day is shrinking until the letter threatens to become a telegram, a telephone message, a post-card. Since the events of the day are transmitted in newspapers with far greater accuracy, detail, and dispatch than they could be by the single effort of even Voltaire himself, the circulation of general news, which formed the chief reason for letters of the stage-coach and sailing-vessel days, has no part in the correspondence of to-day.

Post 1922: 491

Emily Post's 1922 handbook on etiquette attributed the apparent dissolution of the art of letter-writing to the advent of modern, rapid modes of communication. Although she related this decline to the circulation of periodicals, Post also censured a more general degenerescence in good taste, behavior, and intellectual acumen; and just plain apathy. Even worse, the decline in epistolary correspondence apparently contributed to a fracturing network of interpersonal relationships, previously maintained through written acts. Yet it wasn't just the decreased frequency of letter-writing that Post bemoaned, but the lowering of standards in content and aesthetics:

> To such as these, to whom effort is an insurmountable task, it might be just as well to say frankly: If you have a mind that is entirely bromidic, if you are lacking in humor, all power of observation, and facility for expression, you had best join the ever-growing class of people who frankly confess, "I can't write letters to save my life!" and confine your literary efforts to picture post-cards with the engaging captions "X is my room," or "Beautiful weather, wish you were here." It is not at all certain that your friends and family would not rather have frequent post-cards than occasional letters all too obviously displaying the meagerness of their messages in halting orthography. (Post 1922: 491)

Roman Letters, First Edition. Noelle K. Zeiner-Carmichael.

Post was attempting to preserve the artistic form and practice of letter-writing because she regarded the letter as a measure of intimacy, a vehicle for self-presentation, and a symbolic barometer for various cultural changes.

Post saw that letters are more than just a utilitarian mode of communication; they are a vital tool in the creation, maintenance, and preservation of interpersonal relationships, as well as a powerful symbol of cultural identity. She exaggerated the demise of early twentieth-century letter-writing, and one wonders how she would respond to current electronic communications – since email, Facebook, and text messaging have largely replaced not only the long, newsy handwritten letter of a bygone age, but even the more formulaic thank-you or sympathy note. This begs the question: is the letter still dying, ninety years later, or has it merely metamorphosized? In considering the epistolary practices of the near past – and even further the distant past – we must confront our own cultural milieu, which affects how we define and classify (if at all) our modern-day letters. Does an email constitute a letter? Or a text message? What role does the letter, handwritten or otherwise, exercise in today's predominately electronic age?[1]

The ancient Roman epistolary genre offers a useful approach for tackling such questions because it was expansive: it included purely utilitarian forms as well as more literary ones (verse or purely fictional letters). The broad range of ancient letter types, their various historical contexts, and their diverse functions offer lenses through which to view the "letter" in our own world and its roles in connecting us interpersonally – and globally. How do today's epistolary forms function realistically and symbolically, how do they reflect our own values in the spheres of written communication and relationships, and what do they say about our desire to connect across the world? Has email facilitated more intimate relationships, shrinking time and distance through its instantaneity, or has it only created more distance, by depersonalizing words through the absence of tangibility – and of paper and ink? Does today's text message or email replace real face-to-face contact in the same way ancient Romans imagined their letters doing? Moreover, how do instant electronic forms of correspondence conjure up deeper questions about what we choose to write and how, especially when the anticipation of a response is measured by a click – seconds or minutes rather than days, weeks, or even months away? The study of ancient letters tells us much about ancient Roman daily life, yet it also provides insight into our own world. Letters are treasure houses – *thesauroi* – for historical evidence such as of events and people, cultural institutions, literature, and ancient values. But recent scholarship has increasingly focused on letters as *literature*, valuable in its own right and worthy of close reading and appreciation.

This volume's selections showcase the unique features that distinguish the epistolary genre from other types of literature. For example, ancient letter-writers represent a wide range of class and economic strata. Not only highly educated aristocratic men did compose letters, but also slaves, women, and even the illiterate (thanks to professional scribes). Letters thus exhibit widely varying degrees of linguistic competence and styles. The letter's flexibility as a genre makes it particularly well suited to self-presentation and self-promotion: many writers exploit the letter as a way to enhance or solidify their fame. Although most letters are specifically written to a particular recipient, their form allows authors an opportunity to "speak" to broader audiences. The letter thus exploits a dynamic interplay among author/letter-writer, recipient/addressee, and audience. Lastly, as a mode of communication frequently deigned to elicit a response from its reader-recipient, the letter represents a genre of power, capable of effecting change through the replies and responses of its readers. Such change may be manifested, for example, through the creation and maintenance (or dissolution) of relationships, through military or political actions, or through personal emotions. As Post had suggested about letters in the twentieth century, the ancient letter possessed the power to connect individuals through time and space, affirm and solidify social networks, and assert both political and cultural control across large geographical expanses. The letter is a speech act in written form, a conversation maintained across temporal and geographical distances, whether in the ancient Roman Empire or between the ancient and the modern world.

What Is a Letter? A Working "Meaning"

One advantage of an anthology like this one is that it encourages readers to form their own observations and to draw their own conclusions about the nature of Roman letters. Nevertheless, a general overview may assist close readings and thematic explorations of the texts that follow. The question "What is a letter?" was as difficult to answer in the ancient Roman context as it is today; letters resist precise classification and categorization, and strict definitions are limiting. The genre is so elastic, both in form and in function, that it is arguably most useful simply to offer some distinguishing features. At the most basic level, an ancient Roman letter is a written message between two individuals who are physically apart from each other and thus unable to communicate through speech or gesture. Letters may exist on an historical level – being actually sent and received, that is, exchanged between real living beings – or on a purely literary level – being exchanged between fictional characters created by an author. In addition, as noted above, we need to distinguish between letters that have survived physically, as archaeological remains – that is, as "primary, unreprocessed correspondence" (Trapp 2003: 10) – and letters transmitted in published collections, through a manuscript tradition.

As a genre of writing, Roman letters display certain conventions of style and structure. For example, such features include a salutation and a valediction, although these elements aren't required: they can be considered implicit in the letter's purpose and delivery, much like the automatic salutations and valedictions embedded within emails and text messages today. Letters frequently include the explicit or implicit expectation of a response from the recipient (Letters 8, 38, 134, 200), while creating a strong, innate *ego–te* ("I"–"you") relationship between sender/letter-writer and recipient/addressee. The sender can variously emphasize this relationship, and even strategically exploit it when necessary. The ancient epistolary theorist (Pseudo-)Demetrius describes the letter as a kind of written dialogue, one half of a conversation between friends (Letter 215), but he carefully distinguishes between the oral, extemporaneous nature of spoken conversation and its written, epistolary counterpart – a format that is potentially more stylized, more permanent, and serves as an enduring "gift" to one's friend. Demetrius' comparison between oral and written also accounts for the many challenges inherent in conversing with a friend who is absent; notably clarity and eloquence are paramount, since written communication always risks misunderstanding and misinterpretation. The theorist Pseudo-Libanius also comments on the careful attention that goes into preparing a letter (Letter 216). He echoes Demetrius, asserting that the best letters should be written with "great art and precision" – which in turn comes only from truly understanding the nature of a letter and its conventions. He likewise describes a letter as a written conversation, so the sender should communicate "as if speaking to the recipient in person." Seneca the Younger, writing many generations earlier, also emphasizes the conversational nature of letters in a letter to his friend Lucilius: "I want my letters – which have nothing artificial or foreign in them – to sound the same as when I'm talking with you, when we're hanging out together or going for a stroll, you know, casual and natural" (*Moral Epistles* 2.75.1). Seneca's letter, written in clear and eloquent prose, reinforces the point, and his remarks reiterate the theorists' admonitions: letters should be conversational, maintaining a careful balance among precision, plainness, and elegance.

Letters were used not only out of necessity, for instance to bridge physical distance; writers might choose to engage in written exchange for a variety of other reasons, including to establish a written record, to avoid speaking about an embarrassing issue in person, or to fulfill a purpose otherwise considered inappropriate for a different literary genre. The "epistolarity" of a text – that is, its "use of the letter's formal properties to create meaning" (Altman 1982: 4) – varies greatly across samples and presents significant implications for appreciating the ways in which Romans consciously employed the letter for more literary and symbolic purposes.[2] The open-ended, fluid nature of letters offered authors an appropriate – and valued – medium for creating autobiographical self-portraits, for reinterpreting past events in light of the present, and for attaining literary immortality. In substituting for face-to-face communication, the letter bridges a temporal and spatial gap, a function often noted by the sender. Letter-writers frequently make self-conscious references to the passage of time and to their physical separation from the recipient or other loved ones; in doing so they express a variety of ideas and emotions, such as complaints, wishes, hopes, and frustrations. Recollections of a past time or place, narratives of past events, and references to the logistical challenges inherent in sending and receiving letters also appear frequently. Moreover, as Altman has noted (1982: 13), authors may choose to emphasize or de-emphasize their separation from the recipient, depending upon their ulterior literary motives.[3]

The fundamental purpose of the letter, to communicate in writing what might otherwise be communicated orally, led to the categorization of epistolary types: letters of consolation, recommendation or requests, letters from exile, love letters, and ecphrastic letters (descriptions of physical objects that the absent recipient cannot see firsthand). Pseudo-Libanius outlines no less than 40 different types of letters and even includes sample letters as models. Such didactic manuals, perhaps written as guidelines for professional scribes or students (Poster and Mitchell 2007), echo Emily Post's etiquette manual from 1922 and more recent online and print publications offering guidance in epistolary composition and proper "netiquette" within various social contexts. Nevertheless, while these "types" highlight the letter's myriad functions, such divisions are contrived, since most letters serve multiple purposes simultaneously, intermingling different stylistic and literary features. The letter's flexibility, in function and style, means that the letter often incorporates characteristics from other literary genres, such as poetry, history, and philosophy.[4] Thus letters may include features found in other familiar literary forms – say, in historical narrative or in poetry – or they may even embody a genre altogether – through verse, or by taking the form of a philosophical treatise. This innate literary inclusivity is what led a French philosopher like Derrida to declare that the letter is "not a genre but all genres, literature itself" (Derrida 1987: 48) – a sentiment that, in turn, has led Gibson and Morrison to posit: "Where are we to draw the boundary between letters and non-letters?" (2007: 3–4). Their case study, investigating certain Greek lyric poems that at one time scholars identified as epistles, throws into high relief the challenges of classifying ancient texts by genre.

To reinforce the point, this anthology includes not only selections formally identified as letters and pieces surviving within a purposefully collected and arranged letter collection (e.g., by Cicero, Horace, Seneca, Pliny), but also texts with more ambiguously defined boundaries or contexts, including, for example, epistle-like texts transmitted in other literary contexts (e.g., letters from Martial and Catullus, or letters embedded in Suetonius' biographies). As noted above, texts vary in their degree of epistolarity; within the published collection of Horace's (verse) *Epistles*, for example, some pieces appear to be less epistolary than others.[5] Reading epistolary literature demands open-mindedness – a willingness to recognize conventional features identifying a work's epistolarity and to seriously accept an ancient work's "claims to epistolarity" (Gibson and Morrison 2007: 16). Indeed the boundaries of the ancient epistolary genre are as blurred as those between email, texting, and messaging today.

Length and Brevity

Length is a repeated theme among ancient theorists and letter-writers: brevity is the conventional expectation, perhaps developed out of practical considerations for the high cost of writing supplies, especially papyrus, and the letter's original function is to communicate brief messages. Demetrius himself explicitly advocates moderation: letters that are too long – or, worse, too pompous in style – lose their conversational quality and appear as little more than "treatises with 'Dear So-and-So' tacked onto them" (Letter 215). Pseudo-Libanius also promotes brevity, but not at the cost of clarity or content. Significantly, he observes that letters can offer enjoyment to the reader: extended narratives or stories are acceptable when they augment the pleasure of reading, even if they cause a letter to expand. The pleasure that letters potentially offer suggests the role of letters as literature – an intellectual product that not only fulfills a utilitarian or obligatory purpose, but also entertains. This notion underscores Demetrius' recognition of the letter's function to serve as a "gift" to a friend, as noted above.

Aware that recipients would take notice of a letter's length, ancient authors self-consciously referenced this feature by employing both rhetorical and symbolic means. Cicero, for example, occasionally apologizes for exceptionally brief letters at times when he despairs of fluctuating political tides or personal situations (Letter 27). In such contexts, his brevity conveys deeper messages about the political atmosphere and his position within it. Conversely, Pliny the Younger sometimes apologizes for a letter that might appear too long, preempting possible complaints from his recipient (Letters 129, 138). Since letters frequently imply the expectation of a response their length or brevity could serve as a gauge by which recipients assess the length of their own replies. The topos of length sometimes becomes a playful conceit, as an author might jestingly demand a long response, in compensation for the sender's own expenditure of time and attention. Likewise, some authors chastise a correspondent or threaten to send only short letters to a recipient who has written either infrequently or tersely – all in playful retribution (Letter 117). While many of these exchanges are good-humored and friendly meant, they nonetheless hint at the reciprocal nature of letter-writing, in which length and frequency become methods for maintaining or calibrating relationships.[6] There were certainly no strict guidelines for epistolary length, but the texts clarify that letter-writers were acutely aware of compositional length and its deeper implications. Self-conscious statements about length reflect deeper concerns over the expenditure of time, both in reading a (long) letter and in responding to it appropriately. Given the implicit expectation of a reply, letter-writers reveal a perceptive awareness of their recipients' professional and social obligations and time constraints (or lack thereof), and thus of the potential onus or enjoyment that a short or a long letter is likely to bring. Notably, a writer's awareness of and attention to letter length (and the recipient's response to it) operate in a similar manner today, when such preoccupations revolve around email and other social media.

Autobiography and Self-Presentation

The letter is a fluid genre, which enables it to fulfill many different purposes and to reach many types of audience, thus empowering its authors with great freedom in experimentation and self-presentation. One exceptional advantage of the epistolary genre is its potential for autobiographical expression without the overt stigma of conceit often associated with formal autobiography. In one of his well-known letters to a friend, Cicero requests Lucceius to compose a history about him so he can avoid writing an autobiography – something that preserves one's name for posterity but poses challenges of legitimacy (Letter 15). In short, letters offer a suitable backup plan for people not landing a starring role in another's literary work. While the letter is ostensibly written to and for others, thanks to its *ego*centric structure, it can be carefully exploited to direct attention to and for the author. But with this potential comes risk. Once again, Post offers a suitable parallel from the modern era when she explicitly emphasizes the letter as a reflection of self:

> The letter you write, whether you realize it or not, is always a mirror which reflects your appearance, taste and character. A "sloppy" letter with the writing all pouring into one corner of the page, badly worded, badly spelled, and with unmatched paper and envelope – even possibly a blot – proclaims the sort of person who would have unkempt hair, unclean linen and broken shoe laces; just as a neat, precise, evenly written note portrays a person of like characteristics. (1922: 448)

For Post, the visual, aesthetic presentation of the letter is as significant as the content, particularly since she saw poor, careless composition as going hand in hand with poor handwriting. Ancient letter-writers, too, comment upon the visual qualities of letters; for them, handwriting can function as a symbolic gauge of the expenditure of time, care, and attention and as a barometer of familiarity and intimacy. This makes sense, since regular correspondents would recognize each other's handwriting and would authenticate the writer as the legitimate author. Many authors occasionally apologize for a letter written in a scribe's hand and not their own (Letter 20) – a detail that would not have been missed by close friends, with whom they corresponded frequently. Their explanations normally focus on time constraints: pressing political or professional obligations necessitate a speedier method, accomplished by dictating to a scribe, rather than writing by oneself. Such apologies reinforce the general correlation between time, attention, and intimacy. Clearly, though, handwriting functioned as one aspect of epistolary self-presentation, beyond the letter's carefully crafted content. The visual appearance of the letter is important and symbolic.

Many upper-class Romans wrote daily – a task they regarded as a duty or burden. In light of this reality, the more time-consuming act of handwriting a letter becomes an additional way to communicate intimacy and reciprocity. Epistolary handwriting becomes a personal stamp, a signature, and sometimes a symbolic stand-in for the tangible, personal touch otherwise accomplished through a hug or handshake. Even purely fictional letters participate in the epistolary topos of handwriting personalization and emphasis on visual aspects of the letter, noting characteristics such as "ink blots" and "smears" as symbols of emotional distress, for example (Letter 71). These physical signs – whether merely rhetorical or real – further illustrate the epistolary genre's innate autobiographical stance, which is further illustrated through the use of pronouns, self-reflection, recollection, and self-conscious expression. In purely fictional letters this autobiographical posture operates not only at the literary level, where it can manifest itself through the fictional letter-writer's egocentric persona, but also at the authorial level, where the fictional correspondence is both a product and a reflection of the author and his literary expertise.

Materials and Delivery

Letters sent and received between real people (or fictional letters purporting to be sent and received) embody a variety of tangible forms, some of which are found in the archaeological evidence. These "unreprocessed" primary letters survive in the form of wax tablets, wooden tablets, ostraca (pottery shards used for inscribing names on them), and papyri (Muir 2009: 8; Hallo-aho 2009: 3–13). Letters, especially those from an emperor, could also take the form of inscriptions on stone or bronze, intended for an entire community (Letter 85). The unreprocessed letter material of the least permanent kind was the wax tablet, which was often employed for brief messages across short distances. Senders used a pointed instrument called a stylus to make impressions in wax, which had been set into a thin wood tablet; no ink was used (see Figure 1.1; Figure 1.2). The tablet might have a hinged wooden cover designed to protect the inscription, which made the whole object look much like a diptych. Wax tablets were an impermanent, portable medium for letters, since the recipient could reuse the same tablet to send back a reply simply by warming up the wax, smoothing

Figure 1.1 Ancient Roman writing materials: wax tablet, stylus, and papyrus scroll. Ancient Roman fresco. Location: Museo Archeologico Nazionale, Naples, Italy. Source: Scala / Art Resource, NY

Figure 1.2 The baker Terentius Neo and his wife holding a papyrus scroll, a stylus and wax tablet. Ancient Roman fresco. Location: Museo Archeologico Nazionale, Naples, Italy. Source: Vanni / Art Resource, NY

it over and re-inscribing the surface; they were particularly well suited for conveying dinner invitations or similar social requests.

Leaf tablets – such as those discovered at Vindolanda, the Roman military fort in Britain (see Figure 4.3) – could also be used for letter-writing. These tablets, dating from the first to the second century CE, were generally very thin and about the size of a postcard. Ink was used to write directly on the wooden surface, and the tablets were then folded to protect the writing inside (Bowman 1998: 15).[7] Papyrus, another material for letter-writing, was typically more expensive and varied in size and quality (see Figure 1.1; Figure 1.2). Pliny the Elder, for example, notes that quality was graded according to factors such as strength, whiteness, and writing surface (Pliny, *Natural History* 13.24). Surviving examples, most of them coming from the city of Oxyrhynchus in Egypt, show that the letter could be written in columns, and sometimes in more than one hand; if the sender had used a scribe to write the letter, s/he might add a concluding note or valediction in his/her own hand (a "subscript," as in Letters 1, 198).[8] The papyrus letter would then be folded lengthways (or rolled) and secured with a tie and a seal. Papyrus seals could serve as signatures, a symbol of authority and legitimacy, especially for high-ranking individuals or emperors. While initially most papyrus documents comprised scrolls, later on codices developed wherein papyrus (or parchment) was cut and assembled in a manner similar to that of modern books; this format became especially popular during the first and second centuries CE, when Christians nearly universally adopted the codex, preferring it to the papyrus (or parchment) roll (Roberts and Skeat 1983: 37–45).

Surviving epistolary evidence proves that letter-writing was not exclusively reserved for emperors or the upper-class (literate) elite but was used by everyday individuals across a wide section of society, including the middle class, slaves, citizens, foreigners, men and women, rich and poor (see Figure 1.2). Extant examples illustrate a variety of scripts (capital, lower-case, and cursive), in both Greek and Latin, and they showcase different levels of handwriting quality and literacy. They survive in varying degrees of completeness and legibility, often posing significant challenges to papyrologists and paleographers attempting to decipher and transcribe the texts and to philologists attempting to establish their content and meaning.

The address of the recipient(s) was typically written on the outside of the letter. The specificity of the address and/or its accompanying directions could vary considerably, depending on the courier's familiarity with the recipient and the intended destination (Muir 2009: 10). Not only do we find real-life examples of addresses in the archaeological evidence (Letter 205, 210), but even literary passages allude to the discursive way letters might have been addressed. Horace's playful *Epistle* 1.13 (Letter 66; cf. Letters 98, 104) functions as a letter within a letter, giving directions to Vinnius on where to deliver Horace's poetry to Augustus (r. 27 BCE–14 CE) and on the proper, respectful manner in which it should be delivered.

Because Rome had no official postal system for delivering private letters, senders like Horace or Ovid relied on slaves, paid professional couriers, or people who just happened to be traveling to the intended destination. Wealthy Romans might designate a specific group of slaves especially for this role (*tabellarii*, "tablet men"; Casson 1997: 219).

The delivery of a private letter could be a haphazard endeavor, where success depended on the whim of a courier's pace, on travel routes, and on unpredictable factors such as weather, road conditions, and other impediments like wild animals or bandits. Still, as Casson (1997: 221) explains, letters dispatched within relatively short distances could travel quite quickly; he cites, for example, Cicero's correspondence between Rome and Naples as taking approximately four or five days. Yet not all couriers were trustworthy or reliable, and letters could easily fall into the wrong hands or be intercepted. It seems that a shortage of reliable, trustworthy deliverers was a common occurrence and could cause delays. Other times an over-zealous courier might badger a recipient to prepare a response on short notice (Letter 40). Letters across long distances faced much longer travel times and delays, especially if the courier had to wait for a ship heading the right direction. Given the many extenuating factors, travel times were inconsistent: a letter from Rome to Athens could take anywhere from three to seven weeks (Casson 1995: 221).

Many letters explicitly note the logistical challenges of delivery. Complaints about crossed, missing, or late letters and untrustworthy deliverers are frequent (e.g., Letters 7, 177). Such frustrations naturally affect a letter's content by expressing complaints, but they also do so by withholding certain information or by using coded references, repeating the news, or showing misunderstandings and miscommunications. This lack of control, the time lapse in communicating important news, and the long period of awaiting a response influenced the ways in which writers maintained relationships and corresponded across time and space. Without a formal mail delivery system, private senders and recipients were frequently compelled to adjust their letter-writing activities.

When it came to official correspondence – for instance, letters between the emperor and administrators or military personnel, or even letters from the emperor to a provincial city – a slightly more formal system developed. Official correspondence by the emperor and other administrators likely relied heavily on dictation and secretaries. In governing effectively, emperors faced a substantial epistolary burden.[9] The Roman Empire's geographical expanse was vast, and letters were the main vehicle for keeping tabs on matters of imperial administration, the maintenance of borders, finances and taxes, and military activity. The emperor's enormous epistolary responsibilities were, however, mitigated by an official secretary whose job focused on imperial correspondence. The Emperor Claudius (r. 41–54 CE) established a number of imperial secretarial positions, including that of epistolary secretary (the secretary *ab epistulis*), which significantly contributed to the bureaucratization and centralization of imperial administration. This post had already existed in a military form during the late republican period; however, it did not receive official recognition as a title until the early empire.[10]

In fact there were two epistolary secretaries: the Greek epistolary secretary and the Latin one. This possibly indicates an administrative adaptation to the need of writing letters in Greek for the Roman East and in Latin for the Roman West.[11] During Claudius' reign loyal freedmen were appointed for the most part; but, beginning with Domitian (r. 81–96 CE), equestrians – a generally wealthy upper middle class – also held the position. The epistolary secretary was likely responsible not only for transcribing letters dictated by the emperor, to which the emperor might then add a subscript, but also for composing letters (and answering them) at his own discretion (Millar 1967: 14). This means, then, that the secretary himself could make decisions on certain imperial administrative issues, thereby functioning not just as a letter-writer, but as a significant imperial minister.

On especially important issues the emperor might exert more oversight, providing a verbal response that the secretary then drafted into his letter. In these cases the letter sometimes represented a cooperative compositional effort (Sherwin-White 1962: 114–25). Still, even then it is difficult to separate with certainty the emperor's own words from those of his secretary. Regardless of the emperor's degree of autonomy in composing a letter, the epistolary secretary sat at the center of imperial governing, keeping abreast of happenings around the empire; and, as the title indicates, he played a significant role in epistolary correspondence. Even with the help of secretaries, at least until the Severan dynasty (195–235 CE) the emperor continued to be directly and personally involved in imperial administration, and the correspondence required to govern it effectively; he was not a distant and far removed ruler, but rather one who pressed palms and dealt directly with individuals of all social classes (Millar 1967: 18).

The significant role of these secretaries and the social prestige that accompanied their position are suggested in literary and epigraphical sources that explicitly name individuals who held the post. Before Claudius' establishment of the epistolary secretary as an official position, we hear of Augustus requesting the help of Horace, an equestrian poet, to assist in his private correspondence. This request is significant because it represents a forerunner of the secretaryship that became official later; but Horace did not accept. As Lindsay (1994: 459) has pointed out, Augustus' offer suggests that, by the first century BCE, he was feeling the strain of the heavy epistolary correspondence that was needed in order to maintain stable governance. His choice of Horace, who was a well-known poet admired within Rome's literary circle of Maecenas, suggests the importance Augustus placed on keeping up his epistolary obligations – and also his desire to do so well, through someone who was intellectually, linguistically, and stylistically exceptional.

Like Augustus, the Emperor Hadrian (r. 117–138 CE) also wanted a skilled literary man to serve as his secretary, and he chose the ancient biographer Suetonius, who was happy to fill the position (Wardle 2002: 462–480). The instrumental role that the secretary played – not only in writing letters, but also in serving in some capacity as a minister and advisor – is clear from the pride secretaries and their family members expressed; this sentiment was found in numerous literary texts and commemorative inscriptions.[12] Statius, a poet writing under the reign of Domitian, composed a poem at the request of Abascantus, the emperor's epistolary secretary; in it he celebrated Abascantus and his status as epistolary secretary (Zeiner-Carmichael 2007). Statius enumerates a range of letter topics and administrative concerns such as military commands, weather, and agricultural productivity. Abascantus' significance is further symbolized by the vast geographical distances the letters travel as they pass through his hands: his epistolary responsibilities aren't only pragmatic, but symbolically weighty.

The distinction Statius ascribes to the Abascantus' position as epistolary secretary must reflect a parallel reality: the job commanded prestige and fame by virtue of the duties it involved and the central place of its bearer within the imperial court.

The growing Roman Empire demanded the establishment of an official secretarial position for correspondence, yet it also required an infrastructure to facilitate the delivery of numerous regular letters associated with provincial governance. Again, these needs seem to develop concomitantly with the shift from republic to empire through an increasing number of annexed provinces. Suetonius credits Augustus with establishing the first mechanism for transporting official imperial correspondence (*Life of Augustus* 49.3). He explains that the system initially comprised rest stations positioned at modest intervals along major roads such as Via Appia (see Figure 3.1), which were staffed by young men; the letter (or verbal message) would be transferred from carrier to carrier until it reached its destination, much like an ancient Pony Express. Later, as Suetonius tells us, Augustus stationed vehicles such as carts and wagons, so that the same messenger could carry the dispatch from beginning to end, replenishing his animals or equipment along the way. This second phase had the advantage of allowing the original messenger to communicate directly with the recipient when questions or confusion about the message's origin or content arose. Moreover, the vehicles used to deliver messages could serve double-duty by transporting official administrators or goods. Suetonius' description emphasizes the need for increased speed as the impetus for the system's creation – which clearly had political, cultural, and social implications in terms of communications between the emperor and his addressee(s), as well as in terms of disseminating Roman power and culture more broadly. As Kolb (2001: 95) notes, the ensuing delivery system was not a postal service per se, but rather "an infrastructure for use by state officials." Later, under the reign of Diocletian in the fourth century CE, it was given the name of "state delivery" (*cursus publicus*), a phrase often applied to the system, albeit anachronistically, before its official coinage.

Stations along the system supplied food, provisions, and accommodations; but, as a provincial edict from the Roman province of Galatia reveals, it was the onus of local people, who were only partially compensated for it, to keep the stations properly supplied (Kolb 2001: 97). Thus, it would seem, the system was only as efficient and effective as local cooperation allowed. And, as with the delivery of private letters, even official correspondence depended on the whim of the courier.[13] The same edict from Galatia enumerates the types of people entitled to use official transportation vehicles and accommodations stationed along state delivery roads; these included government officials or other people on special official or military business. As Talbert (2012: 244) points out, however, the roads themselves were not reserved solely for official couriers, travelers, and transporters; they also continued to serve private individuals, and they must have been regularly crowded. Authorized users of the state delivery required an official certificate (*diploma*) from the emperor or one of his representatives, which specified the number of wagons or animals to be used for the journey, the itinerary, and the period of time for which the *diploma* remained valid (Kolb, 2001: 97).[14]

The issuing of *diplomata* must have been taken seriously even if its enforcement was difficult to uphold. Talbert (2012: 244) notes that authorities regularly coped with fraudulent use of the state delivery infrastructure by unauthorized persons utilizing its official services (wagons, animals, accommodations). As a specially appointed governor of Bithynia-Pontus, Pliny the Younger writes a letter to Emperor Trajan (r. 98–117 CE) apologizing for issuing a *diploma* to his wife Calpurnia for unofficial family business, carefully noting the unusual personal circumstances and the infrequency of such and action. Pliny the Younger's letter and Emperor Trajan's reply (*Epistles* 10.120–1) are insightful: they reveal that the emperor regularly supplied governors with permits (*diplomata*) to issue on his behalf. Here, of course, Pliny has utilized one such permit in his possession for personal rather than official business. Yet the two letters emphasize in a gendered way the advantages the state delivery offered; for Pliny credits precisely his wife's use of the infrastructure to ensure her own prompt arrival during her family's time of need. Her timeliness (*celeritas*) guarantees the successful fulfillment of familial duty and devotion (*pietas*) – a highly respected Roman virtue. Trajan's response condones Pliny's prior decision and confirms that Calpurnia's *promptness* is an added bonus in her fulfillment of her familial duty. While these two letters upheld the gendered norms that prevailed at the time of their writing, they also illustrate the realities of long-distance epistolary correspondence. Even with an infrastructure like the state delivery to expedite delivery and travel, time lapses could be long, and responses could come too late. Thus we often see letter-writers anticipating or even preempting the responses of their epistolary recipients: they offer answers to imagined questions coming from them, they provide extra clarification and detail, in anticipation of potential confusion or follow-up questions, or, as in this case, they make belated approval second.

Finally, while these two letters prove that Pliny the Younger utilized the state delivery infrastructure, we have no definitive evidence clarifying the extent to which he used it for official correspondence with Trajan. Moreover, our literary evidence provides little information on the infrastructure's exact land routes, the types of messages it was reserved for, or how the system might have operated in relation to other imperial infrastructures, such as bridges, ports, and sea routes. We also lack evidence regarding the methods by which mail was packaged and delivered. In fact there is nothing compelling to suggest that the Romans, especially everyday citizens, conceived of their road system as an elaborate, highly orchestrated network of communication (Talbert 2012: 247). Nevertheless, the roads and seaways facilitating epistolary correspondence comprised an effective, if not always efficient, vehicle for imperial communication and governance. In his speech of praise to the Romans (*Regarding Rome*), the second-century CE Greek rhetorician Aelius Aristides suggests that mail delivery significantly bridged the gap between the emperor and his far-flung provinces. He extols the fact that the Roman emperor can govern wherever he is, relying on letters arriving almost as quickly as they are written, as if carried by "winged messengers" (*Regarding Rome*, 26.33). Aristides does not mention the *cursus publicus* (state delivery) as such, but his comments imply that the Roman emperor was able to govern effectively through letters. Roman imperial administration was thus clearly a portable operation, though Aristides' enthusiasm must be filtered through the rhetorical exaggeration characteristic of speeches given during this period. His praise nonetheless implies that letters, and the Roman infrastructure, allowed Rome to rule "the world" effectively and efficiently and to share its culture and ideals with the surrounding provinces. In sum, state delivery – *cursus publicus* – was an infrastructure, an efficient delivery system whereby official letters, people, and goods could travel throughout the empire relatively successfully, with the help of rest stops and renewable supplies (Kolb 2001: 101). Yet, with all due respect to the empire, the absence of a true postal system meant that most letters were sent and received through a relatively informal system, which relied on sheer luck – among other things.

Audience(s)

Roads connect people, and hence correspondents. A letter, like a road, moves through time and space, joining not only individuals but larger groups, and often in very interconnected, web-like ways. A Roman man might send a letter with a copy of another friend's letter enclosed; that friend may in turn copy the letters and send them on to others, and so forth. A letter from an emperor might take the form of a written inscription – an edict – publicly displayed in a city center, for all to see. Letters written by Christian leaders were often addressed to entire communities and purposely intended for copying and dissemination (Letters 97, 165). The letter's inherent *ego–te* relationship also means that the letter-writer (or author – as the two aren't always the same) can "speak" to an external audience outside of, or apart from, the immediately intended addressee or recipient; and this "dialogue" may occur within the same historical context or in vastly different ones – even years, centuries, or millennia later. The epistolary genre's inherent, regular use of personal pronouns ("I," "you") encourages direct engagement between the letter's reader (whether this is the intended recipient or not) and the text; it is a literary invitation that some letter-writers exploit to their advantage. When in his philosophical letters Seneca the Younger directs advice to his intended recipient, Lucilius, we, the external and much later readers, are implicitly invited either to assume Lucilius' position as addressee and recipient or to imagine ourselves as the letter-writer (Seneca). In other words, the letter's inherent *ego–te* centrality means that an external audience or a group of outsiders (like ourselves, construed as readers of all letters in this anthology) may engage with and participate in the epistolary text in a manner far more intimate and self-conscious than occurs in other literary genres. As the "*te*" ("you") being addressed, we thereby define ourselves in relation to the "*ego*" ("I") of the letter-writer, his/her message, and our own social context. In this way an ancient letter travels not only temporally (across time) and spatially (across geographical space) within its own, "real" historical context, but also beyond, reaching readers in other historical and cultural contexts. It is precisely this literary, interpersonal engagement, this ability to create connections through and across time, this epistolary invitation involving and reaching an audience beyond the immediate recipient that makes the experience of reading Roman letters enjoyable and personal. Yet, when we connect with the ancient world, we must guard against the uncritical assessment of letters as implicitly "true" or "honest"; we should not take them as if they reflected the pure, unfiltered emotions and thoughts of the letter-writer any more than an email or text message does today.

The Romans' habit of copying, disseminating, and formally publishing letters means that they frequently envisioned an external audience. A writer's awareness of the possibility of his or her letters falling into the wrong hands, being copied, or surviving posthumously (with or without intention) prompted natural considerations in the composition, delivery, editing, and publication of letters. Altman (1982: 88) emphasizes the crucial role that the letter's internal reader – that is, the intended recipient (and the imagined external reader) – plays in the actual "generation of the text"; the letter represents a "union of writer and reader" and reflects the reciprocal nature of the epistolary act as one whereby the "letter writer simultaneously seeks to affect his reader and is affected by him." This ever present idea of other eyes reading over the letter-writer's shoulder should caution us when we consider more complex issues of audience and epistolary classifications and our own inclination to label epistolary texts as strictly "real" or "fictional." As has been shown earlier in this chapter, there is no watertight definition for a "letter," and the boundary markers between letter types are blurry. Readers have a natural proclivity to view a letter's contents as a "mirror" of the writer's "honest" inner thoughts and emotions, but such a predisposition can be misguided. The ancient theorist Demetrius might well claim that "each of us writes a letter that is almost like an image of our own soul" (Letter 215), but what he means is that the letter is a reflection of how the letter-writer wants to present a specific image at a specific time. As Rosenmeyer (2001: 5) has noted, every letter-writing act, whether between actual historical people or imaginary ones, is innately fictional: "whenever one writes a letter, one constructs a self, an occasion, a version of truth."

Student readers of this book might take a moment to think about Facebook. Do status updates represent reality or only the reality that the "author" wants his or her audience to perceived at a particular moment in time? Does the Facebook author have an immediate reader in mind or a wider, non-specific one? When we step back and think about it, the Facebook author presents an *image* of emotion or honesty, which may or may not be real. The content, tone, and style of a Facebook status update, even if it is a seemingly general statement, may in fact be consciously directed toward – and generated by – a specific "friend" (or "friends") whom one has in mind; it constitutes, knowingly or unknowingly, an act of deliberate self-presentation designed to elicit a response, no matter whether this is articulated in a "comment" or in a "like." Similarly, when we read letters from the ancient world, we should read the image of how the author presents him/herself at that specific moment in time to a specifically intended recipient and/or imagined external reader. So, whether we deal with so-called "real" letters that were actually sent and received, with collections edited and published by the author (or posthumously), with unreprocessed papyri and inscriptions, or with purely literary letters, we must always tread carefully when it comes to attaching legitimacy to words as signifiers of "pure" emotion, truth, or authenticity. Every letter is a creation, an image of how the writer hopes to be perceived by the recipient – as well as by multiple audiences, imagined and unimagined, contemporary and future.

The caution we must exercise about not making too sharp distinctions between "real" and "fictional" must also be applied to other types of artificial classification, which ignore the complexities of the epistolary genre in its various social and literary contexts. Attempts to construct precise typologies – such as "public" letters versus "private" letters, or even "letter" versus "epistle," as many twentieth-century scholars have done[15] – are too constricting: no letter fits neatly into one single category. Moreover, such classifications limit our appreciation of the genre's fluidity, its autobiographical tendencies, its ability to create literary personas, and its power to construct literary immortality for the letter-writer, the recipient, and those individuals referred to in the text.

Themes

The genre-based fluidity that inhibits our ability to distinguish strict categories of letters is precisely what allows us also to recognize so many different but interrelated themes within letters. If one reads sufficiently many letters of sufficiently different types, he or she easily discerns thematic parallels throughout the entire genre, despite variances in form and style. These themes recur not only in terms of content, but also in expression. Thus, for example, we find similar expressions of grief and consolation in letters about death and in letters about love and exile, where the loss, whether of a lover or of one's homeland, is portrayed as an experience similar to one of death. Similarly, one can trace the theme of slavery throughout the letters, noting the various ways in which Romans conceive of slavery not only as an institution, but as a vehicle of discourse allowing authors to comment upon larger philosophical ideas and ethical principles.

The letters represented in this volume have been carefully selected to showcase such thematic interconnectedness. Student readers might explore, for example, friendship, travel, women, entertainment, literary production, death, exile, art, villas, illnesses – or other topics. And, while we can and should appreciate Roman letters as historical texts documenting ancient Roman life and culture, we can also enjoy them as literature, and we can do so through various approaches. Focusing on one specific author, noting certain features unique to individual writers and their contexts allows readers to become intimately familiar with individual style and purpose. A chronological methodology, in which one reads letters and authors in chronological sequence, offers an opportunity to trace the epistolary tradition and the development and reassertion of literary conventions over time. Tracing one or several different themes among different authors at different time periods can help us appreciate the similarities and differences in style and expression among letter-writers composing on the same topic; such a diachronic approach is particularly useful for close analysis, as in considering how letter-writers use a specific subject (death, slavery, art) for the purposes of self-presentation or for the creation of literary immortality. In reading ancient Roman letters we are encouraged to reflect on our own methods of communicating beyond the spoken word. Whether we do so in handwritten or in electronic forms, our desire to connect with others, who are distant from us, is – and has been for thousands of years – one of the greatest motivators of human behavior.

NOTES

1 See, e.g., Olson 2006. In her analysis of email as an adapted epistolary form, J. Walker (2007: 242) notes the numerous (online) guides to proper emailing – or "netiquette" – that have recently surfaced, which are strikingly similar to Post's etiquette handbook.

2 Cf. Rosenmeyer 2001: 1–16; also Gibson and Morrison 2007: 1–16, who build upon Altman's seminal work.

3 See, for example, Altman's discussion (1982: 13–14) of Ovid's *Heroides*.

4 For a more theoretical approach, see, for example, Jenkins (2006: 1–13), who discusses the epistle as a symbol, i.e., "as one manifestation of writing-within-writing" (p. 10).

5 For a fuller discussion exploring issues of transmission and collections and the identification of texts as "letters," see Gibson and Morrison (2007: 14–16).

6 This kind of compositional barometer is exactly what Post (1922: 491) suggested when she sardonically advised lazy letter-writers to send one-sentence post-cards rather than sloppily written letters: "It is not at all certain that your friends and family would not rather have frequent post-cards than occasional letters all too obviously displaying the meagerness of their messages in halting orthography."

7 "These leaf tablets [. . .] were clearly the counterpart of papyrus in those areas of the empire where papyrus will have been difficult and expensive to obtain" (Bowman 1998: 15).

8 Trapp 2003: 8. See Hallo-aho 2009: 22–3 for the role of both professional and non-professional scribes.

9 For the emperor's personal involvement in letter-writing, see Millar 1967: 9–19.

10 For a historical overview of the function of epistolary secretary, see Lindsay 1994: 454–68.

11 See Townend 1961: 175–81, who challenges traditional assumptions about secretarial organization; and cf. Millar 1992: 224–6.

12 For the imperial sway and rivalries among epistolary secretaries during the third century CE, see Anderson 1986: 65–6.

13 Ramsey (1925: 60–74) estimated that on average a courier traveled approximately 50 miles per day. Compare Eliot 1955: 76 ff.; also Casson 1995 and 1997.

14 "Travelers had to present their warrants [*diplomata*] when exchanging transport at way stations or to other inspecting officials as required" (Kolb 2001: 98). For an example of a military *diploma*, see Mellor 1978/9: 173–84.

15 For a fuller overview of epistolary classification, see Doty 1969: 183–99 and Rosenmeyer 2001: 5–12.

REFERENCES

Adams, C., and Laurence, R., eds. (2001) *Travel and Geography in the Roman Empire*. New York: Routledge.

Alcock, S., Bodel, J., and Talbert, R., eds. (2012) *Highways, Byways and Road Systems in the Pre-Modern World*. Malden, MA: Wiley-Blackwell.

Altman, J. G. (1982) *Epistolarity. Approaches to a Form*. Columbus: Ohio State University Press.

Anderson, G. (1986) *Philostratus: Biography and* belles lettres *in the Third Century* AD. London: Croom Helm.

Bowman, A. (1998) *Life and Letters on the Roman Frontier.* New York: Routledge.

Casson, L. (1995) *Ships and Seamanship in the Ancient World.* Baltimore, MD: Johns Hopkins University Press.

Casson, L. (1997) *Travel in the Ancient World*, 2nd edn. Baltimore, MD: Johns Hopkins University Press.

Derrida, J. (1987) *The Post Card: From Socrates to Freud and Beyond.* Translated by Alan Bass. Chicago, IL: University of Chicago Press.

Doty, W. G. (1969) "The classification of epistolary literature." *Catholic Biblical Quarterly, 31*, 183–99.

Eliot, C. W. J. (1955) "New evidence for the speed of the Roman imperial post." *Phoenix*, *9*(2), 76.

Gibson, R., and Morrison, A. D. (2007) "Introduction: What is a letter?" In Morello and Morrison, pp. 1–16.

Hallo-aho, H. (2009) *The Non-Literary Latin Letter: A Study of Their Syntax and Pragmatics* (Commentationes humanarum litterarum 124). Helsinki: Societas Scientiarum Fennica.

Jenkins, T. (2006) *Intercepted Letters: Epistolarity and Narrative in Greek and Roman Literature.* Plymouth, MN: Lexington Books.

Kolb, A. (2001) "Transport and communication in the Roman state: the *cursus Publicus.*" In Adams and Laurence, pp. 95–105.

Lindsay, H. (1994) "Suetonius as *ab epistulis* to Hadrian and the early history of the imperial correspondence." *Historia*, *43*(4), 454–68.

Mellor, R. (1978/9) "A new Roman military diploma," *The J. Paul Getty Museum Journal, 6/7*, 173–84.

Millar, F. (1967) "Emperors at work." *Journal of Roman Studies*, *57*(1/2), 9–19.

Millar, F. (1992) *The Emperor in the Roman World*, 2nd edn. London: Duckworth.

Morello, R., and Morrison, A. D. (2007) *Ancient Letters: Classical and Late Antique Epistography*. Oxford: Oxford University Press.

Muir, J. (2009) *Life and Letters in the Ancient Greek World.* New York: Routledge.

Olson, E. (2006, March 16) "Write Grandma a what?" *New York Times.*

Post, Emily (1922) *Etiquette in Society, in Business, in Politics and at Home.* New York: Funk and Wagnalls.

Poster, C., and Mitchell, L., eds. (2007) *Letter-Writing Manuals and Instruction from Antiquity to the Present*. Columbia: University of South Carolina Press.

Ramsey, A. M. (1925) "The speed of the Roman imperial post." *Journal of Roman Studies, 15*, 60–74.

Roberts, C., and Skeat, T. C. (1983) *The Birth of the Codex*. London: British Academy.

Rosenmeyer, P. (2001) *Ancient Epistolary Fictions: The Letter in Greek Fiction.* Cambridge: Cambridge University Press.

Sherwin-White, A. N. (1962) "Trajan's replies to Pliny: Authorship and necessity."*Journal of Roman Studies*, *52*, 114–25.

Talbert, R. (2012) "Roads not featured: A Roman failure to communicate?" In Alcock, Bodel, and Talbert, pp. 235–54.

Trapp, M. B., ed. (2003) *Greek and Latin Letters. An Anthology with Translation.* Cambridge: Cambridge University Press.

Walker, J. (2007) "Letter writing in the late age of print." In Poster and Mitchell, pp. 230–43.

Wardle, D. (2002) "Suetonius as *ab epistulis*: An African connection." *Historia, 51*(4), 462–80.
Zeiner-Carmichael, N. (2007) "Perfecting the ideal: Molding Roman women in Statius' *Silvae*." *Arethusa, 40*(2), 165–81.

FURTHER READING

Lendon, J. E. (2001) *Empire of Honour: The Art of Government in the Roman World*. New York: Oxford University Press (esp. pp. 160–75).
Peachin, M., ed. (2001) *Aspects of Friendship in the Graeco-Roman World*. Portsmouth: Journal of Roman Archaeology Supplementary Series 43.
Poster, C. (2007) "A conversation halved: Epistolary theory in Greco-Roman Antiquity." In C. Poster and L. Mitchell, eds. (2007), *Letter-Writing Manuals and Instruction from Antiquity to the Present*. Columbia: University of South Carolina Press, pp. 21–51.
Stirewalt, M. Luther (1993) *Studies in Ancient Greek Epistolography*. Atlanta, GA: Scholars' Press.
Sullivan, R., (2007) "Classical epistolary theory and the letters of Isocrates." In C. Poster and L. Mitchell, eds. (2007), *Letter-Writing Manuals and Instruction from Antiquity to the Present*. Columbia: University of South Carolina Press, pp. 7–20.
Townend, G. B. (1961) "The post *ab epistulis* in the second century." *Historia, 10*, 175–81.

CHAPTER TWO

The Roman Republic (70 BCE–27 BCE)

Cicero

Marcus Tullius Cicero (106–43 BCE) was a Roman equestrian from Arpinum and a *novus homo*, the first in his family to become a member of the Roman Senate. He was conservative by nature, maintaining a strong allegiance to the *optimates* ("best people"), whom he also calls the "honest men" (*boni*, "the good" or the elite). The *optimates* represented the long-standing (wealthy) aristocrats of the late Roman republic, who were intent on holding the reins of power and maintaining control over the Senate. The *optimates* opposed the *populares*, Roman aristocrats who achieved political power through the office of tribune and through the popular assemblies; both Julius Caesar and Publius Clodius Pulcher, Cicero's political rival, were among the *populares*. Despite his political success, Cicero's *novus homo* status meant that he was never fully accepted by the *optimates*.

Cicero served as a lawyer and orator and, as consul in 63 BCE, he suppressed an attempted *coup d' état* by Catiline. Later his political rival Clodius instigated Cicero's exile in 58 BCE for his unlawful execution of the Catilinarian conspirators. Recalled a year later, Cicero found himself embroiled in the mounting tension between Julius Caesar and Pompey the Great. As the political struggle turned into civil war, Caesar openly sought Cicero's support against Pompey; but Cicero fled Rome at Caesar's invasion of Italy in 49 BCE and sided with Pompey. Caesar proved victorious in 48 BCE, and Cicero returned to Rome in 47 BCE, when Caesar pardoned him. He continued being involved in politics, albeit more sparingly during Caesar's dictatorship. In 44 BCE a group of conspirators murdered Caesar; though not involved, Cicero expressed approval.

Following Caesar's assassination tensions arose between Cicero and Mark Antony; as consul, Antony led the Caesarian faction, which vowed to avenge Caesar's murder.

Roman Letters, First Edition. Noelle K. Zeiner-Carmichael.

Caesar's heir and adopted son Octavian also joined the fray, and Cicero hoped to manipulate him against Antony. His plan to drive a wedge between Antony and Octavian failed, however, and the two men, along with Lepidus, formed the second triumvirate in November 43 BCE. Shortly afterwards Cicero's name was added on proscription lists, and he was assassinated on December 7. The second triumvirate eventually dissolved, launching Antony and Octavian – and Rome – into civil war again; Octavian defeated Antony at the Battle of Actium in 31 BCE, subsequently accepted the title *Augustus* offered him by the Senate in 27 BCE, and ultimately became Rome's first *princeps* ("head, leader," – hence "emperor" in later terminology); the Julian–Claudian emperors descended from his line.

Cicero was first married to Terentia and they had two children: Marcus and Tullia. Following their divorce (47/46 BCE), Cicero married the young Pubilia; it was a short-lived marriage. Cicero was especially devoted to Tullia and was devastated when she died in 45 BCE. He was an eclectic Old Academy Platonist, imbued with Stoic ideas, and a prolific author: in addition to many speeches, he wrote many (and voluminous) rhetorical and philosophical treatises. His letters were published posthumously, perhaps by Tiro, Cicero's slave and personal secretary, who was later freed by his master. The collection of Cicero's correspondence includes more than 800 letters by him and 100 letters from others. A substantial portion of the correspondence is between Cicero and his good friend Atticus. As was the custom with most well-educated Romans, Cicero frequently sprinkles his letters with literary allusions, quotations, and expressions in Greek. The letters greatly vary in style, composition, and subject matter.

1 *Cicero to Atticus* (Att. 1.5) *Rome, November 68* BCE

This is Cicero's earliest surviving letter. Pomponia is Atticus' sister, married to Cicero's younger brother Quintus.

Since we're good friends, you can imagine how upset I am over my cousin Lucius' death and how greatly it has overshadowed the enjoyment I normally have, both at work and at home. If you could ever find enjoyment through another person's caring manner, it was through Lucius'. So I'm sure his death is a blow to you, since you always share my pain: now you too have lost a relative and a friend, a man incredibly distinguished in every virtue and office, who adored you both of his own accord and as a result of conversations I had with him about you.

Regarding your sister: she herself can testify to how energetically I've worked to ensure that my brother's feelings toward her are just as they should be. When I realized he might have been offensive, I sent him a letter designed to appease him as my brother, to advise him as my junior, and to reproach him for acting out of line. Here's the upshot: to judge from the frequent letters I've since received from him, I'm confident that everything is back to normal, just as we hoped.

You've got no right chastising *me* about sending letters! Pomponia never informed me about an available courier, and I didn't hear of anyone heading your way to Epirus; moreover, at that time I hadn't heard you were back in Athens. As to the business deal with Acutilius, you've handed that over to me: as soon as I returned to Rome after visiting you, I was planning to finish it up. But it turns out there was no urgency, and, since you had my full confidence, I decided to let our friend Peducaeus write and advise you. Besides, I already let Acutilius talk my ear off for days (you know how he goes on and on). So it wasn't any burden to write you about all his griping: I had already shouldered the burden of listening to him (a rather mind-numbing experience)! Remember, though, that, while you're pointing the finger at me for not writing, I have only one letter from you and *you're* the one with more free time and more opportunities to send letters.

You wrote that, even if "a certain someone" was rather upset with you, I should smooth it over. I'm not ignoring what you're saying, but it's surprising just how offended he is. I haven't overlooked saying all the right words about you, but I think you should guide me as to how far I should push. If there's anything in particular you want me to say, write me with the specifics; you'll find I've tried to be no more thorough than you would be, and no less thorough than you desire. Regarding the property dispute involving Tadius: he told me you had written him and said there was no need to spend any more time and energy on it since the property is secured by usufruct. We're surprised you didn't know that, when a legal guardianship is involved – which applies to the girl, the heir of the property – Tadius has no right to it while she's still a ward.

I'm glad you're happy with your new purchase in Epirus. Yes, please do go ahead and take care of buying what I instructed, as long as it's no trouble, and anything else you think will suit my new place in Tusculum. This is really the only spot where I can clear my head and find some respite from work. I'm expecting Quintus any day now. Terentia is suffering a terrible attack of rheumatoid arthritis. She sends her love to you and your sister and mother. She and my darling Tullia have written a little note below with their best wishes. Be well, love me, and remember I love you like you were my own brother.

2 *Cicero to Atticus* (Att. *1.1) Rome, July 17, 65* BCE

Cicero describes his candidacy for consul for the year 63 BCE (elections to be held in 64 BCE).

I know you're really interested in hearing about my candidacy for the consulship. Here's how it stands, at least as far as I can tell right now: so far Publius Galba is the only one actively canvassing and, with typical good old-fashioned Roman frankness, he's getting a "No," plain and simple. Many think his premature campaign works to my advantage: when people say "no" to him, they admit it's because they're planning on saying "yes" to me. So – I'm expecting to make further headway once word gets out that I've acquired many more supporters who have joined the Cicero Bandwagon! I think I'll launch my official campaign when your business agent, Cincius, confirms your slave is leaving with this letter during the tribunician election in the Campus Martius, where a great crowd will already be assembled. You'll either laugh or cry when you hear that, besides Galba, my other definite rivals include Antonius and Quintus Cornificius. But wait – go ahead, slap yourself silly: some say that even Caesonius is running! I don't think the lawyer Aquilius is going to run; he's swearing it's because of "ill health" and "professional obligations" (!). Catiline will certainly be a rival as long as he's acquitted in his extortion trial. And don't hold your breath for Aufidius and Palicanus: you won't get any letter from me about their candidacy.

As for the current race, Lucius Julius Caesar is considered a shoe-in. Thermus and Silanus count as contenders, though they're so short on friends and reputation that it's plausible Turius will edge ahead as a real challenger. But no one else shares my opinion. From my standpoint, I'd prefer it if Thermus got elected alongside Caesar, because, of all the current candidates, he would be the most competitive rival if he fell into my electoral year and challenged my candidacy; that's because he's currently serving as curator of the Flaminian Road, and by my election year he'll have finished all the repairs. I'm more than happy to see him as consul side by side with Caesar, this upcoming year. So – there you go: that's my sketch of the current state of affairs.

Me? I plan to be exceedingly vigilant by completing every duty of a candidate. Since it's looking like Gaul will be crucial in winning votes, maybe once the forum takes its annual holiday from legal proceedings, I'll set out for Governor Piso and join his staff in September, so I can return by January. I'll write once I've fully scrutinized the inclinations of the nobles. I expect everything else will run smoothly, at least in terms of competitors, here at Rome. As for our pal Pompey, it's up to you to keep an eye on that front: you're much closer to him in Epirus. Tell him I won't be upset if he doesn't show up in Rome for my election!

So, that's that. Oh, wait, there's something else – I really hope you'll forgive me. Your uncle Caecilius was swindled out of a great deal of money by Publius Varius; he's begun legal action against Varius' brother, Caninius Satyrus, who, he alleges, accepted fraudulently acquired items from Varius. The other creditors are also taking action; they count among them Lucius Lucullus, Publius Scipio – and also Lucius Pontius, the one they think will be the custodial receiver, if his property comes to foreclosure. But at this point, any talk about receivers is ridiculous. Here's the point: Caecilius asked me to represent him against Satyrus. Yet nearly every day Satyrus is at my doorstep, paying respects; he courts Lucius Domitius first, me next. He was especially supportive of me and Quintus when we were candidates. I was quite upset, given my friendship with Satyrus – and especially with Domitius (I'm really depending on his political clout). I've explained all this to Caecilius and simultaneously stressed that, if the lawsuit involved only him and Satyrus, then I'd happily say "yes." Now, however, the case involves all the other creditors, incredibly influential men who could easily win the case for Caecilius without my help.

So I've asked Caecilus to sympathize with the loyalty I owe Domitius and with my vulnerable position. I thought he found it harder to stomach this than I would have liked, and certainly harder than a gentleman would have: soon afterwards he completely cut off the friendly interactions we had begun a few days earlier. Please forgive me and believe it was human kindness that kept me from appearing in court against a friend whose good name was at stake at such a stressful time – especially a friend who had already shown me so much loyalty and support. But, if you're feeling less generous toward me, blame it on my candidacy. I, for one, think political ambition is a reasonable justification, "since 'tis not a common hide or a slaughtered beast" that is at stake – to quote Homer: you know the prize I'm after and you understand how I must not only cling to old friendships but even form new ones. I really hope you see my viewpoint – I really want you to.

The Hermathena statue you procured is delightful; it fits in so well that the entire gymnasium in my villa seems to bow to it as an offering! Many thanks!

3 *Cicero to Atticus* (Att. *1.2*) *Rome, July 65* BCE

I'm pleased to inform you that I have became the father of a little son, born the same day Lucius Julius Caesar and Gaius Marcius Figulus were elected consuls!

Terentia is doing just fine.

It's been a while since I got a letter from you. I've already written in detail about my election prospects. Currently I'm thinking about defending my fellow candidate Catiline in his extortion trial. We have the jury we want, and the prosecution has been fully cooperative. If he's acquitted, I hope he'll be more disposed to becoming allies in our quest for office. But, if things turn out differently, I'll bear it with a cheerful heart.

I need you here soon. Many feel strongly that your noble friends will stand in the way of my election. It's clear you'll be a huge advantage winning them over. January is approaching, so make sure you're back at Rome as planned.

4 *Q. Metellus Celer to M. Cicero (*Fam. 5.1*) Cisalpine Gaul, January 62* BCE

As praetor in 63 BCE, Celer had helped Cicero put down the Catilinarian conspiracy; ultimately he was disappointed with how Cicero handled the affair. At the time of this letter Celer was governor of Gaul, a position Cicero had declined and secured for Celer instead. Celer's brother, the tribune Nepos, had sided with the Catilinarians. At the end of his consulship, Cicero followed normal custom by proposing before the Senate to give a formal public address from the Rostra. Nepos, however, vetoed Cicero's request, citing his unconstitutional execution of the conspirators (Celer refers to this veto in his letter as "some remark"). In response, Cicero gave a speech before the Senate that resulted in Nepos being compelled to leave Rome and relinquish his tribuneship. Celer is incensed on his brother's behalf.

Greetings to M. Tullius Cicero, son of Marcus, from Quintus Metellus Celer, son of Quintus, Proconsul.

I hope you are well. Given our mutual affection and restored friendship, I would have thought that, in my absence, you would not have made a laughing stock out of me, or instigated an attack upon my brother's estate and civil rights – all because of some remark. If his own decency wasn't enough to protect him, then at least the status of our family or my support toward you and the republic should have counted for something. Now I see him assailed from all sides and myself deserted by men whom I'd least expect to behave like this.

So I'm in mourning, dressed in black – yes, *I*, a provincial governor, an army commander, who is in the middle of conducting a war! Since you're responsible for all this, behaving recklessly and exercising none of the clemency so characteristic of our ancestors, it will be no surprise if you live to regret your actions. I wasn't expecting *you* of all people to be so capricious toward me and my relatives. Meanwhile, neither personal grief nor wrongful injustice by anyone will distract *me*, at least, from serving the republic.

5 *Cicero to Metellus Celer (*Fam. 5.2*) Rome, January or February 62* BCE

Cicero sternly replies to Celer's letter. Notably, the two continued to be friends – surely thanks, in part, to Cicero's careful epistolary reply.

Marcus Tullius Cicero, son of Marcus, sends greetings to Quintus Metellus Celer, son of Quintus.

I hope you and your army are well. You write: "Given our mutual affection and our restored friendship, I would have thought that, in my absence, you would not have made a laughing stock out of me." What you mean exactly, I have no idea. I'm guessing, however, you heard how I mentioned at a Senate meeting that many people resented my rescuing the republic; and that I declared how your relatives (you couldn't say no to them) convinced you to clam up and not deliver your encomiastic speech, designed to proclaim before the Senate all the accolades that, as you had explicitly stated before, I deserved. But I also added that the duty of maintaining the republic's safety had been shared between us: I protected the City from domestic plots and internal evils; you were to defend Italy against foreign enemies and clandestine conspiracies. I also noted that your close relatives had undermined our partnership, which we regarded as an eminent, weighty responsibility: even though *I* had honored *you* with the highest, most distinguished rewards, they worried that you would return the favor and actually reciprocate with mutual goodwill! When I then merely explained how much I had been anticipating your speech and how sorely mistaken I was about its content, my words seemed to elicit some smiles, and then a little laughter – not at you, but rather at my mistake and my rather frank public admission, confessing as I was my great eagerness to hear you sing my praises. Now my statement can only be interpreted as complimenting toward you, since, even with all my incredibly illustrious, glorious accomplishments, I still yearned to hear such affirmation from *your* lips.

Therefore, when you write, "given our mutual affection," I have no idea what *you* consider to be "mutual" when it comes to friendship. *I*, for one, define it as an equal reciprocity of goodwill between friends. If I were to claim it was for your sake that I turned down my right to govern a province, you might think me a phony: you'd say that self-interest was my driving force, that my decision gave me the better end of the deal. Here's my response: as soon as I renounced my assignment at the assembly meeting, I began strategizing how I could transfer it to you. I'm not mentioning anything about the drawing of lots . . . just that – and here's a hint – in the allotting of provinces nothing was done by my colleague without my full knowledge. Let me jog your memory: remember that day, when the assignments were doled out? Remember how quickly I convened the Senate, for how long I spoke about you? And do you recall how afterwards you said to me that my speech was so complimentary of you that it had made your colleagues look inferior?

Now we come to the Senate's decree; its introduction (provided the document survives) is solid proof of the respect I extended toward you. I also want you to think back and remember how, after you took up your governorship, I spoke highly of you in the Senate; remember what I said in assembly meetings and in the letters I sent you. When you put it all together, I ask you, was your return to Rome to support your brother an adequate – and equally *reciprocal* – payback for all I've done for you? You be the judge.

As for "our restored friendship," it's unclear why you use the term "restored" for a friendship that was never broken in the first place. Regarding your claim that I shouldn't have attacked your brother, "all because of some remark," first, you should know that I applaud your sentiment – one so full of brotherly love, kindness and devotion; second, if in any way I opposed your brother for the sake of the republic, please forgive me: I'm the republic's greatest friend – it couldn't ask for a better one. But if in fact I have protected myself from your brother's incredibly nasty attack, you should fully recognize that I'm not the one complaining to you about his injustices toward me.

Once I realized he was exploiting his position as tribune by scheming and planning for my utter ruin, I appealed to your wife Claudia and your sister Mucia (whose enthusiastic help I was sure I could count on, given my close friendship with Pompey) to dissuade Nepos from his destructive plan. Nonetheless, as I know you have already heard, on December 31 that brother of yours insulted me in such a disgraceful way, as has never, ever before been directed even at the most despicable lowest second-rate citizen: he deprived me of my right to address the people publicly on the conclusion of my consulship – me, the consul, the savior of the republic! This injustice, however, turned into the greatest honor: for, even though he allowed me to do nothing more than swear the oath "The well-being of the state and this city is due to my efforts alone," I went ahead and swore it – the truest and most beautiful oath one can swear – and the people then swore in a loud voice that *my* sworn oath was indeed true.

Although I had been so viciously insulted, on that same day I sent some mutual friends to Nepos to try and convince him to change his mind, but he answered he wasn't budging. In fact, just a little before, he publicly proclaimed that anyone who had punished others without the right to speak at a trial shouldn't himself be allowed to speak. What an upstanding man! What a devoted citizen! For, in his "esteemed" judgment, the person who saved the Senate house from murder, Rome from being burnt to the ground, and Italy from war, that person deserved the *same* punishment the Senate and all the honest men unanimously approved for those conspirators who had planned to set the city ablaze, slaughter the magistrates and the Senate, and incite a destructive war!

So I confronted your brother right to his face. On January 1 I argued with him about the political situation, to make him realize he was going up against a courageous and resolute man. On January 3, when Nepos began his speech, he was either calling me out or threatening me every other word; his sole purpose was to overthrow me however he could – not by legal means, not by debate, but by force and full-on verbal assault. If I hadn't had the guts to stoutly oppose him in all his brazenness, then who would ever believe that the courage I displayed in my consulship was deliberate and not just an accident?

If you didn't know that Nepos felt this way about me, you should realize he's kept you in the dark about the gravest matters; but if he has shared some part of his plan with you, then consider me a lenient, easy-going man for not grumbling to you. If you understand that it wasn't, as you put it, "some remark" by Nepos that got me upset, but rather his plan and incredibly spiteful hatred toward me, then now acknowledge my kindness – that is, if you can call leniency and apathy toward such an outrageous insult "kindness." I never expressed a single negative sentiment against your brother; when a proposal was introduced, I agreed (while still sitting down) with the proposal seeming most lenient. One more thing: though I shouldn't have given a hoot, considering everything that happened, I freely lent my help so that my enemy would, thanks to a senatorial decree, escape the penalty of losing his office – precisely because he was *your* brother.

So obviously I didn't "attack" your brother, but defended myself against his attacks. I haven't been "capricious" toward you, as you write, but consistent, maintaining my goodwill toward you, when you've deserted me and the obligations you owe me. Even right now, while you've written me what virtually amounts to a threatening letter, I'm writing back, responding this way: I not only forgive you for your indignation, but even praise you for it. My feelings remind me how great the bond of brotherly love is. I ask you also to prove you're a fair judge of my indignation: if your friends have been attacking me severely, cruelly, and without any good reason, realize that I was justified in defending myself, and I should have been able to rely upon you and your army for support in a situation like this.

I've always wanted you to be my friend, and I've worked hard to persuade you I want to be your very good friend. I still feel kindly toward you; as long as you want it to be that way, I'll continue to do so. I'd rather end my resentment toward your brother out of affection for you, than allow that resentment to diminish our friendly feelings toward each other.

6 *Cicero to Pompey (*Fam. 5.7*) Rome, June 62* BCE

At the time of this letter's writing, Pompey was in the east, commanding an army in the Third Mithridatic War. Through several military victories, he added four new provinces to Rome's growing empire: Bythinia and Pontus, Syria, Cilica, and Crete. The Senate voted him a third triumph, celebrated in Rome in 51 BCE. While Pompey had been abroad, Cicero celebrated his own victory, uncovering the Catilinarian conspiracy. This letter responds to Pompey's, which expressed less enthusiasm about Cicero's successes than Cicero had hoped. The Laelius and Africanus mentioned at the end of the letter refer to two famous statesmen and friends of the second century BCE, who were also interlocutors in Cicero's philosophical treatise *On Friendship*.

I hope all is well with you and the army. I'm well too. Along with everyone else, I was profoundly pleased with the letter you sent to the Senate and to the people of Rome. You spoke of your expectation of peace in the region, a peace I repeatedly assured everyone that you and you alone would accomplish. Let me tell you – thanks to your letters, your old enemies are now your new friends – and they're down on their knees, completely overthrown, their hopes dashed.

The personal letter you sent me, however, suggested only a small token of your goodwill toward me, though please know it delighted me nonetheless. I derive the greatest happiness from my own good conscience and from knowing I've fulfilled my obligations. If my contributions do not elicit a reciprocal response, then I'm perfectly fine if the greater duty falls upon me.

Certainly if my recent enthusiasm toward you hasn't brought you closer to me, then it will be our mutual concern for the state that will unite us. Let me be frank, so you can fully understand what I found missing in your letter – this is my natural approach and our friendship warrants it. Given my great accomplishments, I expected your letter to convey some kind of congratulations, both because of our close friendship and because of the impact my achievements have had on the republic. I'm assuming you left that part out for fear of offending someone. Still, please know that what I've done to secure the safety of our nation is confirmed by the judgment and testimony of the entire world. When you come back to Rome you'll recognize the profound care I put into these accomplishments and the exceptional personal risk I ran for their sake. Consequently, you'll be inclined to join me in friendship and public interest: I'll be your slightly lesser "Laelius" and you'll be my much greater "Africanus."

7 *Cicero to Atticus* (Att. *1.13) January 25, 61* BCE

At the first Senate meeting of the year the presiding consul, Marcus Pupius Piso, called upon former consuls (*consulares*) to speak; the order of speaking was predetermined, the first place being considered the most distinguished. Cicero was passed over in favor of Calpurnius Piso (consul in 67 BCE). Cicero also writes about Clodius' sacrilege of the Bona Dea festival. Each year Roman women celebrated two festivals in honor of Bona Dea (the "Good Goddess"), a fertility deity whose worship ensured the health of the state. Only upper-class women could participate in the secret rites. In 61 BCE, Caesar was serving as praetor and Pontifex Maximus, and his wife hosted the Bona Dea festival. Clodius was caught sneaking into the rites, allegedly to seduce Caesar's wife. (Caesar divorced his wife shortly after.) The event caused quite the scandal at Rome.

I've now received three letters from you: one delivered by Marcus Cornelius, which I think you gave him at Three-Taverns Town; another that your host at Canusinus gave me; and a third one, which you said you sent off once you had left the coast. They were all, as teachers of rhetoric say, "sprinkled with the salt of humanity and marked with signs of love." You've challenged me to write back, but I've been dragging my feet because I can't find a trustworthy messenger. Is there any courier who can manage to carry a full pack of letters without lightening the load through a little perusal? Besides, I don't really know whether anyone heading to Epirus would actually find you there. I'm guessing that, once you slaughtered your victims at your shrine to the Goddess of Plenty, you immediately "marched" forth to "besiege" Sicyon (to recover the debts that town owes you, no doubt!) – so I'm unsure when you're going to Antonius for his help, or how much time you're spending in Epirus. I don't dare place somewhat confidential letters in the hands of Achaeans or Epirotes!

After you left, some matters came up that really do deserve a letter, but I can't take the risk of sending one containing those particular details when it may be lost, opened, or intercepted. Anyway, I was *not* granted the privilege of speaking first in the Senate. This honor was given to that so-called "pacifist" (ha!) of the Allobroges, Calpurnius Piso. Even though the senators grumbled a little about it, I wasn't disappointed. It meant I was released from having to show respect to that perverse consul, Pupius Piso, and I'm free to maintain my political position in the republic in spite of him. Besides, the second position has nearly the same status as the first and allows a speech that isn't too constrained to do the consul favors. Third to speak was Catulus; Hortensius was fourth, in case you're interested. Consul Piso himself has a petty and deviant mind. He's also a joker, albeit of a mean, sarcastic type – one who manages to provoke a laugh though he doesn't possess an ounce of wit. His face is more laughable than his jokes. He does nothing when it comes to politics and is standoffish with the *optimates*. Don't expect him to do anything good for the republic – he hasn't got the will; and don't expect him to do anything dangerous to it either – he hasn't got the guts. His colleague Niger, however, shows me great respect, is actively engaged with political parties, and is an advocate of "honest men." Currently the consuls' differences of opinion are minor, but I'm afraid this small infection, so to speak, will spread.

I bet you've heard that, during the Bona Dea rites at Caesar's house, a man dressed in drag snuck in. After the Vestals repeated the ceremony from the beginning again, Quintus Cornificus brought up the incident in the Senate (he initiated it, so don't think it was one of us). Later, after the senatorial decree, the matter was referred back to the Vestals and the head priests, who officially declared it an act of sacrilege. Next, by the Senate's decree, the consuls circulated a bill, and Caesar served his wife divorce papers. Piso is being swayed by his friendship with Clodius and is working hard to get the bill rejected – that exactly same bill he is introducing, which was issued by senatorial decree and deals with a religious matter! Messalla is moving forward very sternly. The honest men are dropping their support of the bill, thanks to Clodius' begging; gangs of thugs are collecting. As for yours truly, well, in the beginning I started out as a Lycurgan prosecutor, but I'm softening a little every day. Cato continues putting the pressure on. What else? I'm afraid that the whole matter, which has been ignored by honest men and defended by rascals, may be the start of great political turmoil.

That friend of yours – you know whom I'm talking about? You know, the one who, as you said in your letter, stopped daring to reproach me and began singing my praises? Well, now he's putting on quite a show: he broadcasts his esteem for me, welcomes me with open arms, adores me, and publicly praises me. Behind the scenes it's obvious he's secretly jealous. He's socially inept, problematic, politically lackluster, dishonest, tentative, and insincere; but some other time I'll fill you in with more details. I'm not sufficiently up to date and I don't dare entrust a letter about such important matters to just any old courier.

The praetors have not yet drawn lots for their provinces. The situation is the same as when you left. I'm putting into my speech the topographical portrait of Misenum and Puteoli you requested. "December 3," I noticed, was a mistake. The parts of my speeches you commended, trust me, I really loved them too, but I didn't dare say anything before you read them yourself. Now that you've given these sections your stamp of approval, Atticus, they seem to me even more "Attic" in style! I've added some things to the Metellinus speech and I'll send you the volume, now that your affection for me has turned you into a "logophile."

What else? Oh yes, well, Consul Messalla has purchased Autronius' house for 13,4000,000 sesterces. "Why should I care?" you ask. Only because, by comparison with this sale, it now looks like my purchase of the Palatine house was quite a steal. Also, people have come to realize there's nothing wrong with employing financial help from friends to purchase things that will increase one's social status. When it comes to securing my loan, Teucris is as slow as molasses, but I'm still hopeful of her. Please take care of things. Expect a less guarded letter soon.

8 *Cicero to Atticus* (Att. *1.14*) *Rome, February 13, 61* BCE

News about Pompey and the aftermath of the Bona Dea scandal, for which Clodius faces possible trial.

So maybe it seems a tad tacky to tell you how busy I am, but it's been so hectic I've barely had a second to write this hurried letter – and even then I've had to steal a snippet of time from attending to otherwise fairly critical matters.

I've already written to you about Pompey's first public address since he returned to Italy: it offered small comfort to the poor, little more than empty words to the depraved, no pleasure to the rich, and nothing substantial to the honest men. In other words his speech fell completely flat. Then, at Consul Piso's instigation, Fufius Calenus, that incredibly irresponsible plebeian tribune, called his own public meeting and summoned Pompey before it. The meeting took place in the Circus Flaminius; and there, in that very place, on that very day, we got to watch the very "distinguished" Market Day Pageant! What a spectacle! Calenus asked Pompey if it'd be okay with the praetor handpicking the judges, so that this same praetor could also preside over his chosen panel. (This had been the Senate's original plan for Clodius' sacrilege trial.) So Pompey, in that "wonderful aristocratic manner" of his, replied that, in all matters, he held – and had always held – the Senate's authority in the highest regard. (Mind you, it took him ten minutes to make this one single point).

Afterwards, in a meeting of the Senate, Consul Messalla asked Pompey how he felt about Clodius' sacrilegious act and the proposed bill that had been circulated. Pompey addressed the Senate and evaded the question by generally praising *all* of its decrees; when he sat back down, he leaned over and told me that he thought he had responded sufficiently on the "damn matter." But, when Crassus saw that Pompey had managed to scrounge up a scrap of support by giving the impression he approved of my consulship, he stood up and spoke about my consulship in the most pompous manner: he declared that he was a senator, a citizen, a free man, and even still alive – all thanks to me! He went on to proclaim that, whenever he looked at his wife, his house, his country, it was because of me he could lay eyes on them! Need I say more? He did quite an impressive job covering the whole topic, which I usually paint with various colors in my speeches (you know my palette well) – about fire, sword, and so on and so forth. I was next to Pompey and I could tell the man was irritated, either because Crassus got all the credit that he, Pompey, could have had, or because my accomplishments were great enough for the Senate to be perfectly happy hearing them extolled – and, even more, because the person doing the extolling was the same Crassus I had slighted in my own published speech, where I commended Pompey! The day brought Crassus and me closer together, and I was perfectly content to accept whatever support, overt or implicit, Pompey offered me.

So then: it was my turn to speak – good god you should have heard me! How I paraded myself before my new audience (I mean, Pompey – remember, he didn't get to enjoy my speeches against Catiline)! If ever I could summon elegant periods, turning points, arguments, and reasoning, this was it. Should I continue? Thunderous applause! Yes indeed, I brought down the house! Here's what I covered: the importance and authority of the Senate; the equestrians' cooperation and Italy's total support; the half-dead leftovers from the conspiracy; the markdown on grain prices, peace, and stability. You well know how I can make my voice boom when it comes to such themes: you probably heard me all the way across the Adriatic in Epirus!

So here's what else is happening in Rome: the Senate is virtually an Areopagus. I've never seen it be more consistent, sterner, or steadfast. When the voting day came for introducing the proposed bill (by senatorial decree), all those kids with their ridiculously manicured goatees – the same crowd that used to tag behind Catiline – herded together behind Little Miss Curio, the shepherd, and spoke against the bill. Consul Piso, who was presiding over the Senate and thus responsible for presenting the bill, also spoke against it. Meanwhile Clodius' gang overtook the voting waiting areas and made sure only "nay" ballots were passed out. So then, picture it: Cato bounds up to the Rostra and gives Piso a serious tongue-lashing; his was the voice of reason, a speech full of weight and authority. Our pal Hortensius follows suit, along with many other honest men. Favonius' contribution was particularly noteworthy. During this rally of the *optimates*, the assembly is dismissed and the Senate convenes. Then, even though Clodius was going around kissing the feet of each and every one of us and Piso was fighting for the bill's rejection, a packed Senate house decreed that the consuls should get the people to accept the bill. Curio, who moved that no action be taken, got only 15 favorable votes and 400 "no." So that was the end of that. At this point Fufius just gave in. Clodius was holding his pathetic meetings, where he bitterly attacked Lucullus, Hortensius, Gaius Piso, and Consul Messalla; as for me, he said only that I've "been appraised." Then the Senate passed a decree that they wouldn't do anything about the allocation of praetorian provinces, about embassies, or about any other matters until the bill was put forth.

So there you have it – the latest at Rome. Oh, let me mention one more pleasant surprise: Messalla has proven to be an excellent consul: brave, steadfast, diligent. He sings my praises, shows me affection, and follows my lead. As for his "partner," Consul Piso, that guy is rich – in vices. His one saving grace is his laziness: he's half-asleep, inexperienced, a complete loser, but so evil that, following Pompey's public speech in praise of the Senate, he has turned against him. Naturally, this way he's now alienated all the honest men. You can blame Piso's behavior on his friendship with Clodius as much as on his extremist leanings and on his love for partisan politics. Among magistrates, his only pal is Fufius. We've got plenty of good tribunes, especially Cornutus, who could be called Cato's doppelganger. So what else do you want to hear?

Here's some personal news: "Teucris" (you know whom I mean) has fulfilled her promise in helping me buy the house on the Palatine. Make sure you satisfy my earlier request. Quintus has bought out the remaining three quarters of the building in the Argiletum district for 750,000 sesterces and is in the process of trying to sell his estate in Tusculum so he can come up with enough to purchase the Pacilius house here in Rome. I'm back in favor with Lucceius; I can tell he's just itching to be a political candidate. I'm putting my head down: full force ahead. Tell me each and every detail: what you're up to, where you are, and how things are going in your neck of the woods.

9 *Cicero to Atticus* (Att. *2.14*) *Formiae, April 59* BCE

Seriously, your talk about Bibulus is keeping me in terrible suspense! Same for your conversation with ox-eyed "Juno" [Clodia], and even for that sumptuous dinner party! Hurry up: find a way to get here to quench my ears – they're thirsty for more! There's nothing scarier, I think, than the thought of what our "Fearless Leader of the East" [Pompey] will do when he learns everyone is trashing him and realizes these policies are going to be easily overturned; he may start spiraling downward. I've become so unnerved that I'd prefer peace – even if it means tyranny – over war – even if it holds great hope for the future.

Regarding my literary production you're insisting on, forget it: it's as if I were living in a town square, not in a villa. I've got a constant stream of locals coming by to see me. I won't mention the common mob – after 10 a.m. they don't pester me. But Gaius Arrius is my next-door neighbor – or, better yet, I should say my roommate! He even admits he doesn't go to Rome just so he can stay here all day and wax philosophy with me. Then on my other side is, surprise, surprise, Sebosus, Catulus' friend. Where can I turn? Dear god, I'd go immediately to Arpinum, but obviously it's more convenient to wait for your arrival here at Formiae, at least until May 6. You see the kind of people I have to listen to all day! Wow, though, what a perfect opportunity for a potential buyer of my place – they can make an offer right while they're standing here, in my living room! Easy for you to say, "Let's take a stab at something great, something requiring much thought and time." Alas. Still, I'll make you happy and not scrimp on my efforts! So long.

10 *Cicero to Atticus (*Att. *3.3) Near Capua, late March 58* BCE

In 58 BCE Clodius introduced a law condemning to exile anyone who had executed a Roman extra-legally. Realizing the law applied to him, Cicero tried to garner support from friends and allies. When that failed, he fled Rome. Shortly afterwards an official bill declared him an exile. Cicero writes to Atticus on his way toward Vibo Valentia (Bivone), in the toe of Italy.

If only I'll see the day when I'll thank you for making me go on living! For now, at least, I deeply regret it. I'm begging you, come immediately to Vibo. For various reasons I changed my mind and decided to go there. If you come, I can come up with a comprehensive plan for my itinerary and exile. I'll be surprised if you don't, but I'm confident you'll make it happen.

11 *Cicero to Terentia, Tullia and Marcus (*Fam. *14.4) Brundisium, April 29, 58* BCE

I write you less often than I can, mostly because, though I find every waking minute miserable, when I write to you or read one of your letters, I'm so overcome with tears that I simply can't bear it. If only I had been less determined to live! Then I certainly wouldn't have experienced this kind of despair while alive, or at least not to this degree. But if Fortune has reserved any hope for me of one day recovering some shred of my security, then it wasn't a complete mistake to continue living. If this miserable situation looks like it's permanent, then I definitely want to see you as soon as possible, my life, and die enfolded in your embrace. Neither the gods, whom you faithfully worship, nor men, who received my loyal devotion, have reciprocated. I've been staying with Marcus Laenius Flaccus for thirteen days. He's an exceptional person: in preserving my safety and security, he has ignored the risk to his own fortune and status. Nor has the threat of a completely heinous bill deterred him from following the laws of hospitality and friendship. I only hope that one day I can pay him back for his kindness. I'm eternally grateful to him.

I'm preparing to sail from Brundisium today: my plan is to go to Cyzicum via Macedonia. Oh, I'm done for! I'm ruined! How can I ask you to come, a woman, physically frail and emotionally broken? Do

I not ask? Then am I to live without you? Here's what I think is best: if there's any hope of my recall, then stay and work on that; if it's all done and over, as I fear, then please get here however you can. Just know this: if I have you here with me, I won't feel like I'm dying.

What will become of my sweet Tullia? It's up to you to take care of it – I'm helpless – I can't think of anything to do. No matter what, we must preserve the poor girl's reputation and marriage. Then what? What will Cicero Jr. do? May he forever remain in my heart and soul. I can't write another word: grief paralyzes my hand. I have no idea how you've been getting along, whether you have any possessions left or if, as I fear, you're utterly destitute. I hope Piso will always be our friend, as you wrote in your letter.

When it comes to the manumission of the slaves, don't worry. First off, we already agreed that you'd free each as you saw fit. Orpheus is still loyal, but, beyond him, no one especially. For my other slaves, here's the plan: if my estate should be confiscated, they'd become freedmen, that is, as long as they could maintain that legal status. But, if I retain my property, they'd continue as my slaves, except for just a few. But these are trivial matters.

You advise me to stay strong and keep the faith: I just wish there was a good reason to do so. But now I'm so miserable: when will I receive another letter from you? Who will deliver it to me? I would have waited for one at Brundisium if the sailors had let me, but they didn't want to lose the favorable wind. As for the rest, my Terentia, keep your head up as proudly as you can. We've had a good, prosperous life. We've committed no crime; it's only our virtue that's destroyed us. I've made no mistakes, unless you count not losing my life when I lost my honor and status a mistake. But our children preferred me to live, so let us bear everything as best we can, however unbearable.

So I, the one encouraging you, can't even encourage myself! I've sent back that loyal slave, Clodius Philhetaerus, because his eyes were in bad shape. Sallustius surpasses everyone in his faithfulness. Pescennius is incredibly good to me, and I hope he'll always be considerate toward you. Sica had said he would remain with me, but he left Brundisium. Take care of your health as best you can and trust me when I say I'm more deeply affected by your suffering than by my own. Goodbye, my Terentia, paragon of the faithful wife; and my dearest Tullia; and our last hope, young Tullius!

12 *Cicero to Terentia, Tullia and Marcus (*Fam. *14.2) Thessalonica, October 5, 58* BCE

Cicero is especially concerned about the family's financial situation. Thanks to Clodius, his house on the Palatine hill has been completely destroyed. With reduced resources and cash flow, the family must rely on Terentia's personal assets and the generosity of friends.

Tullius sends greetings to his Terentia, his dear sweet Tullia, and his Marcus.

Don't think I'm writing long letters to everyone – just to those who have written to me at length, and hence deserve a reply. I don't have anything to write about, anyway, and at a time like this there's nothing I find harder than writing. Moreover, I'm simply unable to write you and our sweet Tullia without crying my eyes out. I see you both "reduced to nothing" – you, the very ones I always wanted to be fortunate; I ought to have ensured this and, if I hadn't been such a coward, I would have. I greatly love our Piso for how well he's been handling the situation. I've written him, encouraging him as best I could and expressing my gratitude, which he deserves. I hear you're hopeful about the new tribunes. They'll be a real help if Pompey is on board. Nonetheless, I have my concerns about Crassus.

I see you're taking care of everything with the greatest courage and devotion; no surprise there, but I'm deeply saddened that my troubles require alleviation through the deplorable troubles you must suffer. The diligent Publius Valerius wrote me a letter that made me weep. He described how you were dragged from the temple of Vesta to the *tabula Valeria* [? Valerius' meeting place]. Good god, my light, my darling! You're the one everyone always went to when they wanted my help – and now, my Terentia, now you're being harassed in this way! To imagine you down on your knees, sobbing, dressed in black clothes for mourning, and that all this happened thanks to me – the one who saved other people, only to perish now himself!

As to what you wrote about our house on the Palatine, or rather the spot where it once stood, I can truly say I won't feel completely restored until our home is. These matters are out of my hands. Oh, how I ache that you, already suffering and deprived, must bear any part in covering our expenses! If we can take care of the situation successfully, then we'll recover everything; if the same bad luck afflicting us continues to affect our expenses, let others cover them, if they're willing and able. If you love me, don't strain your frail health. You're on my mind day and night. I see how you're taking on each and every task; I'm afraid you cannot endure it, but I know that everything depends on you! For this reason, take care of your health, so we can achieve what you're hoping and striving for.

I have no idea whom I should write except people who write me, or those you write me about. I won't go farther away, since you ask me not to; but please write as often as you can, especially if there's anything indicating more than just a glimmer of hope. Goodbye, my loves, goodbye.

13 *Cicero to Atticus* (Att. *3.13*) *Thessalonica, August 5, 58* BCE

Cicero writes about his hopes for recall. He's particularly encouraged by the newly elected tribunes, especially Titus Annius Milo.

I know I had written I'd be in Epirus, but, once I realized the hope of recall was fading and vanishing, I changed my plans and stayed in Thessalonica. I decided I'd wait there until you wrote about what you mentioned in your last letter: that, after the elections, some motion would be made in the Senate regarding my situation. That's what Pompey had told you. So now that the elections are over and I still haven't heard from you, I'll assume no letter means that nothing came of it. I'll try not to be irritated that the hope I was clinging to didn't last very long. The positive change in my favor, which you said might occur, well, people coming here don't think it will happen. My remaining hope lies with the tribunes designate and, if I wait for them, there's nothing to make you think I've failed taking into account my own cause or my friends' goodwill.

You often reproach me for taking this so hard; give me a break. You see how my horrible blow is more severe than anyone else's you've ever witnessed. You write you've heard that even my mind is afflicted by grief: I assure you, my intellect is still soundly intact. If only it had been so in my hour of danger, when I realized that the people I thought cared about me deeply were in fact my cruelest and most vicious enemies! When they saw me wilting from fear, they took full advantage, utilizing every bit of their malice and betrayal to cut me down. Now, since I must go to Cyzicus, where I'll receive letters sporadically, please, I beg you, write me in full detail everything I should know. Look out for my brother Quintus and be nice to him. If, despite my own pathetic situation, I leave him intact and unharmed, I won't regard myself as a total failure.

14 *Cicero to Atticus* (*Att.* 4.1) *Rome, September 10, 57* BCE

Cicero was right to be hopeful about the tribunes. With the help of Milo, the Senate passed a decree recalling Cicero, and on August 5 he returned to Italy, arriving at Brundisium.

As soon as I arrived at Rome and found a trustworthy courier to deliver a letter, I decided the first thing I needed to do was congratulate you on my recall. I'll be frank: when it came to advising me, I didn't think you were any braver or more vigilant than I was in advising myself. Nor, given my cautionary warnings to you, did I think you were particularly diligent in safeguarding my well-being. Still, it was you who, from the beginning, shared my mistake (or rather my madness) and proved to be an ally in my unfounded fear; you were the one utterly dismayed over my departure, the one who worked tirelessly, enthusiastically, diligently, and endlessly to secure my recall. So I wholeheartedly assure you that, amid my utter joy and long-awaited congratulations, the only thing that would make my happiness complete is to see you or, better yet, to give you a big hug. Once I've done that, if I ever lose this happiness and don't recoup your delightful company (time accrued over the last months), then I won't consider myself worthy of recall.

I've generally won back (even more than I had hoped for) what I thought was going to be the most difficult things to recover: my illustrious position as a lawyer, my influential popularity in the Senate, and my favor among honest men. As for the state of my private affairs, you know how extensively my properties have been, quite literally, smashed into pieces, dispersed, and plundered. I'm in a bad place; I really need not so much your financial help, which I think of as my own, but your ideas for consolidating and enriching what I still have left.

Now, even though I think you've heard everything from your friends' letters or messengers (or gossip), I'll briefly recount what I think you'll want to hear – straight from the horse's mouth. I left Dyrrachium on August 4, the same day the law for my recall was put to a vote. I arrived at Brundisium on August 5. My little Tullia was there. It happened to be her birthday, as well as the celebration day of the origin of Brundisium as a colony and of the nearby goddess of Salus. These coincidental events aroused great attention and rejoicing from the locals. On August 11 I learned from Quintus' letter that, thanks to the marvelous enthusiasm of people from all ages and ranks and to an unbelievable turnout from voters outside Rome, the law was passed in the centuriate assembly. I continued my journey, accompanied by the most distinguished citizens of Brundisium, who were honoring me, and by various town delegates, who were coming out to congratulate me along the way.

I then arrived outside Rome; anyone and everyone came out to greet me, except those who couldn't conceal or deny that they were my enemies. When I reached the Capena Gate, the steps of the temples were packed with crowds of people delivering congratulations and applauding loudly. The same applause – just as loud and plentiful – followed me all the way up to the Capitol. The crowd that had come to meet me in the forum and on the Capitoline itself was just incredible. The next day, on September 5, I gave a speech of thanksgiving in the Senate.

Two days later: a severe grain shortage caused a spike in prices. At Clodius' instigation a group of men went first to the theater and next to the Senate, all in uproar, blaming the grain shortage on me. For the next two days the Senate met to discuss the situation. The general population and the honest men nominated Pompey to oversee the supply. Pompey was happy to accept, and the crowd specifically demanded that I propose the commission. I did so in a detailed speech. Except for Messalla and Afranius, all the *consulares* were absent (they said it was unsafe for them to express an opinion), and thus, following my proposal, the Senate passed the decree, stating that Pompey was to be put in charge of the grain supply and a law was to be proposed to secure his commission. The Senate's decree was recited right away, and, after the people applauded in their new silly way whenever my name was announced, all the magistrates present – with the exception of one praetor (Clodius' brother) and two tribunes – invited me to give a public speech. And so I did.

The next day, before a packed Senate and all the *consulares*, Pompey was granted everything he requested. He asked for 15 deputies, naming me first and announcing I'd be his alter ego in everything. The consuls wrote up a law stipulating that Pompey be given complete control over the whole world's grain supply; Messius proposed an addendum putting Pompey in charge of the operating budget and giving him a fleet, an army, and power of veto in the provinces. That consular law now looks like small potatoes compared to Messius' (which is unbearable). If you ask Pompey, he says he wants the former, but his friends say he wants the latter. The *consulares* are boiling, most of all Favonius. I'm keeping my mouth shut: the chief priests haven't given an answer about my Palatine house, namely whether they'll deconsecrate the shrine to Liberty that Clodius erected on its site, so that I may actually be able to rebuild on my own property. If they remove the religious bond, I'll have a marvelous spot, and the consuls will estimate the building's worth by senatorial decree. If not, the temple will be demolished and they'll award a contract in their own name, offering an estimate for the whole thing. So that's how it stands: "In good times, unstable, in bad times, good," as the saying goes.

As you know, my finances are in dire straits. There are other private matters, but I won't entrust them to a letter. As for Quintus, he's the epitome of devotion, virtue, and loyalty, and I love him just as he deserves. I'm waiting for you: come quickly so I can take advantage of your advice. I'm beginning my "second life," so to speak. Those who supported me while I was in exile are becoming secretly resentful and openly jealous. I really and truly need you.

*15 Cicero to L. Lucceius (*Fam. *5.12) April 12, 55* BCE

A certain – call it bashful – embarrassment has kept me from speaking to you face to face, although I've often tried to summon the nerve to do it. But now I'll go ahead, since distance makes me bolder: a letter does not blush.

I have a desire burning with an intensity that is perhaps not commendable, but certainly not blameworthy: I want my name to be remembered and celebrated in a literary work of yours. You've often promised this, so please forgive my impatience. Your latest volume is excellent and, although that's no surprise, it still surpassed my expectations. In fact it has so captivated me, or should I say enflamed me, that I want you to create a written monument of my deeds – as soon as possible. It's not just a record for posterity and a certain hope of immortality that justify my urgency, but a desire to enjoy – while I'm alive – the authority of *your* version, the proof of your kindness, and the appeal of your literary genius.

Even as I write this line, I'm fully aware you're saddled with other great burdens, both works in progress and projects you're about to start. But, because I thought your accounts of the Italian War and Civil War were nearing completion and you said you were moving toward subsequent historical events, I'd be failing if I didn't suggest two possibilities to ponder: would you prefer to interweave my deeds with those from the same chronological period or, alternatively, would you rather cover the conspiracy at Rome separately from an account of foreign hostilities and wars? The latter is something that many Greeks have done when distinguishing certain wars from their continuous histories; so did, for example, Callisthenes in his treatment of the Phocian War, Timaeus with the Pyrrhic War, and Polybius with the Numantian War. In my opinion it doesn't make much difference when it comes to my acclaim, but it *does* when my eagerness is at stake: I want you to start immediately on the subject of those historical events that relate to me – rather than waiting until you reach this exact point in your history and composing in strict chronological order. Moreover, if you focus completely on just one event and one single individual, I can already imagine how much richer and more brilliant the work will be.

I'm fully aware of how presumptuous I'm being – first, in making such a request (you can tell me "no" if you're busy); and, second, in asking you to sing my praises. What if, in your opinion, events don't seem to deserve such accolades? Yet, once someone steps over the boundary of modesty, he might as well go all the way to shamelessness. So I'll level with you and be frank: please extol the subject more energetically than you're perhaps inclined. Ignore the laws of history this once and don't frown upon bias – that is, on condition it works in my favor, of course. This is something you wrote about so pleasantly in one of your introductions, where you showed you couldn't be swayed any more than Xenophon's Hercules could be swayed by Pleasure at the expense of Virtue, in the famous allegory. Let our mutual affection make you a touch more liberal even than truth permits.

If I'm successful in persuading you to undertake this endeavor, I'm quite sure the material will be worthy of your ability and readiness. In my opinion, a work of moderate length seems best: something starting with the conspiracy's inception and continuing down to my recall. You'll be able to apply your particular knowledge of changing political tides to expound the origins of the insurrection or the remedies for the turmoil. You'll also censure what needs reproaching, praise what you think merits approval, and explain why it does. If, after your habit, you think you should use a rather liberal hand, I'm confident you'll note many people's treachery, deceit, and betrayal of me. My misfortunes will offer plenty of variety, and the kind of pleasure that – with you as the author – captivates readers' minds as they carry on.

Nothing delights a reader more than the ebb and flow of events and the vicissitudes of fortune. They offered no joy while one was living through them, but now they'll be a pleasure to read: recollecting previous pains is enjoyable once they are out of harm's way. For everyone else (and I mean those who haven't suffered troubles of their own and who contemplate others' misfortunes with detachment) pleasure resides in pity. Who can claim to experience no enjoyment or sympathy in recalling the episode of Epaminondas dying on the battlefield at Mantinea? Remember how he ordered the javelin to be yanked from his body only after hearing, in answer to his question, that yes, his shield was indeed safe; thus, despite the agony of his wound, he'd die honorably and at peace. Whose imagination isn't stirred reading about Themistocles' exile and return? A straightforward chronological survey of history offers about as much inspiration as a calendar. But the varied and unforeseen trials and tribulations of a *prestigious* man, in particular, evoke awe, tension, joy, anxiety, hope, and fear. If these conclude in a glorious death, the mind is fully satisfied by the incredibly joyous delight of reading.

Thus you'll thoroughly fulfill my desire if you take this route: separate the "drama," so to speak, of my accomplishments and experiences from the main part of your work, which comprises a successive history of events. For my story comprises many varied "acts" and "scenes" involving plans and circumstances. I'm not afraid of coming across as someone trying to ensnare you and to win your favor through the trap of trivial flattery when I choose *you*, above everyone else, to praise and celebrate me. You know your own abilities: you're smart enough to distinguish between mere flatterers and those who are envious and thus stingy with their praise. Further, I'm not so foolish that I'd entrust my eternal glory to someone who, in commemorating me, wouldn't also achieve a literary immortality equal to his literary genius. Alexander didn't purposely select Apelles to paint his portrait, or Lysippus to sculpt his image, just to do them a favor, but because he thought their artistic creations would bring immortal fame to them no less than to him. And those portraits became identifiable to audiences who had never seen the subjects in person; but, even if there weren't any artistic images memorializing these famous men, they'd still be famous. King Agesilaus of Sparta is a perfect example: he didn't allow paintings or sculptures to be made of him, but he's no less renowned than those who did. For one brief encomiastic pamphlet composed by the historian Xenophon for this king has virtually surpassed all the paintings and statues celebrating all the others.

But there's another reason why inclusion in *your* work rather than in someone else's would particularly satisfy me and distinguish my name: not only will I benefit from your literary genius, as Timoleon did from Timaeus' or Themistocles from Herodotus', but I'll also benefit from your authority, since you're recognized as a famous public figure, acclaimed as a leader in the republic's most serious public matters. You and your work will not only be the herald of my fame – as Homer was for Achilles; and this is something that Alexander said when he visited Sigeum – but its authoritative voice. I agree with the poet Naevius, whose Hector is happy not just "in being praised," but "in being praised by a man who is himself worthy of praise."

But if I'm unsuccessful in my request, that is, if something prevents you from saying "yes" (for I can't imagine you'd possibly turn me down), I might be forced to do what many often frown upon: I'll write an autobiography. After all, many illustrious men provide a precedent for this. Still, you're aware there are drawbacks to this literary genre: when writing about themselves, people must be more restrained with self-praise and skip over what deserves blame. Autobiography is less trustworthy, less authoritative: many fault it, saying that the announcers at the public games are more modest. That's because, after they've placed victory crowns on others' heads and loudly proclaimed the winners' names, when it's their turn to be presented with the victory garland, they request a different herald to do the job so they're not forced to announce their own name. I hope to avoid this scenario myself and, if you accept my request, I will – hence this letter.

Are you wondering why, even after you've repeatedly assured me you'll accurately recount the events of my consulship in your book, I'm now so zealous and pushy? Blame it on that burning desire I mentioned at the beginning of my letter – the urgency of the situation. My mind is racing with excitement as I think about how others will read your work during my own lifetime and how I'll enjoy a touch of glory while I'm still alive.

If it's not too troublesome, please write back and let me know your thoughts. If you decide to take on my request, I'll collect my notes on all the relevant events. If you postpone until some later date, I'll talk to you in person. Meanwhile, keep up the good work, put on the finishing touches, and continue in your affection for me.

16 *Cicero to Marius* (Fam. *7.1) Rome, October 55* BCE

Cicero writes to Marius at Stabiae, congratulating him for missing the shows hosted by Pompey to celebrate the grand opening of his new theater and its temple dedicated to Venus Genetrix. According to Pliny the Elder (*Natural History* 8.21; 36.115), Pompey's theater was the first permanent one erected in Rome; it was located in Campus Martius and could hold approximately 40,000 spectators.

If gout or some other illness kept you from attending the shows, count yourself lucky, not prudent. But if you consciously rejected what everyone else oohs and ahhhs over, and you purposely chose not to attend even though your health allowed it, then I'm happy for two reasons. First, I'm glad you're not sick. Second, as long as you used your free time wisely, I'm pleased you had the good sense to skip the shows, a pastime that other people marvel at for no good reason. No doubt you can fully enjoy your free time in a remarkable way, since you're practically secluded – you stay in peace and quiet at your lovely villa. While *you*, I'm sure, were tucked away in that little study of yours, enjoying the view of the Stabian Bay and of the port of Misenum through a window designed for exactly that purpose and spending

Figure 2.1 Gladiator fighting lion. Roman fresco from the amphitheatre of Merida, second century AD. Location: Archaeological Museum Merida Spain. Source: Alfredo Dagli Orti / The Art Archive at Art Resource, NY

your morning with some light reading, those of us who left you there were instead dealing with packed crowds and watching pantomimes while we were nearly comatose with sleep. While *you* got to enjoy the rest of your day just as you chose, *we* were forced to endure the "amusements" Spurius Maecius judged enjoyable for us.

If you're curious, the shows were incredibly extravagant, though not to your taste (which I'm extrapolating from my own). First, those actors who came out of retirement just for this special occasion are the same who, I assumed, left the stage to preserve their reputation! In particular, your favorite, our friend Aesopus, was so bad that he'd earn applause – but only if he retired! At the beginning of performing an oath, he lost his voice at that line of the play that goes "If I knowingly deceive." Do I need to continue? You're familiar with other shows that have not an ounce of the charm they usually have. The excessive staging overwhelmed the lightheartedness of the performances – it was an over-the-top lavishness I'm sure you'd happily do without. What's enjoyable about watching 600 mules employed for a performance of *Clytemnestra*, or 3,000 mixing bowls for *The Trojan Horse*, or infantry and cavalry armed with a motley of weapons for some stage battle? The crowds were bowled over at the spectacle, but you? You wouldn't have been impressed.

But if you spent your time listening to Protogenes recite, as long as he wasn't reading *my* speeches (!), you surely had a far more rewarding vacation than we did. I don't think you, at least, would have enjoyed the

Greek dramatic performances or the Atellan farces, especially since you probably observe the same ridiculous skits in your own town meetings at Pompeii! And you dislike the Greeks so much that you actually avoid taking Greek Street on the way home to your villa! Why should I assume you'd enjoy watching athletes compete, since I know how much you despise gladiators? Pompey himself admits he wasted time and money on them. The rest comprised wild beast hunts, two a day for five days; nobody denies their lavishness, but why would a cultured person enjoy watching a weak man savagely butchered by a much stronger animal, or a magnificent beast pierced with a spear? Even if they were worth seeing, you've been there, done that: we certainly saw nothing new. The final day was reserved for the elephants: the unsophisticated crowds were amazed at the show but didn't like it. Quite the opposite, the audience pitied the elephants, sensing something human about them.

So that you may not think I've been completely unhappy or entirely idle, I'll tell you: I nearly ruptured a lung defending your friend Gallius Caninius. Yet, if I thought my audience was as ready to give me walking papers as Aesopus' audience, then, by god, I'd call it quits and spend my time with you and our like-minded friends. Even back in my younger, ambition-driven days, when I could refuse an uninteresting case, I was already growing tired of the lawcourts. Now they offer me no life: I receive little reward for all my effort and sometimes I'm obligated to defend men who don't deserve my talents – all at the request of men who do.

So I'm looking for every reason to live my life the way I want. As for you, I commend how you're choosing to spend your free time – I couldn't agree more. I can more easily tolerate your rare visits lately because, even if you were here, I couldn't enjoy your pleasurable company any more than you could enjoy mine (as much as my company is a pleasure): I'm constantly occupied with endless, tiresome obligations. If I can carve out a little free time (I don't expect to escape all my commitments) then I'll give you some lessons in the art of sophisticated living, although you've been studying nothing else for many years now! So, take care of your delicate health and get strong so you can come to my villas and enjoy the scenery from a chaise lounge!

My rather long letter to you is a not an indicator of my copious free time, but of my copious affection for you. Also, if you remember, one of your previous letters hinted that I should write about the shows, so you wouldn't regret missing them. If I've accomplished this, I'm glad. If not, then I'll comfort myself knowing that in the future you'll come to Rome to see me and the shows, and then you won't be depending on one of my letters for your entertainment!

17 Cicero to G. Julius Caesar (Fam. *7.5) Rome, February 54* BCE

Cicero recommends to Caesar his young friend and mentoree, Gaius Trebatius. Trebatius had been studying law in Rome; Cicero hopes to secure him a position on Caesar's staff in Gaul. At the letter's beginning Cicero alludes to his position as legate for Pompey (prefect of the grain supply, see Letter 14); Pompey was also governor of Spain, but, as Cicero subtly (and disapprovingly) hints, he had not yet left for his post. The recommendation letter is a common epistolary type.

Look how much I've convinced myself you're my alter ego in matters involving not only me, but also my friends. I'd consider bringing Gaius Trebatius with me wherever I might end up, so I could send him home weighed down by all the favors and benefits I could possibly give him. Since Pompey is procrastinating in Italy longer than I had anticipated and a certain something else makes me hesitate (you know what I mean), I'm inclined to call off, or at least postpone, my own departure. Therefore I'm now hoping Trebatius might receive from you all he was hoping to receive from me (see how presumptuous I'm being!). And indeed, I have pledged him your goodwill as enthusiastically as I had been pledging my own.

But an incredible fluke has intervened to corroborate my opinion, and it guarantees your generosity: while our friend Balbus and I were having a serious conversation at my house on this very topic, your letter arrives. At the end you write: "I plan on making Marcus Titinius, whom you recommended, a king of Gaul; or, if you prefer, go ahead and refer him to Lepta and send me someone else who could benefit from my favor." Balbus and I both lifted our hands to the sky: such a stroke of good luck – it really could only be a gift from the gods! Accordingly I send you Trebatius, who I thought was worth sending from the very beginning, on my own initiative: your invitation confirms it! Please show him your usual kindness, my dear Caesar, and bestow on this one individual all the benefits I might convince you to confer on my friends willingly.

So, about Trebatius: I won't respond with that old-fashioned expression I used when I wrote you about Milo – you were fully justified to ridicule me for that one! No, I'll write in plain, straightforward Latin, the way sensible people speak: you won't find a better man, or one more decent and self-deprecating. What's more, when it comes to civil law, he leads the pack: he has an unbelievable memory and his general knowledge is incredibly extensive. I'm not asking you to give him a tribuneship or a prefecture or any other formal office, but just your goodwill and generosity (though, if you want to bestow these little marks of distinction on him, I won't stop you). I hand over the whole man, as the saying goes, "from my hand to your hand" – *your hand* – a symbol of victory and sincerity. Although it's hardly appropriate, forgive me for being a touch effusive. Still, let it pass, as I think you will. Take care and think of me fondly, as I do you.

*18 Cicero to Trebatius (*Fam. 7.7*) Cumae, June 54* BCE

I haven't stopped recommending you, but please let me know what progress I'm making. I have the greatest hope in Balbus and I've been scrupulously – and frequently – writing him about you. I'm frequently left scratching my head because I receive plenty of letters from my brother Quintus, who's also in Britain, but I haven't received any from you. I hear there's no gold or silver to plunder. If this is in fact the case, I recommend you capture for yourself a Gallic chariot and race back home to us lickety-split! But if we can still obtain what we want, even without Britain, then be sure to work your way into the "in-crowd" of Caesar's close friends. My brother will be a great help, as well as Balbus, but trust me: your honorable character and hard work will prove to be your greatest assets. You have a particularly generous leader, you're of the perfect age, and you have a singular recommendation (mine) all working in your favor: the only thing you have to worry about is living up to your potential.

*19 Cicero to Trebatius (*Fam. 7.8*) Rome, June 54* BCE

Caesar has written me a very kind letter saying his own hectic schedule hasn't yet allowed him to get to know you well, but that he looks forward to doing so. I wrote back telling him how grateful I'd be if he'd impart upon you as much generosity, help, and attention as possible. But your letter implies you're very impatient, and I'm surprised that you haven't really taken advantage of all the benefits of your tribuneship, especially when it doesn't involve actual military service. I'll complain to Vacerra and Manilius, since I don't dare say anything to Cornelius; he's the one to blame for your foolishness, since it's from him you confess you learned your "wisdom." Why not squeeze out all you can from this opportunity and good fortune? You won't get anything better again. Regarding what you wrote about the jurist Precianus,

I'm not stopping my efforts in recommending you to him. He writes me that you owe him a "thank you." Fill me in on what he means. I await your letters from Britain.

20 *Cicero to his brother Quintus* (Quint. *2.16*) *August 54* BCE

Quintus is stationed in Britain under Caesar's leadership.

Greetings from Marcus to his brother Quintus.

If you read one of my letters in my scribe's hand, then you know I haven't had a second to spare, and when it's my own handwriting, then you know I've had only a minute! Let me tell you, I've never been this busy with court cases and trials, all at the hottest, most oppressive time of the year! But, since you prescribe it, I must carry on. I don't want to look like I'm failing your and Caesar's hopes and plans – particularly since, despite the challenges, all my hard work will translate into significant appreciation and esteem. So you'll be happy to hear I'm working hard not to offend anyone's sensibilities and to win over even those who are disappointed that we've become so tight with Caesar. At the same time you'll be happy I'm receiving the greatest respect and affection from both Caesar's partisans and his non-partisans. An extremely savage debate over electoral bribery occurred in the Senate for many days, and the candidates for consul have taken their argument to such an extreme level that the situation has become unbearable. I stayed out of it. I've decided I'm not going to stick my neck out to try and heal the republic without powerful backup.

On this very day, the tribune paymasters have acquitted Drusus on the charge of rigging the jury; he scraped by with just four votes (the senators and the equestrians voted largely against him). This afternoon I'm going to court to defend Vatinius, likely an easy win. Elections are postponed until September. Then I've got Scaurus' trial coming up and I won't fail him. I'm generally not a fan of Sophocles' *Dinner Party*, though I see your version is a fun, light-hearted, little one-act play.

Now to what I should probably have started with: I love all your letters about Britain! I found myself fearing the ocean and the island's coastline: I'm certainly not belittling what is yet to come, but your future descriptions offer more hope than fright, and my anxiety comes more from the anticipation of your letters than from any worry. It's clear you have a truly worthy topic: the area's landscape, its natural way of life and its varied topography, its customs, its inhabitants, the battles, and, of course, the general who's leading you! I'm more than happy to help you, as you asked and in the ways you want; I'll send you the verses you requested, though I might as well be sending "sand to the Arabs"!

But come on! Don't keep me in the dark! What does Caesar really think about my poem? He already wrote saying he had read the first book and that he hasn't read anything better, not even in Greek; the rest he described as a bit "slow," to use his term. Be honest, is it the style or the subject matter he doesn't like? No worries, I can handle the truth – I won't love myself any less! Write me frankly as always, my brother.

21 *Quintus to his brother Marcus Tullius* (Fam. *16.16*) *Gaul, end of May/beginning of June 53* BCE

Quintus congratulates Cicero on freeing his slave, Tiro.

As happy as I am at the prospect of seeing you, Quintus Jr., your dear sweet Tullia, and your dear Marcus, you've made me just as happy with your news about Tiro: your determining that he didn't deserve the hand fortune dealt him and preferring us to enjoy him as our friend rather than as a slave. Believe me, when I read your letter and his, I jumped for joy; thank you and congrats! If Statius' loyalty makes me so happy, how much *you* must appreciate these same qualities in Tiro and, beyond his serviceable qualities, his literary talent, great conversation, and kindliness. I love you for many reasons, but especially for this, and also for the way you announced the news: I saw your true heart in that letter. I have promised Sabinus' slaves everything they want and will follow through.

22 *Cicero to Caelius Rufus (*Fam. 2.11*) Laodicea, April 4, 50* BCE

Cicero is now serving (rather reluctantly) as governor of Cilicia. Cicero writes to the Aedile Rufus about acquiring panthers for his upcoming games. The Megalensian Games celebrated the festival of Cybele (Magna Mater), which began on April 4.

Could you ever imagine words would fail me (yes, me!) – not only the words you orators use back in Rome, but even the everyday words I use here? Believe it or not, I am indeed speechless: I'm incredibly anxious about the decrees for provinces. An unexpressible yearning for the city possesses me, an unimaginable desire to see my friends – you especially. I'm tired of being here in my province: I've already attained enough fame: I don't need to enhance it further. Rather, I worry about my good luck changing; or maybe it's because the whole business of governing a province is unsuited to my strengths, since I'm better matched and more skilled for far greater burdens in service to the state; or, perhaps because the fear of a war with the Parthians hangs over my head, and it seems I can avoid it if I leave my province on the appointed day.

About the panthers: I've ordered the regular hunters to put all their efforts into capturing them, but there's a huge shortage; so they're heard complaining that the only traps being set in my province are for them. As a result they've left Cilicia for Caria! Nonetheless, we're fervently working on it, especially Patiscus. Whatever panthers are found, they're for you, though I have no idea how many they'll end up being. Rest assured, by god, I'm very focused on your aedilship. In fact today reminds me of it, since today is April the 4th. Please write and tell me everything about the current state of politics: I'll consider your report to be the most reliable one I get.

23 *Cato to Cicero (*Fam. 15.5*) Late June 50* BCE

Cato writes to Cicero, who is still in Cilicia, "congratulating" him on the thanksgiving (*supplicatio*) decreed to him by the Senate following his military achievements. A thanksgiving is a formal public prayer of thanks to the gods in honor of a military victory or a similar achievement. Cato congratulates Cicero, but also explains why he voted against the decree. Cicero seems to have been hoping for not just a thanksgiving, but a triumph.

Because we're friends and the republic urges it, I congratulate you: the same character, integrity, and conscientiousness you employed as a civilian at Rome during a time of crisis, you have used in Cilicia as a general – and with just as much purposefulness. Accordingly, I did what my conscience allowed me to do: both in speech and by way of supporting the decree once it was passed, I commended your success in defending your province with honesty and sound decision making, in preserving the monarchy and its king for the Ariobarzani people, and in reestablishing our allies' goodwill.

Regarding the decree: this was a situation that depended not on luck, but on your excellent administration in ensuring the republic's security. If you prefer us to thank the gods instead of giving *you* the credit, then I'm happy the Senate voted you the decree. But if you think a thanksgiving gives you the prerogative to celebrate a triumph, and thus it is for *this* reason that you prefer us to credit fortune rather than you, then, quite frankly, remember that a thanksgiving doesn't necessarily guarantee a triumph. Besides, the Senate's judgment that a province has been successfully administered and preserved by its governor's gentleness and integrity (rather than by military force or the gods' benevolence) is a greater mark of distinction than its awarding of a triumph. And this is exactly the point I was making in my speech.

I've written a longer letter than usual, so you may recognize – as I really hope you will – that first and foremost I was looking out for what I thought would most enhance your prestige, and also that I'm happy things have turned out the way you preferred.

Goodbye, think of me affectionately, and stay on course, applying your uncompromising sternness and diligence both to our allies and to our republic.

24 *Cicero to Cato (*Fam. *15.6) Cilicia, September 50* BCE

"I rejoice in receiving praise from you, father, who have yourself been praised." Thus spoke Hector in Naevius' play, as I think it was. Indeed, it's a joy when praise comes from men who themselves deserve it. Personally, after your letter's congratulations and the credit you gave me in your speech, I'm not sure there's anything left for me to achieve; I think it's especially flattering and satisfying that you freely conceded to friendship what you unequivocally conceded to truth. And if many in our city were Catos (though not everyone; but it's a marvelous thing that we have one at all), then what comparison could I draw between a triumphal chariot or a laurel wreath and the praise I've received from you? In my mind, and in light of your genuine and meticulous judgment, there is nothing more flattering than your speech, of which my friends mailed me a complete copy.

But I explained to you in an earlier letter the reason behind my wish (I won't call it a "desire"); if that's a tad unconvincing, let me offer another explanation: I don't think one should excessively covet the honor; at the same time, if the Senate offers it, I certainly wouldn't want to appear as if I'm turning down my nose at it. Moreover, given all my efforts on the republic's behalf, I hope the Senate will judge me worthy of the honor, especially since it's regularly given.

If it turns out this way, I ask only this: that, since you would grant me what, in your view, "you considered to be the most enhancing," you'll be happy if "things turn out the way I preferred" – to repeat the very kind sentiments you expressed in your letter. So your actions, your opinions, your letter, and the very fact that you were present when the decree was drafted seem proof enough to me that you were in fact pleased with the thanksgiving decree in my honor: I'm fully aware that those who draft the decree are usually the honoree's closest friends. I'll see you soon, I hope, and with any luck the political climate will be better then than I fear now.

25 *Marcus Caelius Rufus to Cicero* (Fam. *8.14) Rome, September 50*

Cicero is still in Cilicia (or on his way home). War between Caesar and Pompey is imminent, and Caelius wonders what side to join.

Capturing the king of Parthia or attacking Seleucia wouldn't be a good enough reason for missing the circus that's going on here in Rome! You should have seen Domitius Ahenobarbus' face when he heard the election results – heard that he had lost the augurship to Mark Antony – what a delicious sight! Voter turnout was huge, and it was clear that voters stuck to party lines; only a tiny number dutifully fulfilled the obligations and ties of friendship. Domitius is so hostile to me that even among his closest friends there's none he despises more. That's because he thinks the election was rigged and I'm the one who orchestrated it! He now rages against those celebrating his loss and summons to court anyone who zealously supported Antony. He has personally prosecuted the young Gnaeus Saturninus, whose questionable history makes him an easy target; we're awaiting the outcome and, following Sextus Peducaeus' acquittal, we're now feeling hopeful.

As for national news: I've frequently written that I don't see peace lasting through the end of the year, and the closer we come to this inevitable clash, the more apparent the danger. At the heart of the issue is this: Pompey declares he won't allow Caesar to be elected consul unless Caesar relinquishes control over his army and provinces; Caesar, on the other hand, is convinced his status is threatened if he gives up his troops. He suggests a compromise: they both hand over their armies. So now their love affair, their scandalous liaison, isn't stepping behind the scenes or receding into backstabbing, but exploding into full-scale war! What am I going to do? I don't know yet. I have no doubt you're facing the same conundrum. On the pro-Caesar side, I have influence and connections with these men; on the pro-Pompey side, I love the cause but hate its supporters. I know you're fully aware that men caught in a personal dispute should choose the more honest cause – as long as the dispute involves civil law and not weapons; but when it escalates into war and the battlefield is imminent, they should choose the stronger side – and hence the safer one. In this squabble, as I see it, Pompey will have the support of the Senate and of those who control the courts, while the fearful and the hopeless will align with Caesar. As for their armies, there's just no comparison. At any rate, there's still time to weigh the pros and cons and pick a side.

I nearly forgot the whole point of this letter: have you heard that Censor Appius, that "paragon of virtue," is pulling off the most marvelous feats? He's aggressively conducting inquisitions into fine china and paintings, landholdings and debt, and has convinced himself that his censorship is all about soap and face cream. Here's where he's made his mistake: in trying to wash away the city's scum, he reveals the dirt beneath his own fingernails! Run as fast as your legs can carry you, so you can have a good laugh: Drusus (of all people!) overseeing a trial that cites the Scantinia law on sexual perversion and Appius' investigation of plates and pictures! Trust me, it's well worth the sprint! Our Curio is considered smart for remitting his opposition regarding pay for Pompey's troops.

To conclude, you ask what I think about the future: if one or the other doesn't go off to fight the Parthian War, I predict a huge clash imminently, which will only be settled by sword and force. Both of them are mentally and militarily prepared. If it weren't for the serious danger involved, this would be one heck of a spectacular show that Fortune is now preparing for you!

26 *Cicero to Tiro (*Fam. *16.4) Leucas, November 7, 50* BCE

Cicero writes to Tiro, who had become ill on the journey home from Cilicia. Cicero left him at Patrae with his friend Lyso.

Tullius sends warmest greetings to his dear Tiro, and so do his son, his brother Quintus, and Quintus' son.

I have mixed feelings about your letter: the first page upset me deeply, the second made me a tad relieved. I'm now even more convinced that, until you're definitely well again, you should stay put and not attempt a journey by road or sea. I'll see you soon enough if I see you when you're strong and healthy. You write that the doctor has a good reputation and I hear the same thing, but I completely disapprove of his treatments. He shouldn't have given you broth when you've been nauseous. Nevertheless, I've carefully written to him and Lyso. I've also written at length to Curius, a very pleasant man with the highest sense of duty and humanity. In my letter I asked that, as long as you give the okay, you be transferred to his house; our Lyso, I fear, may be neglectful on two counts: first, all Greeks are like this, and, second, he never replied to my letter. But you approve of him, so I leave it up to you to decide. There's one thing I demand, my Tiro: don't blink an eye at the cost – whatever it takes to make you well again. I've written to Curius that he's to give you whatever you need. I'm thinking the doctor should get some payment in order to become more attentive.

Your help is immeasurable, both at home and in the forum, at Rome and abroad, in private and in public, in my studies and in my writings. You'll outdo yourself if, as hope, I see you again healthy. If everything goes right, I think you'll have a perfectly enjoyable trip sailing home with Quaestor Mescinius. He isn't a total bumpkin and, from what I can tell, he seemed to have a liking for you. When you've given full attention to your health, then and only then, my Tiro, consider returning. There's no way I want you hurrying back right now. You have one job: get better. My Tiro, know there's no one who loves me who doesn't also love you; and, just as you and I worry over your health, so do many others. Until now you haven't had a chance to recover, since you were so concerned about not disappointing me; but now there's nothing standing in your way. Put aside everything and heal your body. I'll measure your affection by how diligently you take care of yourself. Goodbye, my Tiro, goodbye; goodbye and take care. Lepta says hello, as does everyone else. Goodbye.

27 *Cicero to Atticus (*Att. *7.6) Formiae, December 18, 50* BCE

I don't have anything to write. You already know everything and I don't expect anything new from you, but let me keep my habit of sending off anyone going your way with a letter.

I'm enormously nervous about the current political situation; as of now, I haven't found anyone who thinks it would be better to fight than to give in to Caesar's demand. His request is utterly brazen, it's true, and even more drastic than we thought. So why begin opposing him now? The situation is no more serious than when we voted in favor of his five-year extension, or when we allowed him to stand as a candidate *in absentia* – unless perhaps we have given him weapons then only to make him a fully armed enemy to fight now! You'll say: "What, then, are your thoughts?" Well, it's not what you'll hear coming out of my mouth. My honest opinion is that war must be avoided at all costs, but I'll *say* whatever Pompey says and I won't do so out of weakness. To differ from Pompey on such great matters may have huge repercussions on the state, and I can't get away with this like other people.

28 Cicero to Terentia and Tullia, and Marcus to his mother and sister (Fam. 14.14) Minturnae, January 23, 49 BCE

Cicero and his son write to Terentia and Tullia about whether to stay at Rome amid impending civil war.

Cicero to Terentia and Tullia, his two dearest, and Marcus to his wonderful mother and sweet sister, warmest greetings.

If you're well and good, so are we. It's now up to you, not just me, what your plan will be. If Caesar's going to come to Rome on good behavior, then you can safely stay put, with peace of mind; but if he goes nuts and allows the city to be plundered, I fear not even Dolabella himself would be able to give us enough protection. I'm also afraid that, if we're cut off from each other, it won't be possible to leave when you do decide. Another thing – and you're in a better position to judge this: what are other women of your status doing? Are they staying in Rome? If not, think whether you can remain there and still maintain your decorum. As of now, provided I can maintain this location, you can stay comfortably with me here or at another one of our estates. There's also this concern: at Rome basic supplies will run out before long. Please talk it all over with Pomponius, Camillus, and anyone else you see fit. Most of all, stay strong: don't be frightened. Labienus has improved our situation; even Piso is proving helpful by leaving the city and accusing his own son-in-law [Caesar] of treason. My dearest hearts, write me as often as you can about what you're doing and what's going on there. Quintus and his son and Rufus all say hello.

29 Cicero to Atticus (Att. 8.3) Cales, February 18–19, 49 BCE

Cicero wrote this letter during a stopover at Cales on his way to join Pompey at Luceria; but, on hearing about Caesar's actions at Cornifinium (located just east of Rome) and on finding his way blocked, he returned to Formiae the next day.

I'm exceedingly troubled by these terrible, hideous events; although I can't speak to you face to face, I still want your advice. Here's the issue: if Pompey leaves Italy, which I'm expecting, what do you think I should do? To help you out, let me briefly run down my pro/con list for both sides. On the pro-Pompey side: I really owe Pompey for facilitating my recall; we are mutually close friends; and we share the interests of the republic. All these factors lead me to believe that I should join my course of action – or my fortune – with his. But on the other hand there's this: if I stay here and desert the camaraderie of Rome's most illustrious and excellent citizens, I must subject myself to the power of one man [Caesar]; even if in many instances he shows he's my friend (and you know how cautious I was, foreseeing how the clouds of storm begin to gather), there are still two considerations. First, how much can I trust him? Second, regardless of how reliable his friendship may be, is it the character of a brave and respectable citizen like myself to stay in this city – where I once enjoyed the highest offices and power, made huge accomplishments, and held the most distinguished priesthood of augur – when I would become little more than a shadow of my former self, I'd be forced into a dangerous situation, and I could possibly damage my reputation, if Pompey ever restored the Roman republic?

On the other side: Pompey has shown himself to be a foolish coward, and he's done everything contrary to my own advice and authority. I won't bring up the past – how he nurtured, built up, and armed Caesar against the state, how he supported Caesar's laws through force and against religious scruple, how he appended Transalpine Gaul to Caesar's provincial command, how he became Caesar's son-in-law by marrying his daughter, how he appeared as augur in Publius Clodius' adoption, how he showed more enthusiasm in facilitating my recall than in preventing my exile, how he managed to prolong Caesar's governorship and was Caesar's cheerleader during his absence, how he pressured the ten tribunes to propose the bill so Caesar could stand as a candidate *in absentia* (even when he had been consul for the third time, and after he began defending the constitution), how he then sanctioned the same proposal through a law of his own, and how he opposed the Consul Marcus Marcellus, who was setting the end date of Caesar's governorship of Gaul on March 1. But even if you leave out all this: what's more despicable, more disturbing than Pompey's departure from Rome – or rather, I should say, his "utterly shameless escape"? What terms of peace aren't more preferable to abandoning one's country? I'll admit the terms were bad, but is there anything worse than this?

"But he'll recover the republic." When? What's being done to realize this hope? Isn't Picenum lost? Isn't the road to Rome left wide open? Hasn't all money, public and private, been handed over to his opponent? On top of everything, there's no organized cause, no forces, no rallying spot for those who'd be willing to support the republic. Apulia has been chosen, the most sparsely populated region of Italy and the farthest away from the threat of an onset of war: a desperate coastal spot, which is convenient – for a quick escape. I unwillingly took position at Capua, not because I wanted to evade my duty, but because in that cause there wasn't one complaint, either from private individuals or from the political ranks; there was a bit of grumbling from the *optimates* – although, as usual, it was barely audible. But I myself sensed that the general population and lowest classes were leaning to the other side, and that many were ready for change; I told Pompey I wouldn't do anything without protection and money. And there wasn't much for me to do, since I realized that, from the beginning, his sole purpose was to flee. If I follow that escape now, where do I go? It can't be with him: when I headed out his way, I learned that Caesar was positioned nearby and I couldn't reach Luceria safely. I'd have to sail by way of the western sea on an uncertain course in the worst winter weather. Moreover, am I to go with my brother, or without him and just with my son? And how? Either option is hugely challenging and stressful. What kind of attack will he launch on us and our estate while we're absent? It would likely be a more vicious attack than on other people, because he might think he'll gain popularity by ruining us. What about these shackles of mine – I mean these laureled fasces of mine? What a pain in the neck to carry them out of Italy! Even if the waters are calm, where will I find a safe place before reaching Pompey? When it comes to the "where" and "how," I'm clueless.

But what if I stay put and side with Caesar? Then I'll be doing what Lucius Philippus did during Cinna's rule, along with Lucius Flaccus and Quintus Mucius Scaevola – and remember how it turned out in Scaevola's case. Still, he'd say he could predict his end (and he was right), but he preferred *that* to marching against his hometown. Thrasybulus chose otherwise when he left Athens when the Thirty Tyrants came to power, and his choice was perhaps the better one, since he later returned and drove them out. Scaevola's and Philippus' policy were sound: to bide one's time and take advantage of an opportunity when it comes along. But in this case those same power struggles create a sticky situation. If Caesar were to be friendly to me – which isn't certain; but if he were – he'd offer me a triumph. Refusing it would be risky; accepting it would endanger my status and popularity with the honest men. "Oh, you're between a rock and a hard place!" you'll say. Yes, but I need a solution. What can be done? Don't assume I'm leaning more in favor of staying because I've piled up more words on that side; it's possible, as happens in many dilemmas, that one side has more words, the other more validity. In that case, while I'm methodically listing my pros and cons in this crucial issue, please give me your opinion. There's a ship waiting for me at Caieta and another one at Brundisium.

Wait, hold on, messengers just arrived as I'm writing this tonight in Cales – they've got a letter... Caesar is outside Corfinium and Domitius is inside the city walls, with a strong army ready to fight. I don't think Pompey is intent on abandoning Domitius, even though he had sent Scipio ahead to Brundisium with two cohorts and wrote to the consuls that he wanted one of them to lead Faustus' legion to Sicily. But it'd be shameful to desert Domitius while he's begging for reinforcements. There is a certain hope, not a strong one in my opinion, but favorable around here, that Afranius has battled with Trebonius in the Pyrenees and pummeled him, and that your friend Fabius, with his cohorts, has changed sides. The biggest hope is that Afranius is on his way with a large band of troops. If so, maybe we'll stay in Italy. As for me, since Caesar's route was uncertain – for it was believed that he was planning to go either to Capua or to Luceria – I've sent Lepta to Pompey with a letter. To avoid falling inadvertently into a bad situation, I'm returning to Formiae. I wanted you to know all this; I'm concluding the letter on a calmer mindset than when I started, not interposing my own opinion, but asking for yours.

30 *Caesar to Oppius and Cornelius Balbus (at Rome)* (Att. *9.7C) March 5, 49* BCE

Oppius and Balbus sent a copy of Caesar's letter to Cicero, who sent it along to Atticus.

I'm happy at how strongly you approved in your last letter of the events that took place at Corfinium. I'll freely follow your advice, all the more as I had already decided, on my own initiative, to offer clemency and to strive to reconcile with Pompey. Let us, if we can, endeavor by these means to recapture everyone's goodwill and enjoy a long-lasting victory. After all, others haven't escaped hatred or held on to victory by employing cruelty – well, that is, except for Lucius Sulla; and I don't intend to emulate him. Let this be the new policy of conquest: we fortify our strength through clemency and generosity. Many options come to mind, and we can consider how best to accomplish this. I ask you to think about it as well.

I captured Numeris Magius, Pompey's prefect. Naturally, I maintained my established practice and made sure he was released immediately. Now two of Pompey's prefects of engineering have fallen into my hands, and I've let them go. If they wish to express their gratitude they should urge Pompey to prefer friendship with *me* to friendship with those who have always been our arch-enemies and whose scheming was a major factor in bringing the republic to its current state.

31 *Caesar to Cicero* (Att. *9.6A) outside Brundisium, March 49* BCE

Caesar asks Cicero to come to Rome and lend support, authority, and advice.

Although I had seen Furnius, it wasn't convenient to speak with him, since I was in a rush marching to Brundisium and had sent the legions ahead. Nonetheless, I couldn't miss the opportunity to write you; and I send him to thank you, even though I've already done so and will likely do so again and again – I'm that deeply indebted to you. Above all, since I'll be near Rome shortly, I'm asking you to meet me there. I'd really like to take advantage of your advice and popularity, your status, and your help in all matters. I repeat what I said before – forgive the haste and brevity of this letter; Furnius will fill you in on everything.

32 *Cicero to Caesar* (Att. 9.11A) *Formiae, March 19–20, 49* BCE

When I read your letter from our Furnius, in which you asked me to come and meet you near Rome, I wasn't particularly surprised that you wanted to "take advantage" of my "advice" and my "status." But when you also mentioned my "popularity" and "help," I was wondering what exactly you meant. Nonetheless, I stayed focused on my hope that, due to your remarkable and singular wisdom, you wanted – I'm assuming – my input on how to attain peace, stability, and the harmony of our fellow citizens. I considered my nature and public stature to be quite suited for the job. If this is the case and if you're serious about protecting our friend Pompey and reconciling him both to yourself and to the republic, then you'll find no one better than me for achieving this goal. As soon as I could, I pleaded with him and the Senate for peace; and I never took sides, not even when open war broke out. I've also believed that in this war you were treated unjustly when your enemies and jealous others tried to prevent you from holding the office legally granted to you by the Roman people.

Not only did I support your honor at that time: I even encouraged others to help you, and now I'm seriously concerned about Pompey's honor. A number of years have passed since I chose you two as my political associates and – as is still the case – my closest friends. So I ask you, or rather beg and plead with every possible prayer: for all your many other concerns, find a spare moment to think how, through your kindness, I can act with goodness, gratitude, and loyalty in accordance with the serious obligation I owe you. If these matters pertained only to me, then I'd hope to obtain your consent; but, as they also pertain to your loyalty and to the republic, I – I, a friend of peace as well as your friend and Pompey's – I think you should place me in a position best suited for securing harmony between you two and among your fellow citizens.

Although I've already thanked you about Lentulus – for saving the man who had saved me – after I read his letter to me, whereby he gratefully extolled your generosity and kindness, I surmised that the safety you granted him also applied to me. If you recognize how thankful I am when it comes to Lentulus, please, I pray, ensure I can show the same gratitude when it comes to Pompey.

33 *Cicero to Atticus* (Att. 9.18) *Formiae, March 28, 49* BCE

Cicero writes an animated letter to Atticus following his meeting with Caesar. At the end he refers to an epigram by the Greek poet Leonidas: "Now is the time to set sail, for the twittering sparrow has arrived along with the pleasant west wind." Cicero means that, as soon as the weather is favorable, he'll set sail and join Pompey.

I followed your advice in both regards: I spoke so as to earn his respect more than his thanks, and I stuck by my decision not to go to Rome. We misjudged him in one respect: that he would be courteous. He couldn't have been ruder. He said my decision was damning: everyone else would be slower to come if I didn't. I pointed out that their situation was different than mine. We discussed it for a while, and then he said: "Well come, then, and discuss the issue of peace." "And express my own opinion?" I asked. "Am I one to tell you what to say?" he replied. "Okay, then here's what I'll say," I said: "'The Senate disapproves of going into Spain or taking troops over to Greece.' And I'll add many disparaging remarks about Pompey." "Naturally I don't want you saying such things." "I thought so," I said, "but I can't agree to your request: either I come and speak my mind, stating outright what I wouldn't skip over in person, or I don't come at all." The long and short of it was that he asked me to think about it. I couldn't say no to that. Then we went our separate ways. I'm quite sure he couldn't give a lick about me. But I'm happy with how I handled myself and it's been a long time since I felt that way.

As for everything else, holy mackerel! What an entourage! What a "summoning of the dead," to use your expression! And Celer was the hero! What a gang of penniless villains and outlaws! What can be said about the son of Servius, the son of Tullus being in the camp that besieged Pompey? There were six legions! Caesar is extremely vigilant, bold. I see no end to this evil. Now it's time for you to produce your words of wisdom. This was the breaking point. Oh, I almost forgot – he got the last word in and said something totally offensive: "If I'm not allowed to make use of your counsel, I'll use someone else's, and I'll stoop to any level to do so." I bet you're saying: "So, now you've seen for yourself that the Caesar you described in your letter is just as you said. Did you let out a groan of disgust?" I did indeed. "Let's hear the rest," you say. The rest? Well, there's not much left to say. He went on his way to the Pedum district and I went to my villa at Arpinum. Now I'm waiting upon Leonidas' "twittering sparrow." You'll say: "Come on, just let bygones be bygones. Even the man we're following has made many a mistake."

I'm awaiting a letter from you. You can't claim, as you once did: "We'll just wait and see how it turns out." This meeting was the last straw, and there's no question that I offended him. I must make my next move quickly. Please send me a letter, one that's chock-full of political news. I'm anxious to hear from you.

34 *Cicero to Varro (*Fam. *9.1) Late 47 or 46* BCE

A year or so after Caesar's victory, Cicero tells Varro he has taken up reading again.

From the letter you wrote Atticus, I just heard where you are and what you've been up to. But I couldn't tell when we'd next see you. I'm hopeful it will be before too long. I wish that were a comfort, but so many serious matters are oppressing me that only the stupidest person could expect my worries to ease any time soon. But maybe you can help me out, or I can help you! You should know, now that I'm back at Rome I've reconciled myself with my old friends – my books! In truth, I deserted them not because I was angry, but because I couldn't bear to look them in the eye. I was so ashamed. In my mind, ever since I threw my hat into those turbulent events and sided with the most disloyal allies, I had disrespected their precepts. They forgive me and welcome me back with open arms. They say you've been much wiser than I, since you never left *your* books' embraces. So now that we've made up, I think it's reasonable to hope that, once I see you, I'll endure more easily everything that's currently overwhelming me. So, whether it's at your villa at Tusculum or Cumae, or – least preferable – at my place at Rome, a long as we're together in person, I'll ensure we both think that that's the most delightful place to be: in each other's company.

35 *Cicero to Terentia* (Fam. *14.20) Venusia, October 1, 47* BCE

I think I'll be arriving at my Tusculan house on the 9th or the day after. Make sure everything is in order. I'll likely be bringing several others to stay with us for a bit. If there's no basin in the bath, get one. Make sure everything else is prepared for good meals and a comfortable stay. Be well.

36 *Cicero to P. Paetus* (Fam. *9.21) Rome, August 46* BCE

Cicero uses military imagery to joke with Paetus about dinner parties.

Your letter doubly delighted me: first, because it made me laugh; and, second, because I saw you're still capable of laughing. It was like skirmishing in a battle of wits! But I wasn't at all offended being pinned down by your verbal attacks. What I *am* upset over is that I wasn't able to get over there as planned. Otherwise you'd find not a dinner guest but a fellow warrior-in-arms! Oh, and what a hero you'd have had at your table! Not the same guy you used to defeat with your *hors d'oeuvre* platter! No, now I march that healthy appetite of mine right up to the deviled eggs and lead on the charge all the way to the roast veal! The praise you used to give me in days gone by – "Oh what an easy-going guy he is! Oh what a low-maintenance guest!" – are all a thing of the past; I've deserted my concern for the republic, my speeches before the Senate, my scrutiny over law cases. I've surrendered to my old enemy, Epicurus, and I'm now in his camp – to reap not the benefits of today's over-indulgence, but the elegant luxury you enjoy – or, let me say, "used to enjoy" when you still had money to burn (though you've never had more real estate than now!). So, get ready! You're dealing with a man who's got a big stomach and knows a thing or two about eating (you understand how late bloomers can be extravagant!). Forget about your little baskets of dates and muffins! I've now advanced to such skill in the art of fine dining that I often risk inviting your pal Verrius along with Camillus! (What foodies! Their names are synonymous with elegance!) I've even had Hirtius over for dinner, though no peacock for him. For that dinner, my cook couldn't meet his match in anything except the hot sauce.

So this is now the sum of my existence: in the mornings I greet clients at my house – many of them honest men, albeit depressed – along with joyous victors, who are especially respectful and polite to me. When morning visits are over, I surround myself with my books or do some reading or writing. A few come to listen to me as if I were some learned sage, simply because I'm slightly more schooled than they are. Then I devote the rest of the day to my body. I've already grieved the death of my homeland more deeply and intensely than any mother for her one and only son. But if you love me, take care of your health, so I don't take advantage of your hospitality while you're lying sick in bed; I've decided I won't spare your culinary generosity even when you're not feeling well!

37 *Cicero to P. Paetus* (Fam. *9.26) Rome, November (?) 46* BCE

Cicero writes to Paetus during a dinner party at the house of Publius Volumnius Eutrapelus, a friend of Caesar. Volumnius' freedwoman Cytheris, a well-known actress who was Mark Antony's mistress, was also present; social mores meant that, for distinguished people like Cicero, sharing company with actresses was unacceptable.

It's around 2:30. I'm just now reclining for dinner and taking out my tablet to write this note to you. "Where was this?" you ask. At the house of Volumnius Eutrapelus, where your friend Atticus sat in the place above me and your friend Verrius sat below. Are you surprised we're so cheerful in our state of slavery? Well, what else is there to do? I'm asking for your advice, since you're the one attending philosophical lectures these days. Should I cry and torture myself? What's the use in that? And for how long? "Live with your books," you say. Well, what else do you think I've been doing? Could I have managed to stay alive if I hadn't been living with them? But there's a limit, even for reading and writing. Once I've put them down, though, I don't really care about dinner (the question you asked Dio the Epicurean). Nonetheless, I can't find anything better to do with my time before I hit the sack.

Listen to the rest: below Eutrapelus, Cytheris reclined. "Is *this* the kind of party the famous Cicero attends, the Cicero all Greeks turned round to face with wonder and awe?" Honestly, I swear, I had no idea she'd be there. Not even that Socratic Aristippus blushed when he was ridiculed for keeping Laïs as a mistress: "She may be my mistress, but she's not my master." (It's better in the original Greek; translate it yourself if you like.) That kind of thing never really did it for me – not even when I was younger, much less now that I'm an old man. I like a good dinner party. There I can speak by the seat of my pants, as the saying goes, and turn my troubles into boisterous laughter. Are you any better? You're the one who, when the philosopher asked in the early morning, "Do you have any questions?" responded: "Why, yes, I do. Where shall I go to dinner tonight?" The poor fool was thinking you were going to ask him whether there was one heaven or an infinite number of them! But what the hell do you care about that? "But, in god's name," you'll reply: "Was dinner *that* important that you had to go *there* of all places?"

So this is how I'm spending my life. Everyday I read or write something. So I don't blow off my friends, I dine with them and I don't break the sumptuary law (if you can even call it a law). No, I stay well within its bounds! So don't quake in fear at the thought of my arrival! You'll find my joking may be gigantic, but my appetite is modest.

38 *Cicero to Fadius Gallus (*Fam. *7.23) Rome, May 46* BCE

Cicero is unhappy with the expensive statuary Gallus purchased for him from Avianius an art connoisseur. Along with Mars, the purchase included copies of a famous Greek statuary type: Bacchants [Bacchae], female followers of the Greek god Dionysus who took part in the god's drunken and orgiastic revelries as part of their cult practice (they're often depicted in the nude).

I had only just returned from Arpinum when I received your letter from the same courier who delivered me a letter from Avianius. In his letter, Avianius very generously offered to begin charging me the debt and the interest from any date I'd choose. Imagine you're me: is it consistent with my (or your) self-respect to ask for credit in the first place, and, second, to receive credit beyond a year? But this would all be a non-issue, my dear Gallus, if you had actually bought me the pieces I wanted and kept within my price-point. Oh well, I'm still grateful to you for making the purchases. Obviously I realize you expended a great deal of time and effort buying things that *you* liked (and thought worthy of me), and I've always considered you a man of exceptional taste. Nonetheless, I really hope Damasippus follows through and offers to buy the pieces from me: there's not a single one I have any interest in keeping.

Being unacquainted with my buying practice, you purchased four or five for an amount I wouldn't spend on all the statuary in the whole wide world! You compare these awful Bacchants to the Muses Metellus has in his house. Seriously? Where's the similarity? First of all, I'd never think those Muses were worth this chunk of change – and I know they'd share my opinion! Besides, Muses would at least harmonize with my library and interests. Where the hell am I supposed to put statues of Bacchants? Yes, they're beautiful, as you say. I know the type well and have seen them before. But I would have explicitly commissioned statues of a specific, familiar type, if I'd wanted that. What I usually buy are statues I can decorate my palaestra with the way someone usually decorates a space dedicated to philosophical discussions. But come on! A statue of Mars? For *me*, the champion of peace? Thank god Saturn wasn't included in the purchase – otherwise, between the two of them, I'd really be in debt! A statue of Mercury, the god of profit, would have been better. Maybe then we'd have struck a better deal with Avianius.

You said that the table stand was originally meant for you: if you like it, go ahead and keep it. But if you've changed your mind, I'll hold on to it. For what you spent on all these pieces, I'd prefer my money going toward purchasing a little place at Tarracina as a stopover en route to Formiae; that way I wouldn't always inconvenience my host. I blame my freedman: I explained exactly what I wanted him to buy. I also blame Junius, whom I think you know – he's Avianius' friend. I'm having some new sitting alcoves built in my little gallery colonnade at my Tusculan villa; I wanted to decorate them with some pictures, and, if anything, paintings are right up my alley for this sort of thing. If I'm stuck with your purchases, however, tell me where they are and when and how they'll be transported here. If Damasippus isn't going to stick to his offer and buy them off me, I'll find some pseudo-Damasippus who will, even if I lose money.

Regarding what you wrote about the house: as I was leaving I entrusted the matter to my Tullia, for I was just walking out of the door when I got your letter. I had already informed your friend Nicia about it, since he is, as you know, good friends with Cassius. But before I received your most recent letter, I had returned and asked Tullia what she had accomplished. She said she was working through Licinia (but I don't think Cassius is particularly close to his half-sister), who replied that, since her husband was out of town (he had left for Spain), she didn't dare move into a new house without his knowledge. I'm so grateful you value our relationship and daily interaction enough to purchase a house where you'll be not only in the same neighborhood but practically right next door – and that you're in a rush to make the move! I swear on my life, I'm just as eager as you to make this happen, so I'll do everything I can to help. Clearly, it will be mutually beneficial for us both. If I make any progress I'll be sure to let you know. Write back with the latest and let me know when I can expect you.

39 *Cicero to Fadius Gallus* (Fam. *7.26) Tusculum, late 46 or early 45* BCE

I've been suffering for the past ten days from a serious bout of gastritis, but I didn't have a fever and consequently couldn't convince people who were coming to me for help that I really was sick. So I've fled to my villa at Tusculum. And this was after a two-day fast with not even a drop of water! Completely laid low by exhaustion and hunger, I was craving your services more than I thought you might need mine! While I shudder at the thought of any illness, I especially dread the maladies described by your Epicurus: "I suffer from a horrible case of strangury and dysentery." The Stoics attack him for this, attributing the former to gluttony and the latter to even more shameful over-indulgence. I had particularly dreaded the dysentery, but it appears that a change of locale and release from stress (or maybe it just running its course) have made me feel much better.

In case you're wondering how this all came about (or how I let it happen), I have to say the sumptuary law that was intended to effect simple living has been the culprit of my woes. Ever since those elegant foodies decided to bring into vogue all the earthy ingredients the law excludes, they've been concocting the tastiest dishes from mushrooms, herbs, and every possible type of greens. I fell prey to the food at Lentulus' augural dinner, and it gave me such a case of the runs, I think it has only just stopped today. So I, the Cicero who once easily abstained from oysters and eels, I am now victimized by beets and weeds! From now on I'll be more careful.

Once you learned about the situation from Anicius (who saw me starting to turn green), you had good reason not only for sending a concerned letter, but even for making a visit to me. I'm considering staying here until I fully mend, for I've lost both strength and weight. But I expect to recover both – if I get over this bout completely.

40 *Cicero to Cassius (*Fam. *15.17) Rome, January 46* BCE

You have the most backwards couriers. They don't upset me personally, but still, when they're just about to walk out the door, they earnestly demand a letter and when they arrive they have none to deliver. They'd make it a lot more convenient if they actually gave me a second to write. Instead, they come wearing their traveling clothes, saying that their companions are awaiting them at the city's gate. So you'll have to forgive me: once again you're getting another short note. Expect a good, long one soon. But why am I defending myself? Aren't *your* couriers coming to *me* empty-handed and returning to you with a letter in hand?

Well, here you go, so that I have something to send you: we have the death of Publius Sulla Senior; some are saying muggers killed him, others indigestion. The people couldn't care less which it was; they're just happy he's ashes now. With that wisdom of yours I'm sure you'll bear this news with equanimity, but we've lost the city's "main attraction"! People are saying Caesar will take it hard, fearing it will check the sharpness of his spear at the auctions. Mindius the grocer and Attius the paint-seller are really celebrating now that they lost their rival competitor!

No news about Spain, but I'm expecting to hear something big. The rumors are depressing, but uncorroborated. Our Pansa left town on December 29, decked out in all his military garb, so that anyone might now believe your recent doubts: "Good is best for it's own sake." For, since he's uplifted many from their bad luck and proven himself an upstanding man, even in these dark times he received an impressive amount of goodwill from the honest men.

I'm really happy you're still staying at Brundisium and I approve your decision. I wholeheartedly think you're acting wisely if you remain "uninvolved," as the Stoics prescribe. Indeed I, who adore you, will be grateful. And please, next time you're mailing any letters home, don't forget about me. I never allow anyone going your way (if I know about it) to leave without a letter for you. Goodbye.

41 *Cicero to Atticus (*Att. *12.15) Astura, March 9, 45* BCE

Following the death of Tullia, Cicero writes to Atticus in despair.

Please make my apologies to Appuleius every day, since a one-time excuse isn't enough. In my state of loneliness I talk to no one, not a soul. Morning comes and I hide myself away in a thick, overgrown wood and I don't come out until evening. After you, seclusion is my best friend. Alone, I talk only with my books, but then a crying fit comes on, which I do my best to fight against. So far it's a lopsided battle. I will write back to Brutus as you suggest. You'll have the letter tomorrow. You can give it to him then.

42 *Sulpicius Rufus to Cicero (at Astura)* (Fam. 4.5) *Rome, March 45* BCE

Rufus writes a letter of consolation to Cicero following the death of Tullia.

After I heard about the death of your Tullia, I was as deeply distressed as I should have been – it's a tragedy I truly share. If I had been there I would have been by your side and expressed my sorrow to you in person. This type of consolation is bitter and grim, but especially now: the relatives and friends, whose job is to offer comfort, are themselves afflicted with such equal pain and countless tears that they seem to require consolation more than they can offer it. Nevertheless, I've decided to write you whatever comes to mind, not because I think you're unaware of my feelings, but because perhaps you're so paralyzed with grief you're less clearly attuned to them.

What is it about internalized, private grief that affects you so much? Think how fortune has dealt with us thus far. Consider everything you've lost, everything that's just as dear to men as their own children are: country, repute, honor, distinction. At this point what other misfortune could augment your grief? What spirit experienced in such losses as you should not, by now, be thick-skinned and view any other loss as less traumatic?

But tell me, is it her fate you grieve? How often you must have thought – and how frequently it's entered my mind – that at times like these we should grieve least for those who've been allowed to painlessly exchange life for death! Moreover, what made life so appealing for her in this kind of Rome? What did she possess? What hope? What spiritual comfort? That she would spend her life married to some distinguished young man? In this day and age was there any potential son-in-law, do you think, who matched your distinction, to whom you'd feel safe entrusting your child? Or do you think she would have children whom she'd rejoice to see flourishing, who could hold on to their inheritance, have an opportunity to seek public office, and employ their own freedom to help out their friends? Which of these opportunities hadn't already been taken away? True, it's a great misfortune to lose a child, a terrible thing for sure, but to suffer and endure our present situation is even worse.

Let me share with you something that has been a great comfort to me; maybe it will alleviate your own grief, too. On the way back from Asia, when I was sailing from Aegina to Megara, I looked around at my surroundings. Behind me was Aegina, in front Megara, to my right Piraeus, and to my left Corinth, towns that had once greatly flourished and now lie crumbled and ruined before our very eyes. I began thinking to myself: "Wow. Should we, mere humans that we are, be indignant if one of us passes away or is killed? In the grand scheme of things, should we be outraged about our short lives, when the corpses of so many towns lie dead in one spot? Get a hold of yourself, Servius! Remember: you were born mortal." Believe me, I was profoundly encouraged by this thought. If you like, put this same image before your own eyes.

Recently many distinguished men died at once, the Roman Empire suffered a significant loss, and all the provinces were shaken to their core. In this regard, are you so deeply affected when the spirit of one poor small woman is lost? If not now, she would have inevitably died in a few years – since she was, after all, mortal. You must pull yourself together. Remember the things a man of your status shouldn't forget: she had a long life, lived within the republic, and had the pleasure of seeing you, her father, praetor, consul, and augur; she was married to illustrious young men and she enjoyed nearly everything life could offer; and, when the republic perished, her life ended. What can either of you have to complain about? Next, remember you are Cicero, a man who's accustomed to offering guidance and advice to others: don't follow the example of hypocritical doctors who offer their medical expertise to sick patients but can't heal their own wounds. Embrace instead with your heart and mind all those precepts you so often gave others.

Time heals all wounds. You do yourself a discredit if you just sit and wait for time to pass instead of using your own wisdom to hasten it along. If spirits in the underworld are sentient, then she, who devotedly loved you and her entire family, would certainly not want you to act this way. So follow what she would have wanted, for *her* sake, who is now dead, for the sake of all your other friends and family who grieve for your loss – and for the sake of your country, so that, if the republic calls for help, you'll be ready to provide it. Lastly, we've all fallen into the same political hardship, and it's crucial to keep this in mind: don't allow anyone to think that it's the loss of the republic and others' victory that you're grieving instead of your daughter's death.

I'm embarrassed to write more; I don't want you to think I'm disregarding your own sensible discretion. So let me close with one final thought: many times now we've seen how admirably you've handled misfortune and earned great renown because of it. Let us recognize that you can bear ill fortune just as well as the good, and that you consider it no greater burden – lest *this* would seem to be, of all the virtues, the one and only that you do not possess.

43 *Cicero to Rufus* (Fam. 4.6) *Ficulea, April 45* BCE

Yes indeed, Servius, it would have been so nice, as you write, to have had you with me at the time of my dire loss. From your letter I can easily fathom how much your presence would have helped me, both through your consolation and through your sympathy. Your letter gave me a sense of peace: it included all the sentiments that traditionally alleviate grief, and, in offering condolences, you expressed your own deep heartfelt sorrow. Further, the courtesies your son appropriately offered proved how much he valued me and how much he thought his affection would gratify you. Of course, his deferential actions would have been much more welcome under better circumstances, but they have never been more appreciated than now. As for me, however, not only your words and your grief – nearly equal to my own – console me, but also your own person. For I think it's shameful if I do not endure my loss in a way that you, in all your wisdom, think I should.

But sometimes I'm so overwhelmed I can barely stand my own sorrow: I don't have the resources for consolation available to others who have suffered similar losses. For example, Quintus Maximus lost a consular son, a man of great distinction and accomplishment; Lucius Paullus lost two sons within a week; and your relatives, Gallus and Marcus Cato, lost sons of the greatest brilliance and virtue. All of them experienced their loss at a time when their reputation and status, earned through public service, could provide comfort. Me? I've lost all those distinctions that I had acquired through so much effort – you yourself pointed this out. This means that I'm now without the one source of solace I had left.

My friends' businesses or political obligations weren't there to interrupt my dark thoughts; I found no pleasurable distraction being in the forum and I couldn't stand the sight of the Senate house. I believed, as was in fact the case, that I had lost all the fruits of my labor and good fortune. And, even while I knew I shared these political losses with you and other friends and was mastering my emotions and forcing myself to bear everything patiently, I still had a place where I could escape: a refuge where I could find peace and quiet, someone in whose conversation and sweetness I could put aside all my cares and concerns. Now, however, after such a loss, all the wounds I thought had healed over have broken open.

Once there was a home that used to welcome me back when I returned from the forum saddened by its current state: it could alleviate my sorrow. Now there's no longer a healthy, working republic to yield a consoling house of refuge when I leave my home in grief. So I keep away from my house and from the forum, because the former no longer comforts my grief over the current political situation, and the latter no longer offers consolation for the grief I feel at home.

I'm anticipating your visit and can't wait to see you as soon as possible. No amount of rationalizing offers greater consolation than reconnecting and enjoying another's conversation and company. I'm hoping, however, that your arrival is imminent (that's what I heard). There are many reasons why I want to see you immediately – above all, to converse face to face about how to get through this period, when we're entirely dependent on the will of one man, who's both generous and knowing and, as far as I can tell, not at all unreceptive to me (and quite friendly to you). But, even so, it's worth seriously contemplating what approach – not action – to take so as to be able to live a quiet life in a way that allows us to enjoy his kindness and consideration.

44 *Cicero to Atticus* (Att. *13.15) Arpinum, June 25, 45* BCE

Cicero wants Atticus' opinion about sending his current literary work to Varro.

Please mull it over, and then a little more – should I send what I'm working on to Varro? And this also involves you a bit, since you should know that I've written you into my dialogue as a third interlocutor. Therefore I think we should ponder the matter carefully. Even though the names have been assigned, they can still be crossed out or switched around.

45 *Cicero to Atticus* (Att. *13.44) Tusculum, July 20, 45* BCE

Cicero writes about the circus games (*ludi circenses*, namely chariot races) in honor of Apollo, which began with a parade carrying images of the gods. A bust of Caesar was carried beside its "neighbor" – a statue of the goddess Victory. Cotta was one of the Quindecemviri (15 men assigned priestly duties, such as guarding the Sibylline Books); he was interested in making the proposal that Caesar be given the title of king.

What a fun letter! It may have been painful hearing about the parade, in particular – but certainly not about anything else, especially where Cotta is involved! The crowd acted appropriately by not applauding for the Victory float, thanks to her hateful "neighbor"! Brutus came by and really wanted me to write some treatise dedicated to Caesar. I had agreed, but this parade has turned me off. So, did you dare to give it to Varro? I'm waiting to hear what he thinks! When will he read it all the way through? As for Attica, I approve. It counts for something that the spectacle lifted its mood, along with all the talk about it and its religious connections.

I need some reference works: please send me something by Cotta; I have a Libo with me, and I already had a Casca. Brutus delivered a message to me from Titus Ligarius; he said I made a mistake in mentioning

Lucius Corfidius in my speech *In Defense of Ligarius.* But it was nothing more than a "memory slip," as they say. I knew that Corfidius had been very close friends with the Ligarian family, but I realize that by this time he is already dead. Therefore I ask you to instruct your scribes, Pharnacius, Antaeus, and Salvius, to cross out Corfidius' name from all the copies of the speech.

46 *Cicero to Cassius* (Fam. *12.3) Rome, sometime after October 2, 44* BCE

It is now almost seven months since Caesar's assassination. Cicero writes Cassius shortly after delivering his first Philippic against Mark Antony. As dictator, Caesar had appointed Cassius as Syria's governor. Following Caesar's murder, however, the Senate cancelled that appointment and gave Cassius the less important (and less lucrative) governorship of Cyrene; Dolabella was appointed to take over Syria instead. Mark Antony has intervened still further: fearing that Cassius would ignore the Senate's reappointment and go to Syria anyway, Antony has denied Cassius' staff members (legates, *legati*) their traveling money.

Your "friend" becomes more insane with each passing day. First of all, he had the statue he erected on the Rostra inscribed "To the father: for his distinguished service." So now you're guilty of not just murder, but parricide! Yet why do I say "you," when I should be saying "we"? That crazy man claims I was the leader and instigator of your splendid deed. If only! Then he wouldn't be such a pain in my ass. But that was all you and Brutus. Since it's now done and over with, I only wish I had some advice to give you. I don't even know how to advise myself. What can be used against a powerful force when you're yourself powerless?

Their whole plan centers on avenging Caesar's death. On October 2, after Cannutius introduced him to the assembly, Antony gave a poorly delivered speech, which won him a poor reception; he said some words about the "saviors" of the country that are better applied to the country's traitors. He stated in no uncertain terms that you and Cannutius had acted according to my plan. You can further ascertain the situation from the fact that they robbed your legate of his traveling money: what reason do you think they gave? That the money is being conveyed to a "public enemy," naturally!

Oh, what a miserable state of affairs. We couldn't bear living under a master, and now we're enslaved to a fellow slave. Though I have more willpower than hope, I still have faith in your courage. But where are we going to get troops from? As for everything else, it's better if you listen to yourself than to me.

47 *Cicero to Cassius* (Fam. *12.4) Rome, February 3, 43* BCE

Cicero is only half-joking in wishing Antony had been murdered along with Caesar.

I wish you had invited me to the Ides of March banquet: then you wouldn't have any "leftovers"! But now all your "doggy-bags" are harassing me, only me, by god! We have distinguished consuls, it's true, but our consulars are the most rotten lot; we have a courageous Senate, but only the lowest ranked are bravest. For sure, the people and the whole of Italy are most steadfast. On the other hand, nothing is more despicable than our ambassadors Philippus and Piso: after the Senate's decree, they were sent to Antony to deliver specific requests; when Antony refused to comply with one of them, Philippus and Piso returned, willingly conveying some insufferable demands from Antony. So now my house is crowded with visitors, and I've become the people's superstar even though I support the constitution.

As for what you're up to, your plans, and your whereabouts, I have no idea. Rumor has it you're in Syria, but I have nothing to corroborate that. Information seems more reliable for Brutus, who's closer. All the jokers are really attacking Dollabella because he relieved you so quickly – before you had been in Syria a full 30 days! So there's general agreement that he should never have been let into Syria. You and Brutus are being highly praised, because you've put together an army beyond expectations. I'd write more, but I don't know the full situation. What I'm writing now is based only on rumor and general speculation. I'm eagerly awaiting a letter from you. Goodbye.

48 *Cicero to Atticus* (Att. *16.9) Puteoli, November 44*

Cicero has received two letters from young Octavian (the future Emperor Augustus).

Holy smokes, two letters from Octavian in one day! He says I should immediately come to Rome, that he wants to work through the Senate. I said: "The Senate wouldn't be able to convene before January 1," (I really believe it's true), and he added the phrase, "by your counsel." What more? He's pushing – and I'm buying time. I don't trust his youth and I don't know his true character. I don't want to do anything without your friend Pansa. I'm afraid Antony will prevail and I don't like going too far off the coast. Yet I fear some "glorious deed" will happen when I'm gone. Varro doesn't like the boy's plan, but I disagree: if Octavian has loyal troops, he can depend on Decimus Brutus, and he's quite open about the whole thing, gathering recruits in Capua and paying out cash. I see war right on the horizon. Write back your thoughts. I'm surprised my courier left Rome on the 1st without a letter from you.

49 *Cicero to Brutus* (Ad Brut. *1.3) Rome, April 21, 43* BCE

Marcus Brutus and other conspirators were hiding in Macedonia, a province governed by Gaius Antonius (Marc Antony's brother). Brutus and others divested Gaius of the governorship, first allowing him to live – an act of "generosity" that, Cicero warns, may make Brutus appear "weak." Shortly before this letter, pro-republican troops led by Pansa and Hirtius defeated Mark Antony's forces at the Battle of Forum Gallorum in northern Italy. These are the events Cicero refers to as "the latest news." The "state of panic" involves reports that the pro-Antony praetor, Ventidius Bassus, was preparing to march on Rome and to capture Cicero and other pro-republicans. (Instead he went to Vado and joined Antony there.) Five months later, Cicero was assassinated at the command of Antony (and with Octavian's compliance).

Our affairs seem to be in better order. I know for certain you've received letters with the latest news. The consuls are just like I've often described them to you. As for young Octavian Caesar, his innate character and courage are incredible. If only I can continue to guide and manage him (as I've done thus far), while he enjoys his current moment in the limelight! It will be more difficult, but I'm not giving up. It's especially thanks to me that the young boy is convinced our salvation is up to him. It's true: if he hadn't kept Antony away from Rome, all would have perished.

On the third or fourth day before this wondrous event, the entire city was in a state of panic: every man, woman, and child was planning to pour out of the city to join you, but on April 20 they regrouped, and now they prefer that you come here. That was the day I received the supreme reward for my endless toils and sleepless nights, if there is in fact any reward to be gained from real, authentic glory. For the whole city gathered *en masse* at my house, wherefrom the crowds led me up to the Capitol, with much shouting and applause; back down to the forum, they carried me to the Rostra there. I'm not vain: I have no need to be. Still, the unity of all classes in their display of thanks and congratulations moves me, especially because it's a real status symbol to achieve popularity by protecting the welfare of the state and its people. But I'd rather you hear about all this from others.

Please be very diligent in keeping me updated about all your affairs and plans, and take care that your generosity doesn't make you appear too weak. The Senate and the Roman people feel that no enemy has ever deserved every possible punishment more than those citizens who have taken up arms against their own homeland; these are the people I punish and attack in all of my speeches, amid the approval of all the honest men. It's up to you to decide what you think. As for me, I feel the cause of the three brothers is one and the same.

Catiline

Lucius Sergius Catiline (108–62 BCE), the famous instigator of the Catilinarian conspiracy, came from an old and distinguished patrician family. He began his career with the traditional military stint, serving alongside Pompey and Cicero during the Social War (91–88 BCE); he later became a supporter of the dictator Sulla. Prior to the conspiracy he faced other trials: in 73 BCE he was charged with adultery with a Vestal Virgin; in 65 BCE he faced corruption charges following his governorship of Africa. Cicero considered defending him, but decided against it. Catiline was acquitted in both. In 64 BCE Cicero defeated him in his bid for consul.

According to ancient sources, in 63 BCE, during Cicero's consulship, Catiline conspired to overthrow the government by raising an army and planning the assassination of many senators, including Cicero. Forewarned, on November 7, 63 BCE Cicero placed guards outside his home. The following day he convened the Senate at the temple of Jupiter Stator (in the Roman forum) and gave his first speech against Catiline, denouncing him in person. Shortly after Catiline left Rome, ostensibly to obey Cicero's command, but really to raise his army and advance his plans. Cicero obtained letters incriminating five of the conspirators, who, at his command, were put to death without a trial. Many of Catiline's soldiers and supporters consequently deserted him. Catiline fled to Gaul and was forced to engage with Antonius Hybrida's army near Pistoria (north of Rome, in modern-day Tuscany). Catiline was killed on the battlefield.

The letter below is embedded in the *Bellum Catilinae* (*War against Catiline*), an account of the conspiracy composed by the Roman historian Gaius Sallustius Crispus (Sallust, c. 86–35 BCE). Upon fleeing Rome after Cicero's delivery of the *First Catilinarian*, Catiline wrote to one of his supporters, Quintus Catulus. We learn later that Catulus betrayed Catiline by reading his letter to the Senate, which further instigated Catiline and embroiled him in his plot. Some scholars argue that the letter, as it appears in Sallust's work, represents the original, authentic version (rather than a "recreated" literary approximation).

In addition to the *Bellum Catilinae*, Sallust wrote the *Jugurthine War* (*Bellum Iugurthinum*), which documents the Roman war against Jurgurtha in Numidia (112–105 BCE), and the *Histories* (*Historiae*), a history of Rome from 78 to 67 BCE (only fragments remain).

50 Letter embedded in Bellum Catilinae *(Cat. 34–35)*

Upon leaving the city, Catiline sent letters to many of the former consuls, especially to each of the leading nobles. He wrote that he had been assailed with false charges and, since he couldn't withstand his enemies' treachery, he was bowing to fortune and heading into exile to Marseille: in his words, he wasn't leaving because of a guilty conscience, but so that the republic could enjoy peace again and in order to avert any possible insurgency due to his resistance. Yet Quintus Catulus read to the Senate a letter of a quite different nature, allegedly sent by Catiline. Below is a copy of it:

"L. Catiline to Q. Catulus. Your admirable, well-tested loyalty, for which I'm very thankful in these dangerous times, gives me all the more confidence to make this appeal. So, I've decided not to justify my change in plans, but to offer an explanation (not that I have a guilty conscience). So help me god, I'm sure you'll recognize the validity of my position. Incited by injustices and insults, robbed of enjoyment over my just reward for all my efforts, I couldn't attain the distinctive status I deserved. So, doing what I usually do, I championed the cause of the underprivileged. It's not because I couldn't use my assets to pay off my debts (Orestilla's generosity could have fully covered it from her own and her daughter's resources), but because I was watching undeserving men rewarded with honorable distinctions, while unfounded accusations had made me a pariah. So, to preserve what shred of honor I still have, I've pursued plans, which are respectable enough given my current situation. I'd write more, but I've just heard news that an attack is coming my way. I now entrust Orestilla to you and to your loyalty. I entreat you, on the lives of your children, defend her from insult. Be well."

Catullus

Gaius Valerius Catullus (84 BCE–54 BCE), a contemporary of Cicero and Sallust, was a leading poet of the late Roman republic. His 116 poems (including the selections below) comprise 60 shorter poems composed in a variety of meters, 8 longer poems, and 48 epigrams. His poems cover various themes: death and condolence, friendship, political invective (including against Cicero and Caesar), and love (e.g., in the poems about Lesbia, usually identified as Clodia Metelli, the sister of Cicero's enemy, Clodius).

51 Catullus 13

This playful poem reflects a common epistolary type, the dinner invitation; it was written in hendecasyllabics (verses of 11 syllables each), a Latin meter form in which Pliny the Younger also enjoyed composing.

Come in a few days or so, my Fabullus, and, god willing, you'll have a nice dinner at my place. But *you*'ll need to bring along the mounds of good food! Oh, and don't forget the fair-skinned girl, the wine and wit, and lots of deep-belly laughs. Bring all this and, no joke, my charming friend: you'll dine like a king. After all, your Catullus has a wallet bursting at the seams . . . with cobwebs, that is! But don't worry, you'll get a fair exchange: you'll receive pure, undiluted love, or maybe what's sweeter and more tasteful: my girl's perfume, which Venus, and her Graces and Cupids, gave her. And when you get a whiff, Fabullus, you'll pray: "Dear gods, please, turn me from tip to toe into a nose!"

52 Catullus 35

This poem features a theme developed by other epistolary authors: a letter containing instructions to the letter itself. Catullus urges his friend and fellow love poet, Caecilius, to leave his girl behind and visit him; Catullus will offer feedback on Caecilius' latest literary composition.

Letter, please tell my partner in crime, the love poet Caecilius, that he needs to leave New Como and the Larian lake and come to Verona: there's some constructive feedback he'll want to hear from your mutual friend, Catullus. So, if he's smart, he'll hit the road and not look back, even if a stunning girl calls his name again and again when he's got one foot out the door, clasping both hands around his neck and pleading: "Don't go, stay." If the rumors are true, she loves him to death, with unbridled passion: ever since she read his work in progress, *Lady Cybele*, the pathetic little thing has been devoured by flames, deep down to the marrow. I don't blame you, girl: you're as learned as Sappho herself. Caecilius' unfinished work, *The Great Mother*, really is quite charming.

53 Catullus 68

Catullus replies to his friend Manius, who requests consolation following a nasty break-up. Catullus admits he's honored, but his own grief (and limited reference materials) make him unable to fulfill Manius' request. The poem was written in elegiac couplets.

You send me this short letter streaked with tears, letting me know how you've been swallowed up by your misfortunate, sad plight; you ask me to rescue you, shipwrecked as you are, cast out by the sea's foamy waters, and to save you from the brink of death as you lie deserted in an empty bed, deep in sleep (thanks to Venus' departure). The Muses and the sweet songs of age-old poets bring you no joy as you toss and turn, eyes wide open through long nights, filled with anxious thoughts. Since I'm your friend, I'm honored you wrote and I'm glad you seek my poetry and love songs for solace. But, dear Manius, in case you haven't heard about my own misfortunes and perhaps you think I'm fed up with fulfilling a friend's duty, listen. Let me tell you how the waves of fate drowned me as well. You might have a change of heart about soliciting from a fellow sufferer the kinds of gifts that only happy people can really provide.

Ever since I put on the bright-white toga of adulthood and enjoyed youth's endless springtime days, I played around aplenty: she was no stranger to me, that goddess who blends sweet cares with a touch of bitterness. But then everything dissolved: I became grief-stricken over my brother's death. "Oh, brother, stolen away from me so heart-wrenchingly; you died, brother, you died, shattering my streak of good fortune. My house is now a tomb, just like yours; all the joys your sweet affection nurtured during your life are now dead and gone."

His death brought thoughts of playful naughtiness to a screeching halt. So, in reply to your comment – "It's a shame you're at Verona, Catullus: back here anyone who's someone is steaming up the cold bed you deserted" – it's not just "a shame," Manius, but a profound misfortune. So please forgive me if I don't send you the poetic gifts my grief took away. I have nothing to send and I don't have all my books with me here. They're back at Rome: that's where my house is, my home, the place where I spend all my time. Only one small box of books made it here. Since that's the situation, don't think I'm a low class, stingy jerk because I didn't send you a cache of poems: if I had any, rest assured, I would have offered them voluntarily.

FURTHER READING

Cicero

Baraz, Y. (2012) *A Written Republic: Cicero's Philosophical Politics*. Princeton, NJ: Princeton University Press.

Hall, J. (2009) *Politeness and Politics in Cicero's Letters*. Oxford: Oxford University Press.

Hariman, R. (1989) "Political style in Cicero's letters to Atticus." *Rhetorica*, *7*, 145–58.

Hutchinson, G. O. (1998) *Cicero's Correspondence: A Literary Study*. Oxford: Oxford University Press.

Leach, E. (1999) "Ciceronian 'Bi-Marcus': Correspondence with M. Terentius Varro and L. Paprius Paetus in 46 BCE." *Transactions of the American Philological Association*, *129*, 139–79.

Nicholson, J. (1994–1995) "The delivery and confidentiality of Cicero's letters." *Classical Journal*, *90*, 33–63.

Rawson, E. (2009) *Cicero: A Portrait* (Bristol Classical Paperbacks). Bristol: Bristol Classical Press.

White, P. (2012) *Cicero in Letters: Epistolary Relations of the Late Republic*. Oxford: Oxford University Press.

Wilcox, A. (2005) "Sympathetic rivals: Consolation in Cicero's letters." *American Journal of Philology*, *126*(2), 237–55.

Wood, N. (1988) *Cicero's Social and Political Thought*. Berkeley: University of California Press.

Catiline

Cairns, F. (2012) "Lentulus' letter: Cicero *In Catilinam* 3.12; Sallust *Bellum Catilinae* 44.3–61." *Historia*, *61*(1), 78–82.

McGushin, P. (1977) *Sallustius Crispus*, Bellum Catilinae: *A commentary* (Mnemosyne Supplements). Leiden: Brill.
Waters, K. H. (1970) "Cicero, Sallust and Catiline." *Historia*, *19*(2), 195–215.

Catullus

Giasser, J. H. (2002) "Picturing Catullus." *The Classical World*, *95*(4), 372–85.
Hansen, W. (2007) "Caecilius' response to the invitation in Catullus 35." *The Classical Journal*, *102*(3), 213–20.
Levine, P. (1976) "Catullus c. 68: A new perspective." *California Studies in Classical Antiquity*, *9*, 61–88.
Skinner, M., ed. (2007) *A Companion to Catullus*. Malden, MA: Blackwell.
Stroup, S. (2010) *Catullus, Cicero, and a Society of Patrons: The Generation of the Text*. Cambridge: Cambridge University Press.

CHAPTER THREE

The Augustan Age (27 BCE–14 CE)

Augustus

Gaius Julius Octavius (63 BCE–14 CE; r. 27 BCE–14 CE), more commonly Octavian, came from an equestrian family. Julius Caesar, his maternal great-uncle, adopted Octavian in his will. Although initially he formed a coalition with Mark Antony and Lepidus known as the second triumvirate, his relationship with them disintegrated and civil war erupted. Octavian emerged as the victorious at the battle of Actium (31 BCE) and shortly after, in 27 BCE, he became *Augustus* by senatorial decree. As the first *princeps* (or, for some scholars, the first Roman "emperor"), Octavian ushered in a new Golden Age of peace and a return to traditional moral values. During his rule Augustus designated several heirs; but it was Tiberius, the son of his second wife, Livia, who introduced the new imperial government and started a dynasty of Julio-Claudian rulers. Many authors provided biographical accounts of Augustus' life, and Gaius Suetonius (c. 69 CE–c. 140 CE) was one of them.

Suetonius practiced law and, as noted in the Introduction, he was chief secretary *ab epistulis* to Emperor Hadrian (r. 117 CE–138 CE). He wrote prolifically, but his collection of the biographies of the first Roman emperors, *The Twelve Caesars*, is his only work that survives in its entirety (some fragments from his *On Famous Writers* have also survived). In addition to other biographies (e.g., *Lives of Famous Prostitutes*, or *Royal Biographies*), Suetonius composed encyclopedic works such as *The Physical Defects of Mankind*, *The Roman Year*, and *Roman Festivals*. Suetonius was a close friend of Pliny the Younger.

Roman Letters, First Edition. Noelle K. Zeiner-Carmichael.

54–55 Suetonius, *Life of Augustus*

The first two selections come from Suetonius' *Life of Augustus* and, according to Suetonius himself, represent authentic letters written by Augustus to his stepson, the future Emperor Tiberius Claudius Nero (r. 14 CE–37 CE).

54 *Augustus to Tiberius* (Aug. *71.2*)

Dear Tiberius: I dined with the same people, except this time Vincius and Silius Senior joined the party. All throughout yesterday's and today's meal we gambled like old men. Whenever someone threw a "dog" or a "six," he put one denarius per die into the pool, and whoever threw a "Venus" got to take it all.

55 *Augustus to Tiberius* (Aug. *71.2*)

We had quite a pleasant five days during the Feast of Minerva, my Tiberius. We gambled all day and kept the seats nice and warm. Your brother Drusus made a big stink complaining about his bad luck; in the end he wasn't out much, since, after some early big losses, he was able to make an impressive comeback little by little. I lost 20,000 sesterces, but that's because, as usual, I played so freely and generously. If I had made everyone else ante up the same wagers as myself or had kept what I gave to others, I would have easily taken home 50 grand. But this way is better, since my profuse kindness will win me the biggest prize: immortality!

56–58 Suetonius, *Life of Claudius*

The subsequent three selections come from Suetonius' *Life of Claudius* and comprise letters by Augustus to his wife Livia; these focus on young Claudius, the future emperor (r. 41 CE–54 CE), whose stammering and unbalanced gait caused the family grave concerns about its public image. The Latin festival mentioned at the end of this letter celebrated the union of the Latin peoples; all the Roman magistrates participated in the procession to the temple of Jupiter on Mt. Alba (southeast of Rome). The presiding consul chose a young man from the imperial household to serve as his stand-in city prefect, while he himself was engaged with the procession. Augustus implies that, if Claudius were to join in the procession, that would call attention to the embarrassing fact that he wasn't considered capable of standing in as temporary city prefect.

56 *Augustus to Livia* (Claud. *4.1–3*)

As requested, my Livia, I've spoken with Tiberius regarding your grandson Claudius and the upcoming games of Mars. As far as we're concerned, we both agreed we must decide once and for all what policy to follow. The central question is whether he is, how should I put it, "wholly whole." If so, why hesitate advancing him through the same stages of office as his brother? But, if we feel he's impaired by intellectual and physical disabilities, we must not present any opportunity to the public (prone as it is to ridiculing such things and sneering at them), to make fun of him – or us. Otherwise, if we don't agree on a plan we establish in advance, we'll always find ourselves in a quandary, deliberating at each and every occasion whether or not he's capable of fulfilling a particular duty.

As to the current situation that you wrote about: I'm not opposed to him presiding over the dinner of priests at the games, so long as he agrees to let his relative, Silvanius' son, keep an eye on him, ensuring he doesn't do anything idiotic to elicit negative attention and laughter. Nonetheless, I don't want him watching the games from our official box seat: it's in clear view, right up front, visible to every spectator. I also don't want him accompanying his brother in the procession up to Mt. Alba during the Latin festival; if he did, then people would wonder why we hadn't appointed him city prefect, as one would expect.

So there you have it: that's our opinion, my Livia. I'd like to establish a firm policy: that way in future situations we won't always have to waver between worry and hope. If you want, you can show this part of the letter to our dear Antonia.

57 *Augustus to Livia* (Claud. *4.4–5*)

Yes, Livia, I'll definitely ask young Tiberius Claudius to dine with me daily while you're away, so he won't be left alone eating just with his pals Sulpicius and Athenodorus. I wish he'd be more thoughtful and diligent in picking his friends and he'd choose someone whose movement, demeanor, and gait he could emulate. Poor little guy, it's really too bad – because, when he's focused on serious pursuits and doesn't let his mind wander, the splendid quality of his intellect is obvious.

58 *Augustus to Livia* (Claud. *4.6*)

Well, I'll be damned! Your grandson Claudius gave an impressive speech! I don't understand how the hell someone who stammers so incomprehensively in conversation can then speak so clearly in a public declamation and say exactly what needs to be said. Amazing.

Horace

Quintus Horatius Flaccus (8 December 65–27 November 8 BCE) was a poet of the Augustan Age whose most famous works include four books of *Odes* (published between 23 and 13 BCE) and two books of *Satires* (published in 35 and 30 BCE). He is largely credited with adapting the Latin language so as to produce poems modeled after famous Greek lyric poets such as Sappho, Alcaeus, and Archilochus. Like Propertius (see below), he enjoyed the friendship and literary patronage of Maecenas, who provided him with an estate (the Sabine villa, in modern Tivoli). Horace's two books of *Epistles* in verse (published in 20 and 14 BCE) reflect their historical and cultural context and explore philosophical ideals espousing simple, honest living. The following selections come from the first book of Horace's *Epistles.* (See the book's website, www.wiley.com/go/romanletters, for additional letters, including Horace's *Epistle* 1.1 – a programmatic piece that introduces many of the themes explored in the subsequent letters.)

*59 Horace to Florus (*Epist. *1.3)*

Horace writes to Julius Florus, a staff member accompanying Tiberius (Augustus' diplomatic representative) in Asia Minor.

Julius Florus, tell me, where in the world is Tiberius campaigning? What distant land detains you? Is it Thrace, where snowy shackles fetter the Hebrus river? Or the straits, flowing between the parallel towering peaks? Do Asia's fertile plains and hills keep you? And what literary work is his learned staff composing? Who is undertaking the task of recording Augustus' accomplishments, of publicizing for all posterity the *princeps*' feats in war and peace?

What about Titius, who will soon be all the talk of the town? He didn't blanch drinking from Pindar's fountain, boldly proving his contempt for more easily approachable lakes and streams. What's he working on these days? Is he doing well, and does he ask about me? Do the Muses celebrate his attempts to adapt Pindar's Greek meters to the Latin lyre, or is he ranting and bellowing through tragedies? And how's my friend Celsus? He's been warned time and time again to seek material of his *own* and to keep his hands off the library books collected in the temple of Apollo Palatine. Otherwise, one day when the flock of birds arrive to reclaim their feathers, they'll strip the poor little crow of the colorful plumage he stole, and he'll end up a complete laughingstock.

And what are you up to? What flowers and herbs are you busily buzzing over? Your brilliant genius is refined – not at all weedy and overgrown. Whether you're exercising your sharp tongue in the courtroom, sharing legal advice with fellow citizens, or composing charming poetry, you'll win the gold, the victor's ivy crown. But if you'd stop nursing your worries, you'd reach that pinnacle where godly wisdom will lead you. It's *this* work, *this* pursuit (big or small) we should strive for if we want to secure our own self-respect and our country's admiration.

Write back and let me know: do you care about Munatius like you should? Has the poorly stitched gash in your friendship healed, or has it reopened? You're both wild, untamed beasts; is it hot tempers or just inexperience? Whatever it is and wherever you are, both of you have better sense than to let a brotherly bond be shattered. I'm fattening up a heifer so we can all enjoy a meal together when you're both back.

*60 Horace to Torquatus (*Epist. *1.5)*

A common epistolary theme: Horace invites a friend to a quiet dinner without the luxurious, expensive food often appearing at dinner parties.

Dear Torquatus:

If you can handle reclining on one of Archias' simple couches and don't mind eating salad on clay dishes, then I'll expect you for dinner this evening. You'll enjoy a nice wine from the region between marshy Minturnae and Mt. Petrinum, vintage 26 BCE. (If you've got a nicer bottle, send it over – or you're stuck with mine!) I've made sure the hearth is spick and span and the furniture nice and tidy. So quit worrying about pointless things like trying to get rich quick, or your big-time court case defending Moschus. Tomorrow is Caesar's birthday, so we can sleep in: "It is hereby permitted to prolong a summer night in pleasant conversation." Why should I care about money, if I'm not allowed to spend it? The man who's so frugal and selfish just to secure his kid's inheritance is a raving lunatic. I'll start drinking and scattering flowers now: I'm fine being called reckless.

What can't wine do? It unlocks secrets, turns hopes into realities, induces a coward into battle, frees the mind of burdens, and teaches new arts. Who can't deliver a winning speech with a full wineglass in hand? Or is there anyone wine hasn't liberated from tight times? I'm ready and willing to follow my own orders: you'll find no messy covers, no dirty napkins to wrinkle your nose at; every goblet, each dish will be so polished you'll see your reflection in it! Beyond these doors no one repeats what's spoken among loyal friends: we come together as equals and as equals we sit and drink. I'll be sure to invite your friends Brutram and Septicius, and Sabinus too – as long as he doesn't have a previous dinner engagement or some girl as a more attractive option. Bring along a couple of friends, but remember: too many armpits stink in tight quarters! Write back and let me know how many of you are coming. Then drop everything and sneak out the back door and slip past the client awaiting you in the courtyard.

61 *Horace to Numicius* (*Epist. 1.6*)

Horace explains to Numicius (otherwise unknown) that riches and fame are ephemeral, but the rewards of philosophy are everlasting. Toward the end of the letter Horace refers to the city Caere and its "wax tablets." Caere had been a leading Etruscan city, a symbol of Etruria's past glory and present decay. According to Livy, its citizens rebelled against Rome in the third century BCE and were disenfranchised as a punishment. Thus when Horace envisions Numicius and himself earning a spot on "Caere's wax tablet lists" he is sarcastically suggesting that decadent, depraved living merits a loss of voting rights.

"Admire nothing," Numicius, except one thing and one thing only: whatever makes and keeps you happy. Some gaze up at the sun and the stars, measuring the passing seasons and feeling little fear or apprehension. What's your opinion about the gifts of earth and sea, enriching faraway Arabia and India? What do you think about public shows, the audience's applause, and Rome's magisterial offices? What's your reaction? Do you frown or do you smile when you see them? The fear of losing what you have is almost the same feeling as admiring what you don't have: both involve an aggravating anxiety about the future, and the surprise appearance of either is disappointing in similar ways. Joy or pain, desire or fear – what does it matter? What's the difference, if one sees something better or worse than his own situation and stops – paralyzed in mind and body, staring emptily into space? If anything, even virtue, is pursued beyond the proper limit, the wise man becomes insane and a just man unjust.

Go ahead, admire silver, marble, bronze and antiques; feast your eyes upon Tyrian purple and gemstones. Rejoice when thousands of eyes stare in rapture while you speak. Be the eager beaver: arrive at the forum at dawn and stay 'till evening, otherwise Mr. Silent might reap better profits from his farm (acquired through his wife's dowry) and, god forbid, you'd find yourself admiring *him* more than he admires *you* (How *could* you? He's lower in rank!). Whatever lies buried underground, time will bring to light, and whatever shimmers brightly, time will bury and hide. You're a constant fixture at Agrippa's portico and on the Via Appia, but you'll still make that final trip to the underworld just like everyone else, even the great King Numa and King Ancus.

If some acute illness afflicts your lungs or kidneys, you go see the doctor. You want to live life after a moral compass. Who doesn't? If virtue alone is the path, then get on with it and take a risky step: surrender the pleasures. But if you think a sacred grove is just a spot to collect firewood and virtue is nothing more than a name, then, by all means, make sure nobody else reaches the port first. Otherwise you'll lose money on all your imports from Cibyra and Bithynia and destroy your business. Count your money, round it off to 1,000, multiply by 2, add 1, and then another 1,000. Hail to Queen Money! She can buy a wife, credit, friends, a high birth, and good looks, while Prince Persuasion and Lady Sex make a rich man even richer.

The king of Cappadocia is loaded with slaves but light on cash: don't be like him. Then there's Lucullus: when asked if he could supply a hundred cloaks for the theater, supposedly he answered: "That many? I'll see what I can do and send what I have." Not long afterwards he wrote back: "I can give you five thousand – take as many as you want." A house is "poor" unless it has a duplicate of everything (the owner forgets what he already has) – it's a burglar's dream! So, if money is the one and only source of your happiness, be a slave to your work. If appearances and popularity make people rich, well then, let's purchase a slave whose sole duty is to remember peoples' names and whisper them in our ear, who will poke us in the ribs so we'll offer a handshake across the stepping stones. "This one here, he's got clout with the Fabian tribe, that one with the Velians; this man can get you a high-ranking position or take it away when he's in a bad mood." Add a "Bro" or a "Sir" and deftly adopt whichever title suits the voter's age.

If good food dictates good living, well, it's morning, the day has started! Let's go where our palate leads us. Let's "fish" and "hunt" à la Gargilius: at the sun's rising he'd order his slaves to carry nets and spears through the jam-packed forum and Campus Martius, just so that all eyes would see one of his thousands of mules carrying home a boar captured . . . at the butcher's shop! Let's go to the baths; no matter that our bellies are sagging with half-digested food, or we forget what's decent and what's not. We might earn ourselves a spot on Caere's wax tablet lists. Or maybe we'll earn a comparison with Odysseus' vile shipmates, who preferred illicit pleasures to their own homeland. If, as Mimnermus believes, nothing is delightful "without love and laughter," then "May you spend your life amid love and laughter." Live on! Farewell!

Oh, and if you have any better ideas than what I've written here, please let me know. If not, join me in putting these suggestions to good use.

62 Horace to his Muse (and to Celsus) (Epist. *1.8*)

Horace admits that living a virtuous life isn't always so easy.

Muse, bring greetings and best wishes to Celsus Albinovanus, one of Tiberius' staff members and secretaries. If he asks how I'm doing, let him know that, despite the promises I've made to myself, right now life isn't as pleasant or as proper as I'd like. No, it's not because a hailstorm has devastated my vineyards, or because the summer heat has stunted my olive trees, or because I've got cattle lying sick in distant fields. No – it's because my body is perfectly healthy but my mind is less so, and I don't feel like listening to possible remedies. I'm rude to the doctors who're just trying to help, and I'm angry because I don't know why my friends try so hard to rid me of this dark and dismal apathy. I follow what's harmful, avoid what's helpful; I'm as fickle as the wind. At Tibur I ache for Rome, and at Rome I ache for Tibur.

After you've repeated all this, ask Celsus about his health, how he's managing his job, whether he's taking care of himself, and how he's fitting in with the young Tiberius and the rest of his staff. If he says "I'm well, thank you," first congratulate him and then open up his ears by infusing the following drops of advice: "How *you* steer your success, Celsus, will guide how *we* handle you."

63 Horace to Tiberius Claudius (Epist. *1.9*)

> Horace explains why he's a bit hesitant to recommend a friend to Tiberius Claudius.

Apparently, dear Claudius, Septimius knows best how much you hold me in regard. So when he requests (or, more like it, begs) "Please, oh please, Horace, sing my praises. I'm begging, write me a recommendation letter," so he'll win favor and connection with a Nero (who selects *only* honorable additions to his home), and when he counts me among your closest friends, apparently he knows me and my capabilities better than I do. Indeed, I gave Septimius many excuses as to why I should be let off the hook (although recommendations are a friend's duty), but I was afraid he'd think I was downplaying my role, hiding my own influence so that nobody else gets a piece of the pie in winning your favor. So, in choosing the lesser of two evils, I've put on my city face in order to exploit the advantages of my other persona: City-Slicker Horace! So, if it's okay by you that I've relinquished my modesty for the sake of a friend, please give him a welcome and trust me when I say he's honorable and worthy.

64 Horace to Fuscus (Epist. *1.10*)

> Horace writes to his friend and urbanite Fuscus about the joys of country living. He dictates the letter while sitting next to an old dilapidated shrine dedicated to the ancient Sabine goddess Vacuna.

Greetings to Fuscus the city-lover, from Horace the country-lover!

It's obvious that only in this one thing we're complete opposites; in nearly everything else we're practically twins, sharing the same fraternal heart. You say "no," I say "no;" you nod "yes," so do I. We're like little doves sharing equal affection for each other. You stay and guard the nest, I praise the streams, the woods, and the moss-covered rocks of the peaceful countryside. In short, as soon as I've left behind everything you and your fellow urbanites praise to the heavens, *that*'s when I really begin to live and can be my own king. I'm like the priest's slave who prefers freedom to food given for free, however delicious and otherwise expensive it may be: I'll take good old plain bread over croissants any day.

If we live in harmony with nature, as we should, we need in the first place to choose the site for constructing our house: is there any better spot than the blissful countryside? Where can you enjoy a more temperate winter? Where else can you welcome pleasant breezes that soften the dog days of summer and its blazing heat? Where are anxious worries less likely to keep you up all night? Is the scent of fresh grass or the shine of its glossy blades any less gratifying than the artificial shine and perfumed bouquet of marble tiles imported from Africa? Do you really think Rome's lead pipes, nearly bursting from the pressure, carry purer water than the gurgling currents that flow gently down the winding river?

Naturally, a forest can be cultivated even amid marble columns, and a house that overlooks even distant fields can win accolades. Go ahead, try to banish nature with a two-pronged fork: she'll still come running back. She'll stealthily make her way past your disdainful treasures, a victor wearing a scornful smirk on her face. The man who can't discern between wool dyed with local purple from Aquinum and the exotic purple of Sidonia won't suffer a deeper loss than the man who can't distinguish falsehood from truth. Anyone who exults too much in his or her good fortune is shaken to the bone when his or her luck changes. When you admire something, you'll be reluctant to relinquish it. Spurn treasures. You may live in a shack but you can still live like a king, outstripping patrons and clients in the race of life.

Once upon a time there was a stag and a horse. The stronger stag was always driving the horse out of their shared pasture, until the loser in that endless battle begged man for help and submitted to the bridle. But, once the horse defeated his antlered enemy and left the battleground victorious, he couldn't shake the rider off or spit the bit from his mouth. In the same way, the man who fears poverty sacrifices his freedom, a treasure more precious than gold; forever a slave, he shamefully lugs around his mistress, Lady Avarice, because he refuses to figure out how to survive on just a little. If a man's circumstances don't fit him, either they'll trip him up, like a shoe that's too big, or they'll give him a blister, like one that's too small. If your shoe fits, Aristius, then you'll live wisely, not letting me off without a scolding when you notice I'm accruing more than I need and ignoring my own advice! It doesn't matter who we are: when we hoard our money we let it rule us and enslave us. *We* should be the ones holding the reins, not the other way around.

I'm dictating this letter while I sit behind the crumbling shrine of Vacuna, perfectly content except for one thing: you're not here.

65 *Horace to Bullatius* (Epist. *1.11*)

What were your impressions, Bullatius, of Chios and famous Lesbos? What did you think of elegant Samos and Croesus' royal city, Sardis? What about Smyrna and Colophon? Did they all live up to their reputations and your expectations? Do they pale in comparison to our Campus Martius or the Tiber? Were you hoping to visit one of Attalus' cities, like Pergamum or Ephesus? Or are you sick of sea and roads, and looking to visit Lebedus? (You're familiar with Lebedus, right? It's a dirt road ghost town, more deserted than even Gabii or Fidenae!) I'd be ready to live there, forgetting all my friends – and letting myself forgotten by them – happy as a clam to stand on the shore and gaze out into the distant raging sea. The man from Capua traveling for Rome, spattered with rain and mud, wouldn't want to live forever in an inn; the man who's got a cold wouldn't praise the saunas and the heated bathhouses as the key to a happy, healthy life. And you – if a strong southerly gale pitched you every which way when you were crossing the Aegean Sea, you wouldn't sell your ship the second you reach shore. For a man who's healthy, lovely Rhodes and Mytilene would be as attractive as wearing a hooded fur coat (however gorgeous) in the heat of summer or running in shorts in the middle of a snowstorm, and as tempting as a dip in the Tiber in the dead of winter or cooking over a hot stove in the middle of July. While you can – while Fortune smiles upon you – go ahead, sing the praises of Samos, Chios, and Rhodes, but do so from a distance – at Rome. Whatever hour the gods bless you with, accept it gratefully and don't postpone the pleasures for next year. That way, wherever you happen to be, you can say: "I've lived a happy life." For, if it's reason and knowledge that dispel worries and not some lookout point over the wide, open ocean, then those who rush to the other side of the sea get only a new view – not a new viewpoint. Laziness wears us out, makes us tired, and we tend to look to yachts and sedans for the better life. But what you're looking for is right here at Rome – or, if you've got a well-adjusted mindset, in remote and deserted Sticksville.

66 *Horace to Vinnius* (Epist. *1.13*)

Horace sends a playful note to Vinnius, instructing him on how to deliver his poetry to Augustus. Vinnius' inherited family name is Asina ("donkey," a name likely indicating ancestral agricultural ties).

Vinnius Burro, Vinnius Burro, if I've told you once, I've told you twice: make sure my poems are signed, sealed, and delivered to Augustus, but only if he's healthy, happy – and asking for them. I know you're excited for me, but do try to avoid being a blundering klutz. You take your job seriously, I realize, but don't act like a clown, or you might find a door slammed in your face. If you can't handle the hefty bulk of my pages, go ahead, just chuck 'em; that's better than crashing through the door, throwing your knapsack down right at his doorstop, like some wild beast, and disgracing your honorable family name "Burro" by making an *ass* of yourself and heading up the front page of Rome's gossip column. Across mountains, streams, bogs – push on, steadfast and strong, until you've reached your destination. Then, *then* you can shout "VICTORY!" Hold the little bundle of volumes just so: don't stick them under your smelly armpit or, like a country bumpkin, heave them over your shoulder like a sack of potatoes, or stumble like the character Pyrria in that play (she got caught stealing a ball of wool because she was so drunk she was tripping all over herself). And don't carry them like you would your own shoes and cap, when you're trudging home from some dinner party at some distant relative's home. And, for god's sake, don't go telling everybody and everyone how much sweat and tears you've spilled transporting poems enthralling enough to captivate the eyes and ears of Caesar Augustus. You've got your instructions. Go on now, adios. But, I beg you, *be careful*! Don't trip and fall, breaking the precious cargo placed in your hands.

67 *Horace to Quinctius (*Epist. *1.16)*

Horace describes his Sabine farm to Quinctius and then defines what makes a "good man."

In anticipation of your questions about my farm, excellent Quinctius – whether the ploughed fields furnish food for its master, or whether it is fruity olives, apples, pastureland, or vine-entwined elms that bring in a hefty income – I'll recreate it all for you on paper.

The surrounding mountains would be uninterrupted, were it not for the shady valley parting them – so that the rising sun shines down on the valley's right slope, and then, as it flies away in its chariot, warms the left. You'll write back: "Wow, what a temperate climate!" What would you say about the abundant bushes and their ruddy berries? And the plums? What will you say about the various species of oak trees with their equally copious acorns and shade, delighting the pigs and their master alike? "Verdant Tarentum has returned home!" There's even a spring you could call a river (as cold and pure as the Hebrus winding its way through Thrace), and its flowing waters can alleviate a headache and soothe a nauseous belly. I'm sure you'll be happy to hear how charming this secluded haven is, how much I love it, and how it keeps me safe and sound during the malaria-ridden month of September.

You'll be living life right if you live up to the praise everyone gives you. All of us at Rome have long been calling you "happy." But I'm afraid that you might trust others' opinions more than your own, or that you assign happiness to people other than the wise and good man. I worry that, if people repeatedly say "You're so healthy and sensible," even when you head to the dinner table – and later, when your greasy, food-covered fingers begin trembling as you shiver – you'll still pretend you don't have a fever. Foolish men with false decorum hide the wounds they leave festering. If anyone mentions the wars you fought on land and sea and tries to flatter your ego by saying, "I hope Jupiter, protector of both you and Rome, never divulges whether you worry more for the public's safety or the public for yours," you'd recognize that this praise was directed at Augustus. When you allow people to call you "wise" and "faultless," tell me, do you confirm their assessment with a "Yup, that's me"?

"Surely you like being called 'good' and 'prudent' just as much as I do." Yes, but the praise the public offers today can be snatched away tomorrow if its members choose. *They* are the ones who bestow the fasces of power, revoking them if the officeholder proves unworthy. "Put it down, it's mine," they say: I put it down and sadly walk away. If the same public declares me a thief, or charges that I've committed lewd acts, or alleges that I've strangled my father's neck with a cord, should I feel stung by these false charges and blush in shame? Does phony honor help, or false dishonor frighten, anyone except the guy who's already flawed or in need of a doctor? "So who *is* the good man?" you ask. "The man who obeys the Senate's decrees, laws and oaths, who settles lawsuits through his judgment, secures property through his surety, and wins cases by serving as a witness." But back at home, away from the forum, his whole household and even the whole neighborhood see his inner wickedness under his handsome coat. If my slave says, "*I* haven't stolen anything, *I* haven't run away," I'd say, "Good. As your reward I won't flog you." If he says, "*I* haven't killed a man," I answer, "Well, then, you won't be food for the crows while rotting on the cross." "I'm good and upright." Our old-fashioned Sabellan friend knows better; he shakes his head, denying it.

The wary wolf avoids the hidden pit, the hawk stays away from a suspicious net, and the kite-fish swims clear of the open hook: *truly* good men hate to err out of love for virtue. *You*, however, avoid committing a crime because you're afraid of the punishment: if you think you can escape getting caught, you'll make no distinction between sacred and profane. Even if you steal only one bean from a whole bushel, the financial loss may be insignificant, but not the crime. Your so-called "good" man is famous in the forum and lawcourts, and, whenever he appeases the gods with a pig or a heifer, he prays loudly, for all to hear, "Father Janus . . . " or "Apollo . . . " while under his breath it's rather "Beautiful Laverna, grant that I can keep my cheating a secret and appear to be moral and righteous: conceal my sins under the cloak of night and shroud my deceit under a misty cloud."

How is a miser "better" or "freer" than a slave who stoops at the crossroads to pick up a penny stuck in the mud? I don't get it. The man who desires also fears. A man living in fear will never, in my opinion, achieve freedom. Whoever scurries around, burying himself under a heap of riches, loses his weapons and deserts virtue's post. Don't kill your captive: you can sell him for a profit. He'll be a useful slave, so let *him* be the one who sweats while shepherding his flocks or plowing the fields. Let *him* be a merchant, let *him* sail the winter sea amid all the waves, or be the one to reduce our grain prices and lug all the food and provisions! A good and wise man will boldly ask: "Pentheus, ruler of Thebes, what disgrace will you make me endure? How will I suffer?" "I'll take away all your possessions." "You mean my herds, my money, my furniture, my silver? Go ahead, take them all." "I'll restrain you with handcuffs and shackles and a cruel guard." "The god himself will grant my freedom if I only say the word." What he really means, I think, is "I will die." Death is what awaits us after we cross the finish line of life's race.

68 *Horace to Lollius* (Epist. *1.18*)

Horace advises Lollius, a wealthy and distinguished younger friend, on how to behave properly toward friends and patrons.

If I know you as I think I do, most honest Lollius, once you've professed yourself a friend, you'll be sure not to come across as a fool. Just as a matron differs from a whore in behavior and dress, a friend should steer away from the disingenuous parasite. Even worse, however, is uncultured, boorish rudeness. How can you recognize it? It looks like the hick from the boondocks, you know, the guy who's dull and crude, sports a cheap buzz haircut and black teeth, and tries to pass himself off as the real thing – truly candid and virtuous. Virtue is the mean between vices, the middle road between two extremes – two opposite ends of the spectrum. On the far left is the one who approaches servility, a jester sitting beside his host; he waits with bated breath for the rich man's nod of approval, repeating what the latter utters to make sure everyone hears him. You'd think he was a schoolboy regurgitating lessons back to his cruel teacher; or a supporting actor in a mime; the one who mirrors the star's role. On the far right is the guy who often squabbles about "goat's wool" ("Is it hair or fur?") and puts on full armor to defend trivial matters: "What do you mean you don't believe me?" and "What's wrong with asserting my true opinion? A second life would be cheap reward for frank honesty." So, what's the issue he's up in arms about? Whether Castor or Dolchis is the more skillful gladiator, or whether Minucius Street or the Appian Way is the best route to Brundisium.

The man stripped naked, penniless from wasteful spending and reckless gambling, can't stop looking in the mirror and buys clothes and cologne beyond his means; he's gripped by an unremitting thirst and hunger for money and seized by the fear and shame of poverty. His rich friend (who is ten times more experienced when it comes to vices) hates and abhors him; if he doesn't hate him, he acts like his devoted mother, urging his buddy to outdo him in virtue and knowledge. He *nearly* speaks the truth when he claims: "My wealth – don't even try to compete – condones stupidity. In comparison, your assets are pathetic. So a simple, inexpensive toga suits you as a client just fine: forget about competing with me." Eutrapelus, a.k.a. "Mr. Jokester," always gives expensive clothes to someone he hopes to harm: the lucky bastard, wearing his handsome new outfit, now dons new hopes and plans, sleeps in late, lays aside honest duties for a whore, fattens his debt with interest payments, and, worst of all, becomes a gladiator or a hired wagon driver for the local vegetable grower.

Figure 3.1 The Appian Way. Source: Album / Art Resource, NY

Just as you should never poke your nose into your friend's secrets, Lollius, don't violate his confidence, even if you're tortured by wine or wrath. Don't praise your own pursuits or criticize others'; when he wants to go hunting, don't decide *that*'s the time to write poetry. This clash in interests is what caused the brotherly bond between the twins Amphion and Zethus to break, at least until Amphion put down his lyre and gave in to his brother's sterner temperament. So, follow the gentle commands of your influential friend: however many hunting dogs he leads into the countryside, however many mules loaded down with Aeolian traps, get up! Say goodbye to your antisocial gloomy Muse, and your efforts will win you an appetizer at his next dinner party. Hunting is the regular sport of Roman men: it benefits their reputation, life, and body (especially when, like you, one is in good shape, can outrun the dogs, and can use his strength to defeat the boar). Who else handles those manly weapons more adeptly than you? Don't you recall how spectators cheered for you when you competed at the Campus Martius? And remember when you were younger? You endured a tough war fighting in Spain's Cantabrian campaign under that general who now fights to recover the Roman standards from the temples in Parthia and adds them (and anything else missing) to the Roman Empire. Don't say "no," and if you absolutely have to, make sure you have a good excuse; even though you're careful never to do anything tacky and gauche, I know you sometimes like to enjoy free time out on your father's country estate. Two armies of boats are divided on either side of the lake, which is renamed the "Adriatic Sea"; you play the role of the general, your brother that of the enemy, and the slaves are all the other soldiers. Thus you recreate the Battle of Actium in hostile fashion, until swift victory crowns one of you. If your patron believes you'll join in his pursuits, he'll praise your pastimes and give you a thumbs up.

One last piece of advice (if you need any): be careful about what you say, not just *to* your friend, but *about* him. Avoid the guy who asks questions: he's the one who never shuts up, and his big open ears can't be trusted to keep a secret. Once a word is spoken, it flies away and can't be recalled. When you're past the marble entry and inside your venerated friend's house, don't allow any slaves, male or female, to make your heart ache with lovesickness. That handsome boy or girl might become your one and only big gift; otherwise, if he's annoyed by your heartsickness, he might torture you by withholding presents altogether.

Whomever you recommend to him, mull it over carefully, to ensure you won't injure your own honor through someone else's faults. On occasion we're deceived, and sometimes we recommend someone unworthy. So, if you do happen to be taken in for a fool, don't vouch for the man whose downfall stems from his own missteps. That way, when someone you know inside and out is falsely accused and turns to you for protection, you can offer help and legitimately defend him. If he's bitten by the so-called "tooth of envy," isn't it always the case that you, too, hear threats coming your way not long afterwards? When the wall you share with your next-door neighbor is on fire, your own interest is at stake: flames left ignored are apt to gain strength and engulf the whole building. To the inexperienced, cultivating the friendship of a powerful man seems appealing. The experienced dread it. As for you, while your ship is at sea heading home, concentrate! Make sure a change in wind doesn't turn your around and set you back.

The morose hate the jovial, the jovial hate the morose; the swift hate the slow, the lazy hate the active and diligent; even though they swear they hate hangovers, drinkers hate teetotalers who lift a hand and say: "No, thank you." Dispel that cloud hanging over your brow: a modest man can often be interpreted as secretive, the quiet as a sourpuss. Amid all this, closely read and study the philosophers, who will teach you how to live serenely – so you can determine whether it's constant poverty and greed tormenting you, or fear and the desire for things only marginally useful. Can virtue be learned, or is it innate? Figure out what can minimize your worries, what can make you your own best friend, and what can put you truly at peace, whether that be public office, a satisfying, modest profit, or a private journey along the path of quiet retirement.

69 *Horace to his* Epistles (Epist. *1.20*)

Horace jokingly writes to his book of *Epistles*, which are now ready for publication, personifying the book as a young male (slave) prostitute. The letter reflects the potential dangers – and advantages – of publication, for instance the attainment of literary immortality. The references to Vortumnus and Janus (Roman gods of change, renewal and commerce) allude to an area in Rome popular with booksellers. Roman "books" consisted of rolled papyri ("volumes") whose ragged, uneven long ends would be neatened and polished with a pumice stone.

Book, you seem to be eyeing Vortumnus and Janus, so I'm guessing you want to be put up for sale, smoothed and polished by the pumice of Sosian Publishers, Inc. You despise modesty's keys and seals, which keep bookcases locked up tight. You're sad at the prospect of being explored by just a few and prefer life in the public eye; but I didn't raise you to think this way. Oh well, off with you, head where you've been itching to go. But, once you leave, that's it: don't come back. "Oh, poor me, what have I done? What was I thinking?" you'll say when someone hurts you, when you're rolled up tight and boxed away after your lover grows bored with you.

Suppose this diviner (I mean, your's truly) is annoyed at your mistakes and issued the wrong prophecy. Rome will love you – that is, of course, until youth deserts you. After countless hands have pawed and fondled you, you'll start feeling dirty. When you're overlooked and forgotten, worms will silently gnaw at you and you'll flee to Africa or be wrapped up, shipped off to Spain, and sold at half-price. Your mentor warned you, but you ignored him. Now he's chuckling like the man who pushed his donkey off a high cliff, in a fit of anger, when it refused to budge. Who should bother saving someone against his will? Oh, and here's what else you can look forward to: some lisping old man in back alleys will use you as a cheap textbook, to teach schoolboys their ABCs.

When the warm evening sun brings you a bigger audience, explain that, even though I'm a freedman's son of modest means, my wings stretched too widely for the nest. And, although my family tree may be a shortcoming, you can replace the deficit with my worth: tell your listeners that, in both war and peace, I won accolades from Rome's most powerful. Tell them I'm short, prematurely gray, always cold, and prone to anger (though easily soothed). If anyone happens to ask my age, tell them I turned 44 on December 8, 21 BCE – the year Lollius took Lepidus as his fellow consul.

Propertius

Sextus Aurelius Propertius (c. 50 BCE–15 BCE), like other famous poets of the Augustan age, enjoyed the patronage of Maecenas. He was probably from Assissium, but little else is known about him. Four books of *Elegies* are his only surviving work (published between 25 and 16 BCE); they cover many themes, including his torrid love affair with the fickle Cynthia (which is the main theme of Book 1). The following two poems, originally written in elegiac couplets although not formally identified as "epistles," exhibit epistolary qualities.

70 Propertius 1.11

Propertius writes to Cynthia, who's vacationing at the famous resort town of Baiae (near the Bay of Naples). He worries about her fidelity, given Baiae's reputation as a party town.

While you're at Baiae, basking beachside in the sun, gazing at nearby Hercules Boulevard (the hero's own masterpiece), or oohing and ahhing at how the waters of Lake Avernus flow into the sea and reach famed Misenus' tomb, do I, perhaps, cross your thoughts late at night, when you're all alone? Any chance your heart still has a little room left vacant? Or does some rival with his phony "I love you" steal you away from me – and my poems? Instead, I'd like to imagine you're rowing around Lake Lucrino in a little one-person dinghy fitted with tiny oars, the perfect size – for one. I'd prefer it if Teuthras' calm waters were stroking you as you practiced your freestyle swimming; that's better than picturing some guy whispering "sweet nothings" in your ear while you sunbathe on a secluded strip of beach, known to keep secrets hush-hush. It's not unusual for a girl who's sidestepped her guardian to loose her footing and let those god-sanctioned bonds slip her mind. No, I haven't forgotten your tried and true reputation as "Miss Faithful," but when it comes to love (and Baiae) a lover always finds reason to worry.

So: forgive me if my letter seems a little . . . gloomy. Blame it on nerves. Could I look after my own dear mother less devotedly? Is anything worth living for without you? Only you, Cynthia: you're my home, my parents. You're my everything, all happiness – you. Friends ask: "Why so cheerful?" "Why so sad?" I have one answer: "Cynthia." As soon as you can, leave Baiae, that fishy resort. Its beaches don't make absent hearts grow fonder: they're an honest girl's worst enemy. Damn the beaches of Baiae – a lover's kiss of death.

71 Propertius 4.3

This poem assumes a more explicit epistolary form. Arethusa writes to her husband Lycotas, who's been campaigning in Parthia. Many scholars consider this poem the inspiration for Ovid's *Heroides* (see below).

Arethusa sends this letter to her Lycotas (well, that is, if you are in fact still *mine*, seeing that you've been gone for so long). If some parts are hard to read, blame the smears and ink blots on my tears. If some words are indecipherable, it's because I'm dying here, my hand trembles as I write. Last I heard, Parthian Bactra saw you on its eastern shores; the Persians on their armored horses say they've seen you, as do the Getae far up north; the Britons, who ride on painted chariots, and the dark-skinned inhabitants of India, pummeled by eastern waters, all say they've seen you, too. Is *this* what a "faithful" marriage is? Is *this* what I get for giving myself to you when I was just a naïve virgin, conquered by your forceful arms? Is *this* where the marriage torch has led me? It must have been lit with black fire from a scorched funeral pyre, accompanying not just me, but an omen of the future. Water from Lake Stygia was what they sprinkled on my soft hair, where the veil sat on my head . . . crookedly. The god of marriage was certainly not my friend that wedding day, and my vows, posted on every city gate, were nothing more than graffiti.

This is now the fourth cloak I've woven to send to your outpost. Whoever it was who first chopped down an innocent tree to make stakes for forts and used cacophonous bones to construct the battlefield's woeful trumpet, whoever you are: go to hell! This evildoer can satisfy your hunger, dear donkey. Let him replace Ocnus, relieving him of his perpetual punishment in the underworld: let this deadly inventor now be the one weaving braids of hay for all eternity. Tell me, does your breastplate chafe your soft shoulders? It does, doesn't it? Does your heavy spear blister your smooth, untested hands? These abrasions are, however, preferable to some girl giving you love bites on your neck – I'll scream and cry if I see one. I hear your face is thin and drawn, but I hope your pallor comes from missing me. Evening brings bitter nights: that's when I find myself kissing not you, but the weapons you left behind. Then I sob seeing your cloak missing from my bed, and I weep some more when morning songbirds usher in the day – with dead silence. I spend winter nights spinning wool for your martial coat, cutting expensive Tyrian purple wool for your badge of stripes. I read up on the places where you're fighting, learning about the currents of the Araxes river and how many miles a Parthian horse can run without water. I study maps and teach myself where the learned gods placed each country, discovering which land is icy cold, which one crumbles in the heat, and which wind will return you safe and sound to Italy. My sister sits beside me; my nurse is pale with worry and she swears – though I know she's lying – that the winter is what delays you.

Lucky Hippolyta, queen of the Amazons! She got to go to battle, bare-breasted, hiding her soft hair under a helmet. I just wish Roman girls could fight! I'd be your ever trusty field pack, ready to tackle Scythia's hills where cold turns water into ice. Every love is great, but even greater is the love binding husband

and wife: Venus herself fans the fire keeping love alive. I couldn't care less about my expensive dresses, the purple cloth from Africa; my diamond rings are worthless. There's no point in wearing any of them. Everything is quiet and still. Sometimes, on the first of the month, a girl comes by to open the Lares' small shrine, but only little Woofie's cute whimpers and licks can make me smile as he jumps up and plops down on your side of the bed. I cover shrines with flowers, crossroads with fragrant shrubs, and throw Sabine herbs into the crackling fire. Whenever an owl hoots on a neighbor's roof beam or a flickering lamp requires a drop of wine, I sacrifice a year-old lamb at the temple, and the priests eagerly collect their fee.

I wish there were less glory in scaling Bactra's walls or in stripping a perfumed chief of his costly linen clothing, as lead missiles from slingshots fly by and devious bowstrings twang, while arrows swoosh past as their horsemen gallop away. But, once you've defeated those Parthians and march your horses in an official triumph, proudly displaying your medal of honor, make sure you come home guilt-free: don't taint my bed and our marriage pact – that's the only condition I demand for your safe return! I hereby vow to hang your armor up on Rome's Capena Gate, along with this inscription:

"A GRATEFUL WIFE, IN HONOR OF HER HUSBAND'S SAFE RETURN."

Ovid

Publius Ovidius Naso (20 March 43 BCE–17 CE) came from an equestrian family in Sulmona, Italy and wrote during the Augustan age, though he was significantly younger than other Augustan poets. Ovid studied rhetoric at Rome and held minor magisterial positions, but he focused his energies full-time on poetry. He was a prolific author: in addition to his famous *Metamorphoses*, he produced love elegies (*Amores*), mock-didactic poems – e.g., *The Art of Love* (*Ars amatoria*) and *Women's Cosmetics* (*Medicamina facei femineae*), and a work on the festivals of ancient Rome (*Fasti*), which survives unfinished. The following selections come from Ovid's three different epistolary works: the *Heroides* (*Heroines*), the *Tristia* (*Sorrows*), and the *Epistulae ex Ponto* (*Letters from Pontus*). Ovid began the *Tristia* in 8 CE, when Augustus banished him to Tomis (modern-day Constanta, Romania) on the Black Sea (in the province Pontus). Ovid doesn't fully explain the reasons for his exile, telling us only that *carmen et error* ("a poem and a mistake") were to blame. The "poem" refers to his *Ars amatoria* (which challenged Augustan moral legislation), but the "error" isn't clear. Ovid's epistolary efforts to gain recall (or a change in location) were unsuccessful: he died at Tomis, in 17 CE.

72 Ovid, *Heroides*

The following selection comes from Ovid's *Heroides*, elegiac verse letters composed in the voice of Roman and Greek heroines writing to their absent lovers. The collection comprises two parts; the first 15 (composed around 25–16 BCE) are single letters, and the remaining six consist of three paired epistles (the heroine's letter and the recipient's reply). These letters rely largely upon the reader's familiarity with famous figures and myths to create an ironic tension between the audience's foreknowledge and the letter-writer's ignorance. (For an additional example, see *Heroides* 7, Dido's letter to Aeneas, on the book's website: www.wiley.com/go/romanletters).

72 *Penelope to Ulysses* (Her. 1)

The iconically faithful Penelope writes a letter to her husband Ulysses (the Latin form of the Greek name of Homer's Odysseus), who still hasn't returned from the Trojan War.

Dear Ulysses, I'm resorting to letter-writing since you're taking so long to come back. Don't bother replying: just come home. Troy is dead and gone, much to the relief of every Greek girl. Priam and the whole city of Troy weren't worth it, that's for sure. God, how I wish the furious sea had crushed that adulterer, Paris, when he was on his way to steal Helen! Then I wouldn't be lying here in an empty bed, cold and lonely, constantly complaining how the days pass at a snail's pace. I wouldn't be spending every night like a widow, monotonously weaving and weaving until my hands are about to fall off. Every minute my imagination goes wild, inventing the worst possible scenario. Love involves constant worry. In my mind I picture violent Trojans attacking you; and the mere mention of Hector's name makes me nearly faint.

If someone was describing how Antilochus died, I imagined it was you. If someone told of how Patroclus fell dead wearing Achilles' armor, I wept: clearly wily deception doesn't always turn out well. Or, if someone was recounting how Heracles' son Tlepolemus died, I envisioned you pierced by the Lycian's sword, dripping hot red blood. It didn't matter what Greek had his throat slit: my loving heart went cold as ice imagining it was you. But a sympathetic god rewarded my chastity: Troy was burnt to ashes and you survived unscathed. Our Argive leaders are home, the altars smoke with offerings, and Trojan spoils hang from temple doors. Young wives give thanks for their husbands' safe return, and they in turn tell stories of how their own fate conquered Troy's. Anxious girls and distinguished elders listen with rapt attention; a wife hangs on to her husband's every word. Someone else dips his finger in wine and traces a map of Troy on the table, pointing out where all the fierce battles took place: "Here's the Simois river, here's Sigeum, here's where old Priam's lofty palace stood. And there's Achilles' position, and right over there is Ulysses'. And this is where galloping horses dragged Hector's mangled body around and around the city."

Old Nestor gave all the details to Telemachus – I sent him out to find you – and he repeated them to me. Wow! How daring to use your wiles like that and to sneak up on the Thracian camp in the dark of night, slaughtering so many men – and all with only one other person's help! I know you were very careful, thinking of me first and foremost. I was holding my breath the whole time, up until that point in the story where I heard that you (and the Thracian horses you took) had returned safely to the Greek camp.

But what's the point? What does it matter that Troy is just a pile of rubble, thanks to you and your comrades, if I'm still here, waiting and wondering just like I was when Troy was still standing? What good if Troy is gone but so are you, and I'm still sitting here twiddling my thumbs with no end in sight? For everyone else, Troy's just a memory; for me it's still a reality. Victorious colonists till Troy's soil with captured oxen. City streets are now fields; it's no longer the sword that's at work, but the sickle, slashing dense wheatfields enriched by Trojan blood. Ploughs turn over the soil, and with it heroes' half-buried bones, while vines and grasses grow over destroyed houses, burying them. Even though you were on the winning side and you survived, I have no idea why you're still gone or where the hell you (and your cold heart) are hiding out. Whenever some foreigner visits, I put him through a thousand questions; I send him away with a letter that I've written myself, just in case: maybe, just maybe, he would run into you soon. I've sent Telemachus to Pylos, to find out if wise old Nestor has heard anything, but he came back empty-handed. I've sent him to Sparta, too: nothing.

Where are you now living? What's making you take your sweet old time getting back? It'd be more to my advantage if Troy's walls still stood! I'm now kicking myself for making all those prayers! If the city still remained, then at least I'd know where you're fighting, and my fears would be only about war. Then I wouldn't be the only one still complaining about her husband's absence! What do I fear? I don't know. But I'm crazy with worry and everything is a cause for concern. Sea or land, whichever: both have countless dangers, making me anxious about your delay. But while I'm home (stupidly) worrying about your safety and well-being, maybe I should really be worrying that some girl's holding you up; maybe you've been "captured" by some foreign lover.

Perhaps you're explaining (to her?) what a silly provincial housewife you have, the kind who likes everything coarse and unrefined (except wool). I really hope I'm wrong and my allegation doesn't hold water – that it's not that you don't *want* to come home, but that you *can't*. Back here my father Icarius tries forcing me to leave my "widowed" bed, as he calls it, and chastises me for my infinite excuses for postponing remarriage. He scolds me again and again, and wants to repeat himself until I'll agree. But I always retort that I'm yours and yours alone, forever. "Penelope is and always will be the wife of Odysseus. End of story." He finally relents, swayed by my loyalty and entreaties, and gives up.

Dulichians, Samians, even men from Zacynthus – they descend upon me like lions, and each acts like he's king of the den; they're tearing us to pieces. Should I mention Pisander, Polybus, and savage Medon, or the greedy hands of Eurymachus and Antinous? How about I list all the others? Don't you think it's a tad disgraceful that in your absence you're feeding and housing everyone trying to steal your hard-earned possessions (me included)? And the ultimate disgrace, you ask? Your very own slaves, Irus and Melanthius, only contribute to your financial loss and shame by carrying in the goats and sheep for the dinner table. And there we are, the three of us – an old man, a powerless woman, and a boy – your dad, your wife, and your son. We three sit and watch, unable to do a thing about it. To top it off, I almost lost my son when these suitors treacherously ambushed him, trying to stop him from going to Pylos. Dear gods, I pray, let the Fates proceed in due order, let Telemachus outlive us, let *him* be the one to close our eyes at death, not the other way around! We have only three loyal slaves left: the herdsman Philoetius, the swineherd Eumaeus, and your very old nurse Eurycleia. Laertes can't fight: he can barely hold up his own scepter. Telemachus can't: he'll be strong soon enough (please, gods, just let him live), but right now he needs his father's help to protect him. I can't fight: I'm not able to drive these enemies from your home. So who's going to protect your kingdom? You better come quickly. *Here* is your safe harbor, your sanctuary. Think of your son (just hope he'll still be here by the time you get back) – your son, who should have been trained under his father's guidance. Think of Laertes: he's holding on, resisting death just so you can be the one to close his eyes when he takes his final breath. And finally me, think of me: you left me a young girl and, if you returned right now, you'd find me an old lady.

73–78 Ovid, *Tristia*

The following selections come from the *Tristia* (*Sorrows*) and *Epistulae ex Ponto* (*Letters from Pontus*), elegiac verse letters Ovid wrote from exile. The five books of *Tristia*, addressed to unnamed friends, were published between 9 and 12 CE; the *Epistulae*, published between 13 and 16 CE, comprise four books and were addressed to named friends. Throughout the *Tristia* and *Epistulae ex Ponto* Ovid frequently refers to the *Getae*, a foreign tribe inhabiting what is now modern Romania and Bulgaria.

Figure 3.2 Goddess Fortuna and Pontos. Graeco-Roman marble, late second century BCE, from Tomis, Romania. Location: Muzeul din Constanţa, Romania. Source: Gianni Dagli Orti / The Art Archive at Art Resource, NY

73 *Ovid to his little book (*Tr. *1.1) 8* CE

Like Horace in Letter 1.69 of his *Epistles*, Ovid addresses the first book of *Tristia*, which he's about to send to Rome.

Dear little book, go without me. I'm not jealous, so go to Rome, where your master's forbidden! Go, but not in your fancy clothes – they're unfit for an exile. Wear what suits our miserable situation. No purple cover for you: that's not the color of mourning. No title printed in red or paper with anti-rotting cedar oil; you'll have no white knobs to decorate the black ends of your volumes: these bells and whistles belong to lucky books. Remember my misfortune. Brittle pumice won't polish your two ends, no, you'll have to show up with your "hair" all disheveled and uncombed. Don't be embarrassed by ink blots: people will recognize my tears. Go, book, be my spokesperson: say hello to my old beloved stomping grounds. I'll walk there by the only "feet" actually allowed to tread there (my metrical ones!). If anyone by chance remembers me (as is likely to happen among crowds) and asks what I'm up to, tell him I'm alive and *not* well. Tell him the fact I'm still breathing is a gift from god. Beyond this, keep your mouth shut: if they want to know more they'll need to *read*! Beware! Don't say anything outside what's necessary! If you jog his memory, he'll immediately recall my mistakes. Then I'll be put on trial, pronounced guilty by public opinion.

Even if you're pricked with stinging words, don't defend me; I don't have a strong case; it's too weak to stand up in court even with a lawyer's help. Find someone who sadly sighs over my slow death, who can't read those verses dry-eyed, who prays silently (lest the spiteful hear) for Caesar's dwindling anger to lighten my punishment. I'll pray that, whoever hopes that gods are sympathetic to sufferers, he not also suffer – let his prayers come true! And let the *princeps*' wrath vanish, granting me the possibility of dying in my homeland!

Perhaps, book, in carrying out my instructions you'll be chastised, judged inferior to the reputation of my genius. It's the critic's duty to investigate a book and its context. If you're asked about your origin, rest easy, you've got a good excuse: fine-spun verses radiate from a calm mind, but poems formed under a dark cloud of unpredictable misfortune are foggy and dim. Poetry demands seclusion, peace and quiet, but I'm tossed by the sea, winds, and fierce wintry storms. When it comes to my poetry, every fear intrudes. Ruined, I'm constantly thinking a sword is about to pierce my throat. These verses will come as a surprise even to an impartial critic, and, however inferior, he'll read them with an eye to leniency. Take Maeonian Homer and inundate *him* in all these perils. See how a touch of *his* genius dissipates when he is surrounded by such evils.

Remember, my book, don't worry about fame and don't feel embarrassed that you don't provide much reading pleasure. When it comes to fame, Fortune isn't smiling so much on me now. While I was still safe and secure, I was smitten by the love of glory, burning with desire to make a name for myself. Now it's enough that I don't hate poetry and writing it: that's what got me to this place. I can thank my own brilliance for this exile. Nevertheless, go on my behalf, *you*'re allowed: go and lay eyes on Rome. If only the gods could change me into my book, how I'd love that metamorphosis! Do you think just because you're entering the great metropolis as a foreigner you can arrive incognito? You may lack a title, but they'll recognize your face: your style is uniquely yours. You'd like to deceive them, but it's obvious you're mine. Still, assume a secret cover when you enter the city, so my poems don't incriminate you: they aren't winning any accolades these days. If there's anyone who declares you shouldn't be read just because you're mine, and then throws you on the ground, proclaim: "Take a look at the title. I'm not the *Art of Love*. That work has already paid its penalty."

Maybe you're wondering whether I'll send you to the high Palatine hill and order you to scale the steps to Augustus' house. Let those august places and their gods forgive me! That's the citadel from which this lightening bolt struck my head! I'm well aware that extremely merciful deities live there, but I'm still afraid of the gods who hurt me. Once injured by your talons, oh hawk, a dove flinches at the slightest rustle of feathers. Once a lamb has escaped the wolf's hungry teeth, she doesn't dare wander far from home. If he were alive today, Phaethon would avoid the sky and wouldn't dare touch those horses he so foolishly desired. I'll admit, I'm afraid of Jupiter's weapons, since I've experienced them firsthand. When thunder rumbles, I think I'm the bull's eye for a dangerous lightning bolt. Any Argive who escaped the Capherean rocks always turns his sails away from Euboean waters. My ship, once smashed to pieces by a huge storm, now shudders at the approach of the place where it was wrecked. So beware, book: stay alert, keep your eyes open, and be content with a middle-class readership. It's because Icarus sought heights too high with wings too weak that we now have the Icarian Sea, his eponym.

Nonetheless, from my standpoint it's hard to say whether you should employ oars or breezes. You'll be given the time and place: if you can be put into his hands while he's relaxing, when everything seems low-key; if his anger's mellowed, if there's anyone who can hand you over while you're timidly hesitating, who's willing to introduce you, then go ahead: approach him. May you arrive on an auspicious day and have better luck than your master, alleviating his misfortunes! Either nobody can do this or only one who's given wounds can heal them – like Achilles. Just be sure that, in trying to help, you don't make things worse. Fear outweighs hope, so beware you don't add fuel to the fire and become my second source of punishment!

But, once you enter a safe refuge, that is, you own house and the rounded bookcases inside, you'll see your brothers arranged in order: they're the product of the same skill and attention, the same wakeful nights. The others will openly flaunt their titles, showing off their names printed on their ends, but you'll see three hiding in a dark corner. Doesn't matter, everyone knows who they are: instructions on how to love. Either avoid them or, if you have the guts, re-title them. Give them names like "Oedipus" or "Telegonus" – famous parricides. Lastly, I'm warning you, if you care about me at all, me, your Dad, don't give one ounce of love to those three, although they were your teachers. You'll also find on the bookshelf 15 volumes on changed forms, the *Metamophoses*. They were recently rescued from my burning funeral pyre. Tell them my fate looks a lot like those metamorphosized shapes. My face suddenly looks quite different from what it was before: it's been transformed from one of happiness and joy into one of tears and weeping. I've got more instructions if you ask, but I'm afraid they'll only delay you. Besides, if you took all my instructions with you, dear book, you'd become just a heavy suitcase to lug around. It's a long trip back to Rome: get going! I'll continue sitting and waiting here, at the ends of the earth, in a place far, far away from *my* home(land).

74 *Ovid to his wife* (Tr. *1.6) 8* CE

Ovid thanks his wife, who's protecting his financial interests and working on securing his recall.

The poet Antimachus loved his wife Lyde and Philetas loved his wife Bittis, but neither of them loved the way I love you, my wife. You are an ever present fixture in my heart. You deserve a happier, but not a better husband than me. I'm an eroding building, a crumbling ruin, and you're my support, the plank that props me up from beneath: if I'm still anything at all, it's thanks to you alone – your gift to me. It's because of you that I don't become a spoil of war, stripped bare by people looking to steal the timber from my shipwreck. There was that faithless rat who would have exploited my sorry situation and seized my property – just as a bloodthirsty, hungry wolf seizes a lamb who's escaped the sheepfold's protection, or as a greedy vulture scans all around, looking for a rotting corpse – were it not for you.

But your courage and the help of our brave friends drove this vulture away; there aren't enough ways to thank them as they deserve. So I'm the witness of your proven loyalty, one who's as misfortunate as he is loyal (if such a witness means anything anyway). Hector's wife, Andromache, can't surpass your virtuous integrity, nor can Laudamia, who took her own life to be her husband's companion – even in death. If it had been your fate to appear in Homer, Penelope's fame would be second to yours. Either it's just who you are and no teacher taught it to you, or you acquired such virtues the moment you were born. Or (if I can compare great with small) the imperial first lady Livia, whom you've honored all these years, has served as your model, teaching you how to be an ideal wife, and you became just like her through regular practice. My poems don't have great enough power and my mouth isn't skilled enough to sing your praises! If my lips had ever possessed any innate vitality, it's now died, totally suffocated by these never ending sorrows. Thanks to your virtuous heart, you've earned first place among the blameless heroines, and everyone knows it. As long as my public tribute retains its power, you'll continue to live – through my poetry – forever and ever.

75 *Ovid to his readers* (*Tr. 1.11*) *8* CE

Each and every letter you've read in this little book I wrote during my difficult journey. First it was the Adriatic Sea that witnessed my writing these letters, while I shivered during the ice-cold days of December. Then, once I had passed the two seas of the Isthmus and was on ship number two heading into exile, I think it was the Aegean Cyclades that marveled at my composing verses amid all the sea's wild howling. I really can't believe I managed to keep my head among such waves of mental turmoil and buffeting seas. Call it writer's dedication, or writing in a trance, or just plain stupidity: it was the torturous act of writing that in fact alleviated my torture.

Some days the storm-bearing Hadis constellations made me keel this side and that; often the constellation Steropes made the sea turn threatening, or the Arcadian bear's guardian changed day into night; or sometimes the south wind pulled a late November downpour from the Hyades. Often the sea poured into our ship and, although my hand was shaking, I continued writing my poems, such as they are. Even right now the north wind pulls the ropes taut and they screech, and the curved waves rise up and over like a hill. The captain himself is lifting his hands to the stars, praying for help, forgetting he's the captain! Wherever I look, all I see is the image of death: my mind is rocking, I fear death – and yet in my fear I pray for it.

I'll safely reach the port, and then it'll be the port I fear: the land holds more dangers than the hostile seas. For the snares of men and sea combined ravage me: sword and waves present a double trouble. Men, I'm afraid, will spare no drop of blood while hunting for plunder, the sea may want to gain fame through my death. On my left is the uncivilized coastline: voracious acts of robbery are an everyday occurrence and the land hosts bloodshed, murder, and wars. And, although wintery storms stir up the sea, my heart is even more turbulent than the waters.

So, be fair, reader: forgive me if these verses disappoint your expectations. It's not like in the old days, when I'd write sitting in my garden or on my little comfy old couch. No, it's a winter day, and here I am, writing, pitched side to side by the brutal deep sea, my paper sprayed with the dark blue waters. The insolent storm fights me, incensed that I dare to write while it hurls its uncompromising threats at me. Let the storm conquer the man! But let the storm come to its own end at the exact same time I conclude my poem.

76 *Ovid to a silent friend* (*Tr. 4.7*) *10–11* CE

It's been two years: twice the sun has approached me after the chill of icy winter, twice completing its journey by entering the constellation of Pisces. In all this time, what happened to your faithful hand? You can't write even just a few lines? Where's your loyalty? People whom I barely knew still write. Why not you? So often I've broken a letter's seal expecting to find your name on the paper. I hope the fact is you *have* written letters, but they simply haven't reached me. It's perfectly obvious what I pray for: I'd rather believe that the Gorgon Medusa's face really is framed by locks of snakes, that the part-dog virgin Scylla exists, that there *is* a Chimera, that four-footed horse-men Centaurs really do exist, and that Geryon the Giant lives, along with the three-headed dog Cerberus; I'd rather believe in the Sphinx, the Harpies and the snake-footed Giants, the hundred-handed Gyes and the half-bull man, the Minotaur. I'd much rather believe all these were real than that you, dearest friend, have changed, deserting your affection for me. Endless mountains lie between you and me, countless roads, rivers, fields, and many seas. There're a thousand possibilities why frequent letters of yours reach my hands infrequently. Trump these thousand of reasons by writing more often: that way I won't always have to make excuses for you, my friend.

77 *Ovid to a friend* (*Tr.* 5.7) *11–12* CE

This letter you're reading comes from the land where the broad Hister empties into the sea. If your life is good and happy, then that's a bright spot, the only one, in my life. As always, dearest, you ask how I'm doing, though I don't have to utter even one word for you to know: I'm miserable. This is the sum of my existence, and it will be for anyone surviving Caesar' wrath. What are people at Tomis like, what kinds of customs surround me? There's a mix of Greeks and Getae here, but a greater number of the latter. The roads are crowded with Samartae and Getae coming and going on horseback. Not one is without a quiver and bow and darts tinged yellow with viper poison. Gruff voices, fierce expressions (clearest evidence of their manner), and hands inexperienced in trimming beards or hair, but quite practiced when it comes to thrusting and stabbing knives (every barbarian keeps one fastened by his side): *these* are the "people" your poet lives among – good god, can you believe it? Among these savages he lives, forgetting his playful Cupids; these are the men he must look at, listen to. If only he'd live and not die among them: then his shade would be free from this hateful place.

You say, dear friend, my poems are being danced to in a packed theater, receiving much applause. As you know, I haven't composed anything for the theater purposefully. My Muse has no ambition for standing ovations. At the same time, I won't refuse anything that might thwart my oblivion and could potentially return my name – the name of an exiled man – to people's lips. Sometimes I curse the poems, recalling how they've hurt me; I curse the Muses; but, when I've had my fill swearing at them, I still can't live without them. I continue pursuing poetry, the "weapons" still bloody from the wounds they gave me. A Greek ship recently smashed by Euboean waves still dares to sail the waters of Capharea.

Nonetheless, I don't stay up all night working to ensure my name for posterity – better if my name were forgotten. I keep my mind busy and outwit my grief, and I try to translate my cares into words. What else should I do all alone on these deserted shores? What other therapy should I seek for my depression? When I look around, the place is ugly, no other place in the world could be gloomier. I look at the men and they barely deserve the name: they're more savage and cruel than even wolves. They don't fear the law: right yields to might, and the laws lie conquered beneath the belligerent sword. They defend themselves against the cold with animal skins and loose pants, protecting their scraggly faces with long bushy beards. You can hear traces of Greek among a few, but even they sound foreign, thanks to their Getic accent. There's not one single person in this whole damned population who can speak even a word of basic Latin. I, the Roman poet, yes – forgive me, Muses! – I'm forced to speak mostly Sarmatian. I'm ashamed to admit that long disuse of Latin words means they no longer come tripping off my tongue. I'm sure in this little book there are countless verbal barbarisms – not the fault of the man, but of his locale. But, so that I don't lose my ability to communicate in the Ausonian tongue, so that my voice in my native language doesn't go mute, I talk to myself, dragging out rarely used words, seeking again the perverse linguistic currency of my literary pursuits.

This is how I wile away my time, my life; how I pull myself out of thinking too deeply about my troubles. Through my poems I seek to forget my wretched state of existence: if these are the rewards I attain through my work, so be it.

78 *Ovid to an enemy* (Tr. *5.8) 11–12* CE

Ovid chastises a man who disparages him back at Rome, warning that misfortune can strike anyone, anytime.

I've been demoted, for sure, but I haven't fallen so low that I'm also beneath *you* – nothing could be lower than you. What do you have against me, you bastard? Why do you laugh at my misfortunes? It could be you! I'm down and out: doesn't this deserve your sensitivity and sympathy? I've got troubles that even wild, untamed beasts weep over. Don't you fear Fortune standing atop her uncertain wheel, or the hateful goddess' haughty words? Avenging Nemesis demands punishment from the deserving; why do you trample my fate with your stomping foot? I've witnessed a person who laughed at another's shipwreck drowning in the sea later on. Know what I said? "The waves were never fairer." The man who once wouldn't give even a crust of bread to the poor now himself eats food he begs for. Fickle Fortune wanders around directionless: she never remains still and focused in one place. Now she radiates with happiness, now she wears a bitter expression. She's constant in one thing: inconstancy.

Once upon a time I flourished, but my pinnacle was short-lived. My flame had straw for fuel and burned out quickly. Don't get used to the joy you feel in that inhuman heart of yours. Stay tuned: I'm still holding out hope of appeasing the god. I fell short of committing a crime, and, while I'm certainly ashamed, my fault doesn't amount to treachery. Moreover, from east to west, the whole wide world considers no one to be more compassionate than the ruler it obeys. Of course, he can't be swayed by any power, but he's sympathetic to the prayers of the fearful and, following the gods' example (he'll join their company one day), he'll pardon my punishment and even fulfill extra requests. Go through a year. Compare days of sun with days of clouds: you'll find more sunny days. So try to contain your excitement about my ruin. Think about the fact that one day I might even be restored to Rome. Remember: if the *princeps* is mollified, one day you may be sorely disappointed to run into me in the forum. And maybe one day I'll see *you* exiled – for a more serious infraction. After the first prayer, this is my second.

79–83 *Epistulae ex Ponto*

79 *Ovid to Cotta Maximus* (Pont. *1.9) 12–13* CE

Ovid expresses consolation to Maximus over the death of their mutual friend, Celsus. Ovid is unable to attend the funeral, but commends Maximus for his loyalty to Celsus, urging him to show the same to Ovid.

Your letter informing me about Celsus' death is now completely soaked in my tears; It's a horrible thing to say, and I never thought I'd say it, but I wish I hadn't gotten it. My ears haven't heard such terrible news since I arrived here in Pontus, and I pray they never will again. The image of him, as if he were still right here, alive and well, hovers before my eyes. He's dead, but my love for him imagines he's still living. I recall his typical lightheartedness, how his seriousness always played out with true fidelity. Still, my strongest, most profound memory is when I think back to the day my household fell into sudden ruin, crushing me. He was right there, right there, Maximus: when nearly everyone else abandoned me, he was there, even though he had nothing to do with my misfortune. I saw him weeping my death as if his own brother were on the funeral pyre. He hugged me tight and consoled me as I lay face down crying, and his tears mixed with mine. Oh, how often he assumed the role of the hateful guardian to preserve my bitter life, restraining my hands when they were all set and ready to end my life. How many times he said: "The wrath of the gods can be placated! Live! Don't give up hope! You may be forgiven!" But I especially remember him saying: "Think, think what a great help Maximus will be to you. He'll work hard on your behalf: he's devoted to you. He'll ask Caesar not to let his earnest anger persist forever. To his own resources he'll add those of his brother and will leave no stone unturned to help you and lighten your suffering."

His words, how they eased the tedium of my sad life. Maximus, be sure they're not in vain! Celsus often swore he'd come here if you, and only you, gave permission for the long trip. For he worshipped your house's private sanctuary the way you worship the gods, masters of the world. Believe me, although you deserve all the friends you have, he was the best – as long as it's neither property nor a famous family name that make men great, but honorable character and intellect. Therefore it's right that I make an offering: a libation (of tears) for Celsus, who's now dead and who, when alive, did the same for me as I was leaving my old life for a "life" of exile. It's fitting that I write these verses to testify to his rare character, so that one day future readers will know of your name, Celsus. This is it, this is what I can send you from Getic lands; this is the only thing of mine permitted back at Rome. I wasn't able to join your funeral procession or anoint your body; an entire world separates me from your pyre. The man who *was* capable of doing all this for you, the man you treated like a god when you were alive, has carried out every duty on your behalf. Maximus oversaw your funeral and ensured its great honor; he poured the balsam upon your icy chest. In his grief he diluted the perfumed ointments with his falling tears and covered your bones in a nearby plot. Since he's so dutiful in paying out debts to deceased friends, let him count me as good as dead.

→ this is his funerary offering

*80 Ovid to Flaccus (*Pont. *1.10) 12–13* CE

Naso the Exile sends you, Flaccus, good health. Well, that is, if one can send something he doesn't actually possess. Longstanding weariness doesn't allow my injured, suffering body to maintain its strength. There's no pain, I'm not burning with fever or gasping for breath, my blood pressure remains steady. Rather it's my mouth: it's dry. The dishes placed before me make me squeamish, and I can't help complaining when dinner time arrives with its disgusting food. Offer me anything from the sea, land, or air – not one is enticing. The gods' maid, tireless Hebe, could offer me nectar and ambrosia, the food of gods, with her beautiful hands, and not even that taste would awaken my listless palate. A dead weight will continue to sit in my inactive belly. I'm being honest, but I wouldn't dare write this to just anyone or send it to just anywhere – I wouldn't want to be called a spoiled brat. But these are my circumstances, and my situation is such that there's not even the *possibility* of becoming spoiled rotten! I pray these local so-called "delicacies" will be the punishment for anyone thinking Caesar's wrath toward me is too lenient!

Nor does sleep, frailty's nourishment, fatten my deprived body: I'm awake all night – and so, too, is my endless suffering: my surroundings supply plenty of food for that! If you saw me you'd barely recognize my face. You'd ask where all my earlier healthy color disappeared. A lot less blood runs through these scrawny limbs of mine; my skin is whiter than brand new wax. It's not my fault, I'm not binge drinking: you know that almost always I drink only water. Nor am I being gluttonous: even if I wanted to, there's no chance of that happening here in Getic land. The damning passion of Venus isn't to blame for my weakness either – she's not prone to visit sad, depressed beds. It's the water and my surroundings that are making me sick and, even more than that, constant mental anxiety. If it weren't for you and your brother lightening my load, I could've barely endured the burden of my sadness. You're a welcoming land for a shattered dinghy; you deliver the help many refuse to offer. Do so always, I beg, because, as long as divine Caesar's wrath is upon me, I'll always need your help. May each of you approach the gods as suppliants, begging that he lessen (not necessarily end) his justified anger.

81 To Maximus (Pont. *3.3) 12–13* CE

Ovid recounts a dream in which Venus' son, Cupid, visits him. As the personification of love, Cupid had been the inspiration for many of Ovid's earlier poetic works. He credits Cupid as his guide in writing the *Amores* by playfully punning on the word "feet": "I placed five feet after six," a reference to the poems' elegiac meter – couplets consisting of a dactylic line of 6 feet (measures) followed by a pentameter line of 5 feet. Ovid compares his relationship with "Love" (Cupid) to other famous mythological teacher–student relationships. He cleverly plays with the contradiction between Love as the "teacher" of Ovid's early elegiac poetry and Love as the student, whom Ovid instructed through his handbook *The Art of Love.*

If you have a second, Maximus, star of the Fabian family, lend an ear to an exiled friend. Listen while I tell you what I saw. I'm not sure it was a ghost, a real body, or just a dream.

It was night; the brilliant full moon was shining through the double-shuttered windows as usual. Sleep, the universal escape from cares, consumed me, and my lazy limbs were stretched out the length of the couch. Suddenly the air quivered, stirred by fluttering wings, and the window lightly creaked open. I jolted awake, up on my left side, heart thumping, chest trembling: sleep immediately departed. Love was standing there not with his usual dapper appearance, but with a sad expression, holding his left hand upon the maple bedpost, no necklace around his neck, no hair ornament, hair all a mess and disheveled. His soft locks were hanging down over his scruffy face, his feathers seemed messy and unpreened, like what you'd expect on the back of a wind-tousled dove that many fingers have handled. As soon as I recognized him (for no one's more familiar), I untied my tongue and spoke:

"O boy, cause of your beguiled master's exile – better if I hadn't instructed you. Have you really come here, where peace is ever absent, where the savage Danube's waters freeze? Why else have you made the trip, unless to witness my woes for yourself? In case you didn't know, they're all thanks to you. You first dictated to me the poems of my early career: following your lead, I placed five feet after six. You forbade me from writing Homeric epic or the deeds of great generals. My intellectual powers may have been small perhaps, but they were something, and then your bow and fire destroyed them: for, as long as

I was singing about your and your mother's domain, my mind had no time for greater works. And that's not all: thanks to my stupid poem I ensured you wouldn't be ignorant when it came to the *Art of Love*. As a result, I was rewarded with exile. Poor me! What's more, it's exile in the boonies, in a place that's always at war. Chionian Eumolpus never got Orpheus exiled, nor did Olympus and his teacher, the Phrygian Satyr Marsyas; Chion never received this kind of "reward" from Achilles, and Numa reputedly never harmed Pythagoras like this. I won't go through the long list of names collected over time: I'm the only one who's been ruined by his own student! I gave you weapons and instructions, insolent boy. Is *this* the thanks I get? You know I've never undermined legitimate marriages – you can swear it's true! I wrote those lines for a specific audience, for unchaste women who don't wear ribbons in their hair or the long stola past their ankles. Tell me, I beg of you, have you ever learned from *my* lessons how to deceive married women and throw a question mark upon paternity? The law protects every woman from smooth-talking Casanovas – haven't I also strictly forbidden them to get near these books? But what good is it if people believe I wrote instructions for adultery, a crime subject to severe penalty? May your arrows continue to always hit their mark, may your torches never lose their flickering flame, and, as for Caesar Augustus (your brother via Aeneas), may he rule the world and maintain power over all lands; make sure his anger toward me isn't unrelenting, so I can serve my time in a more forgiving place." I heard myself saying all this to the winged boy, and in my mind he answered:

"I swear by my torch and arrows, and by my mother and Caesar, I've learned from you only what's permissible: your *Art* committed no crime. I can defend you in this regard, but I wish I could do it for everything else! But you know as well as I, there's something else, something far more serious, that has injured you. The very pain of it keeps me from stating it, and you can't say you're free from guilt; whatever it is, you may cover up your crime under the name "mistake," but the extent of your punisher's wrath was completely fitting. Nonetheless, I wanted to see your dejected face for myself and console you; so my wings glided over far-reaching roads and highways. I first saw these regions eons ago, when, at Mom's bidding, I pricked Medea with my arrows. Now, after so long, I'm making a second trip for you, oh friend and soldier in my camp. Put away your fear. Caesar's wrath will soften, a gentler breeze will blow in your favor. Don't worry about a delay: the time is approaching, and Tiberius' Germanic triumph has brought everything to a happy state. While the house, its children, and their mother Livia rejoice, while you, great father and leader of our country, rejoice, while all the people give thanks and every altar throughout the city burns with sweet-smelling flames, while the holy temples have open access, we must hope our prayers make a difference."

He spoke and either slipped away into thin air or I woke up. Oh Maximus! I'd sooner believe that swans were as black as the Ethiopian Memnon than doubt your approval of these words. But white milk can't be changed to black pitch, and shining white ivory never becomes turpentine. Your family tree suits your spirit: you have a noble heart and Hercules' honesty. Jealousy is a pointless vice: it has no place in a superior nature, and like a hidden snake it creeps along the ground. Your lofty mind surpasses even your birth, since your disposition is as noble as your name. Therefore let others hurt the unfortunate, and enjoy being feared; they can carry darts tipped with corroding poison. *Your* house is accustomed to helping suppliants – I beg you, count me among them.

82 *Ovid to Maximus* (Pont. 3.8) 12–13 CE

I was thinking what gift I could send from Tomis as a token of my affection. You deserve silver, and especially gold, but these presents are more likely to please you when you're the one giving them! Besides, there aren't any precious metals to be found here: the enemy hardly allows even the farmer to do any digging! Flashy purple has often bordered your clothing, but you won't find that dye in the Sarmatian sea.

Here the sheep's wool is rough and the young girls of Tomis haven't learned the art of weaving. Instead of working wool, women mill grains and carry heavy water jugs on their heads. You won't find intertwined vines covering elm trees here, or fruit weighing down tree branches. The ugly fields produce bitter wormwood – the land's proof of its hostile nature.

So there wasn't anything in the whole entire region of awful Pontus worthy enough of you. Nonetheless, I've sent some Scythian arrows in their quiver – I hope they become stained with your enemy's blood! These are the "pens" you'll find in this neck of the woods, these are the "books." This, Maximus, is the kind of "Muse" flourishing in my "home" here. I'm embarrassed to send them since they seem so cheap, but I hope you'll think they're adequate.

*83 Ovid to Carus (*Pont.* 4.13) 14 CE*

Ovid describes a new literary composition honoring Tiberius and Livia. By now Augustus has died and Tiberius is the new emperor. In Latin *carus* means "dear."

Dear Carus, greetings, oh friend!

You're one of my loyal buddies – you live up to your name! This letter's style and poetic structure signal who's saying "hi," not necessarily because my words are so impressive, but because they are at least not mundane: whatever this letter has going for it, there's no doubt it's from me! Likewise, I can tell what you've authored even if you scratched out the title page. It doesn't matter how many other books sit on the shelf with yours, you're still recognizable: familiar stylistic consistency gives you away. A work's literary strength reflects its author, and yours is worthy of Hercules, its very subject. My Muse gives away her identity by her blotches (take a look at her complexion). Thersites' ugly face kept him from going incognito the same way Nireus' dashing good looks turned heads. Don't be surprised if my poem reveals some flaws – I've nearly turned into a Getic poet! (Wow, how embarrassing.) I actually composed a work in Getic, conforming its vocabulary to Latin meter! I even won some admirers (*kudos* to me!) and began making a name for myself: a poet among the barbaric locals. What's the topic, you ask? You'd approve: Caesar. The god's spirit assisted my literary experiment. I described how Father Augustus' body is mortal, but his spirit's gone to live among the celestial gods; that Tiberius equals his father in virtue and, when the time came, he accepted the reins of leadership that earlier he had so often refused; that you, Livia, are the Vesta of virtuous mothers – it's debatable whether your son or your husband deserves you more; that there were two young men, steadfast supporters of their father, who gave definitive proof of their own spirit.

When I gave a public reading of the work (keep in mind, it's not in my Muse's native Latin) and my fingers came to the very last page, all the Getae moved their heads and their arrow-packed quivers: there was quite a bit of murmuring. Then one of them said: "Since your poem's about Caesar, he should order your recall to Rome." Indeed he said it, but look at me now, Carus: it's the sixth winter since I've been banished here beneath the North Pole. My poems are no help. They're the ones that hurt me, that caused this miserable exile in the first place. As for you, I pray Germanicus' subjugation of the enemy offers a subject for *your* talents, and may his boys be well – those boys whose education you've been asked to oversee (a great feather in your cap, by the way). I pray that, by the shared bond of our sacred pursuits and in the name of friendship, which you value, you give my cause a little push, in whatever way you can. Otherwise I'll be at an unhappy standstill forever – that is, unless I find some other way of getting the hell out of here.

FURTHER READING

Augustus

Leon, Ernestine (1948) "The *imbecillitas* of the Emperor Claudius." *Transactions and Proceedings of the American Philological Association, 79*, 79–86.

Wallace-Hadrill, A. (1984) *Suetonius: The Scholar and His Caesars*. New Haven, CT: Yale University Press.

Horace

Armstrong, D. (1989) *Horace*. New Haven, CT: Yale University Press.

Davis, G., ed. (2010) *A Companion to Horace*. New York: Wiley-Blackwell.

Freudenburg, K. (2002) "Poetry, philosophy, politics and play: *Epistles* 1." In T. Woodman and D. Feeney, eds., *Traditions and Contexts in the Poetry of Horace*. Cambridge: Cambridge University Press, pp. 141–57.

Houghton, L. B. T., and Wyke, M., eds. (2009) *Perceptions of Horace: A Roman Poet and His Readers*. Cambridge: Cambridge University Press.

Leach, E. W. (1993) "Horace's Sabine topography in lyric and hexameter verse." *Journal of American Philology, 114*, 271–302.

Lowrie, M. (2009) *Writing, Performance, and Authority in Augustan Rome*. Oxford: Oxford University Press.

Mayer, R. (1986) "Horace's *Epistles* 1 and philosophy." *The American Journal of Philology, 107*(1), 55–73.

Walter, A., Carlson, S., Clarke, W., Gross, N., Hall, R., Hatch, D., Kopff, E. C., Payne, M., Simms, L., and Zartarian, R. (1972–1973) "Horace's first book of *Epistles* as letters." *The Classical Journal, 68*(2), 119–33.

Propertius

Cairns, F. (2006) *Sextus Propertius: The Augustan Elegist*. Cambridge: Cambridge University Press.

Dee, J. (1974) "Arethusa to Lycotas: Propertius 4.3." *Transactions of the American Philological Association, 104*, 81–96.

Fantham, E. (2006) "The image of woman in Propertius' poetry." In H. C. Günther, ed., *Brill's Companion to Propertius*. Leiden: Brill, pp. 183–98.

Janan, Micaela (2001) *The Politics of Desire: Propertius IV*. Berkeley: University of California Press.

Keith, A. (2008) *Propertius: Poet of Love and Leisure*. London: Duckworth.

Maltby, R. (2006) "Major themes and motifs in Propertius' love poetry." In H. C. Günther, ed., *Brill's Companion to Propertius*. Leiden: Brill, pp. 147–82.

Ovid

Claassen, J.-M. (2008) *Ovid Revisited: The Poet in Exile*. London: Duckworth.

Drinkwater, M. (2007) "Which letter? Text and subtext in Ovid's Heroides." *American Jouanal of Philology, 128*, 367–87.

Farrell, J. (1998) "Reading and writing the *Heroides*." *Harvard Studies in Classical Philology, 98*, 307–38.

Jacobson, H. (1974) *Ovid's* Heroides. Princeton, NJ: Princeton University Press.

Kennedy, D. (1984) "The epistolary mode and the first of Ovid's *Heroides*." *Classical Quarterly*, *34*, 413–22.
Knox, P., ed. (2009) *A Companion to Ovid*. Malden, MA: Blackwell.
Lindheim, S. (2003) *Mail and Female: Epistolary Narrative and Desire in Ovid's* Heroides. Madison: University of Wisconsin Press.
McGowan, M. (2009) *Ovid in Exile: Power and Poetic Redress in the* Tristia *and* Epistulae ex Ponto. Leiden: Brill.

CHAPTER FOUR

The Roman Empire (14 CE–third century CE)

Emperor Tiberius (14–37 CE)

The following reply letter survives as a stone stele written in Greek, dating to 15 CE. It's a reply from the Emperor Tiberius to the leaders (ephors) and inhabitants of Gytheion, a city located in Laconia, Greece (previously Sparta's port). During the Roman Empire the city gained prestige thanks to a nearby marble quarry (see Cancik and Schneider 2004: 1070). The original letter from Gytheion requested permission to establish special honors for Tiberius, Augustus, and Livia. Among other things, the Gytheionites wanted to erect statues of the three in the city's theater and to establish festival days devoted to each. The Gytheion letter reflects typical Roman religious customs, especially in the eastern empire, whereby the emperor (or his deified person) were worshipped as deities. Reverence to the imperial cult included monuments and statues, holidays celebrating the emperor's birthday, and complimentary decrees. Cult worship was reciprocal: not only did the emperor receive honor and prestige through these accepted offerings, but provincial cities considered them a source of pride and status. These cities regularly competed for permission to honor the emperor, in order to distinguish themselves from other regional cities through piety and patriotism. The emperor carefully limited the number of requests he accepted, with a view to maintaining a delicate balance of reciprocity and to avoiding "squandering his capital" and thus "cheapening the honour by handing it out too widely" (Lendon 2001: 172). In the letter from Gytheion Tiberius refuses the divine honors offered to him, but accepts those offered in honor of Augustus. The personal response from an emperor could itself function as a status symbol, even if the reply denied the request; the Gytheionites had Tiberius' letter inscribed below the original request and publicly displayed. Compare Tiberius' letter with Claudius' letter immediately following. Letters like these display great formality and many conventional features.

Roman Letters, First Edition. Noelle K. Zeiner-Carmichael.

84 *Tiberius to Gytheion* (SEG *IX 922) 15* CE *(stone stele)*

Tiberius Caesar Augustus, son of Divus [deified] Augustus, Pontifex Maximus, holding tribunician power for the 16th time, sends greetings to the ephors of Gytheion and to the city.

The ambassador Decimus Turranius Nicanor, whom you sent to me and my mother, delivered your letter along with the attached ordinances voted by you to enact the pious reverence of my father and the honoring of us. I'm much obliged, but it's my belief that it befits all men in general, and particularly your city, to keep in reserve honors more suited to gods (especially since my father bestowed great public benefits upon the entire world). I'm content with honors more appropriate to mortals. My mother, however, will give her reply once she learns about your decision regarding the honors you voted for her.

Emperor Claudius (41–54 CE)

The same Claudius who was the topic of Augustus' letter to Livia (Letters 56 and 57) was declared emperor by the praetorian guard following Emperor Caligula's assassination. Not only was he a fairly effective emperor; Claudius proved himself intellectually talented, especially in law and literature. He was a prolific writer, alhough none of his works survives. It's widely asserted that Claudius died from poisoning, perhaps at the hands of his last wife, Agrippina.

85 *Claudius to the Alexandrians* (Sel.Pap. *2.212) 41* CE

This letter begins with a proclamation by the Egyptian prefect announcing he'll publicly display an inscribed copy of the emperor's letter in order to make it more widely accessible. The letter illustrates Claudius' careful attention to maintaining peace in the region. As is typical of letters from the region, the months correspond to the Egyptian calendar system. Claudius' letter was originally written in Latin, but the surviving inscription is a Greek translation of the original (Greek was the official language of the Roman east). Toward the end of the letter Claudius refers to two provincial magisterial positions: the gymnasiarch (head of the gymnasium) and the *cosmetae* (cosmetes, civic magistrates in Hellenistic Egypt).

Lucius Aemilus Rectus proclaims: Since the entire city, given its large population, couldn't be present for the reading of this most revered and generous letter to the city, I have decided it is necessary to exhibit the letter publicly so each one of you, upon reading it, may marvel at the grandeur of our god Caesar and give thanks for his kindness toward the city.

Year Two of Tiberius Claudius Caesar Augustus Gemanicus Imperator, the 14 of the month Neus Sebastus.

Tiberius Claudius Caesar Augustus Germanicus Imperator, Pontifex Maximus, with tribunician power, Consul designate, sends greetings to the city of Alexandria and its inhabitants.

Tiberius Claudius Barbillus, Apollonius son of Artemidorus, Chaeremon son of Leonidas, Marcus Julius Asclepiades, Gaius Julius Dionysius, Tiberius Claudius Phanias, Pasion son of Potamon, Donysius son of Sabbion, Tiberius Claudius Archibius, Apollonius son of Ariston, Gaius Julius Apollonius, Hermaiscus son of Apollonius – all these ambassadors of yours delivered the decree to me and said much about the city, clearly indicating to me your friendliness toward us, which, rest assured, I've been keeping track of for quite some time. I well know that you are naturally pious toward the Augusti, showing particularly earnest interest toward my house – and I toward yours; the greatest testament to this, regarding this last point specifically, is the fact that my brother Germanicus Caesar previously addressed you in your native Greek language.

I gratefully accept the honors you offered me, although I set no great store by them. First, as you proposed, I permit you to retain my birthday as a feast day and to erect statues of myself and of members of my family, since I recognize your eagerness to memorialize everywhere your reverence to my house. Of the two golden statues: the one made to represent Pax Augusta Claudiana – which my most distinguished Barbillus proposed and then insisted about, after I refused in order not to cause offense – this one will be set up at Rome. The other will be carried in parade on eponymous feast days in your city, as you requested. With it there will be a seat to go, and it will be decorated as you like. As I accept such honors as these, it would perhaps be foolish to refuse the establishment of a Claudian tribe and Egyptian-style sacred gardens: I therefore permit you to carry out these honors and, if you want, to set up the equestrian statues given by my procurator Vitrasius Pollio.

Regarding the four-horse chariot statues, which you want to raise in my honor around the points of entry into the country, you may erect one at Taposiris in Libya, another at Pharos in Alexandria, and a third at Pelusium in Egypt. But I respectfully decline the establishment of a chief priest and temples to me, since I don't want to offend my fellow contemporaries and I think that temples and similar tributes throughout the ages are gifts allowed for gods alone. About the requests for which you've been anticipating my response: I approve and preserve Alexandrian citizenship, with all the honors and benefits of the city, for those who have become ephebes from the beginning of my rule, except for those who have managed to become ephebes even though they are sons of slaves; it is equally my will that all the other benefits that were given to you under earlier rulers, kings, and prefects continue, as the deified Augustus also ratified them.

I've decided that the manager of the temple of Divus Augustus in Alexandria be appointed by lot, just as is done for the managers of the temple of Divus Augustus in Canopus. As for limiting the city magistracies to a three-year term, this seems a very good idea; for the magistrates will conduct themselves more moderately during their term if they fear any potential charges of corruption. Regarding the senate: I cannot say what your tradition was under the ancient kings, but you know well that there was no senate under the Augusti preceding me. Since this is a matter just now being introduced and its benefit to your city and my state affairs is not entirely clear, I've written to Aemilius Rectus to investigate it and to apprise me as to whether it's appropriate to establish a senate and, if so, in what manner we should go about it.

As for the question of who was responsible for starting disturbances and factions – or, if we are being honest, the *war* with the Jews: although your ambassadors, especially Dionysius son of Theon, valiantly argued against the Jews who opposed them, I was nonetheless unwilling to conduct an official investigation. Instead I've been storing up inside me an immutable wrath for whoever stirs up trouble again. I'm telling you, plain and simple: if you do not end this deadly, stubborn hatred toward each other, I'll be forced to prove to you what happens when a kind-hearted ruler transforms it into justified outrage. So, yet again, I earnestly demand that the Alexandrians behave tolerantly and kindly toward the Jews, who have been inhabiting the same city for many years, and that they don't dishonor any of their religious customs but allow the Jews to practice their own rites, as they did during the time of Divus Augusus – rites that I myself have approved, now that I've judged both sides. On the other hand, I explicitly demand that the Jews not vie for more benefits than they held before and not send their own ambassadors, as if they lived in a different city – an action never done before; and I demand that they not sneak their way into the athletic contests run by the gymnasiarch and the *cosmetae* (in which they are not allowed to participate, as they are not citizens), since they enjoy their own advantages and share in the benefits that come from living in a city – a city belonging to others; and that they themselves not lead or welcome any Jews who sail down from Syria or Egypt, or they'll make me greatly suspicious. If they do not abide, I'll use every means to go after them, as if they were stirring up a plague that is universally spreading all over the inhabited world.

If you are, both of you, willing to live showing patience and kindness to each other, then I will act with longstanding care toward the city, as if old family ties connected me to it. I stand witness to my friend Barbillus for the consideration he has always shown for you in my presence: now he most earnestly pleads your case. And I also stand witness to my friend Tiberius Claudius Archibius. Goodbye.

Seneca the Younger

Lucius Annaeus Seneca (4 BCE–65 CE) was the son of Seneca the Elder (54 BCE–39 CE), a prominent rhetorician. Originally from Cordoba, Spain, Seneca the Younger went to Rome to be trained in rhetoric and philosophy. In 41 CE Emperor Claudius exiled him to Corsica on a charge of adultery. There he spent the next several years, studying literature and philosophy and composing three *Consolationes*. In 49 CE, at the request of his fourth wife, Agrippina the Younger, Claudius recalled Seneca and appointed him tutor to Agrippina's son, the future Emperor Nero. When Nero became emperor in 54 CE, Seneca served as his imperial advisor until 62 CE, when Nero's behavior became increasingly erratic and malicious. In 65 CE Nero forced Seneca to commit suicide following allegations that he was involved in an assassination plot. The conspiracy, usually referred to as the Pisonian Conspiracy (after Gaius Calpurnius Piso), involved several other prominent Romans; of the approximately 41 named conspirators many were either executed or forced to commit suicide, like Seneca himself.

In addition to his *Consolationes*, Seneca wrote treatises of Stoic ethics, a satire of Emperor Claudius (*The Pumpkinification of Claudius*), nine tragedies, and a collection of 124 letters addressed to his pupil Lucilius: the *Moral Epistles*. The letters explore various Stoic topics and encourage simple, virtuous living.

86 Seneca to Lucilius (Ep. *1.2*)

Seneca advises quality over quantity.

From what you write and from what I hear, I've got high hopes for you: you're not running all around, moving from place to place, unsettling yourself. That kind of jumpiness signals an unhealthy mind: the main proof of a calm mind is remaining in one spot and lingering awhile with your self. Be aware, however, that reading many authors and genres also involves roving and instability. You must linger and absorb a few select literary masters if you want to draw from them ideas that you retain permanently. Being everywhere means you're nowhere. When someone spends life traveling the world, s/he acquires many hosts, but no friends; it's the same for those who hurriedly and superficially peruse every author instead of spending quality time becoming intimately familiar with the genius of just one. Food is pointless when it leaves the body immediately after being swallowed; nothing impedes healing like switching medicines frequently; no scar heals over a wound when various ointments are tried; a plant doesn't grow and thrive when it's frequently transplanted. Nothing is particularly useful when it's constantly altered, and reading a large quantity of books is distracting. So, since it's impossible to read everything, own only as many books as you can read.

"But," you say," I want to take a look at this book now and at that one later." Sampling many dishes is the sign of a fastidious palate, for foods provide not nourishment when they're too numerous and diverse – only distaste. Always read the canonical authors; and, when you want a diversion, return to the ones you've already read. Every day gather something helpful to arm yourself with against poverty, against death, against every kind of plague. And when you've run through many a food for thought, pick one that you can chew on that day. This is something I do: from the many passages I've read I pick one excerpt and ruminate on it.

Today's daily thought comes from Epicurus (I often cross over to the enemy's camp – not as a traitor, but as a scout!): "Happiness in poverty is an honorable enterprise," says Epicurus. In fact that kind of "happy poverty" isn't poverty at all. The poor person isn't the one who has too little, but the one who desires too much. Who cares how much you have stashed away in your safe or stored in your warehouse, how large your flocks are, or how big your revenues? What's the point in eyeing others' possessions, calculating the value not of what you've *already* earned, but of what you *hope* to earn? You want to know the proper limit to riches? To have, first and foremost, what is necessary, and, second, what is enough. Goodbye.

87 Seneca to Lucilius (Ep. 1.4)

You've sent me a letter through "your friend," as you call him. Then you continue by warning me not to discuss anything about you, since you yourself don't usually confide in him. So in the same letter you've both confirmed and denied that he's a "friend"! If you've employed this particular word with its more formal meaning in mind, referring to him as a "friend" the way we refer to all political candidates as "good men" or the way, when we run into someone whose name we forget, we greet them with "Hello, *sir*!" – so be it. But if you call a "friend" someone whom you don't trust as a friend, you're making a big mistake and don't understand the true meaning of the word "friendship." Let's consider everything involving "friendship," starting with the notion of "friend." After a friendship is established, there must be trust; even before that, you must act as a judge. Those who judge *after* they've already formed a bond, instead of assessing the individual *first*, are people who do everything backwards, mixing up their obligations contrary to Theophrastus' precepts. Think carefully when you're considering becoming friends with someone. Once you've decided to do so, fully welcome them into your heart: talk to them as openly as with yourself. Behave so that you entrust to yourself nothing you can't entrust even to a personal enemy. There are certain things social convention demands you keep private, but share with a friend all your thoughts and worries: if you think that friend's trustworthy, this is exactly what you'll do. Some people, afraid of being deceived, have taught others to be deceitful and, by being suspicious, they give their friend the right to do wrong. Why shouldn't I be frank with my friend, speaking exactly what's on my mind? When I'm with my friend, why should I think I'm alone?

Some people share intimate details, reserved only for friends, with any person they run into on the street, unloading their worries onto any Joe Schmo. Then there are others who abhor confiding in their nearest and dearest and keep their secrets under lock and key if they can. Neither extreme is good. Trusting everyone and trusting no one: both are vices. Still, the former I'd say is more honest, the latter less risky. Also avoid being either of these two: the guy who lives in permanent seclusion and the guy constantly in the thick of things. Reveling in the hustle and bustle isn't "industry," but the sign of a restless, agitated mind; avoiding lifting a finger isn't "rest," but laziness and apathy.

Let me share something I read in Pomponius: "Some hide away in such deep corners that what they think is as clear as day is actually as dark as night." Find a balance and integrate the two: the man living quietly must act, and the man who acts must live quietly. Talk it over with nature. She'll tell you she created the perfect balance between day and night. Goodbye.

88 *Seneca to Lucilius* (Ep. *1.7*)

You want to know what you should avoid? Crowds. You're not yet at the point where you can safely trust yourself among them. Me? I'll admit, I become weak around crowds. I never return with the same good habits I left; if I've calmed down about something, I get all riled up again and, whatever vice I've avoided, it returns. Just as long-term infirmity debilitates sick people, so they can't ever be taken outside without suffering a setback, the same can happen to those of us who have healed our minds and souls from a prolonged illness. Mingling with crowds is dangerous: there's always someone making some vice appealing, or imprinting us with it, or secretly smearing it on us. The larger the mob, the greater the danger. But the thing most damaging to good character is sitting at some spectacle: that's when vices creep in more stealthily, along pleasure's path. What do I mean? That, if I go, I return home greedier, more power-hungry, more materialistic? Yes, definitely! What's more, I'm more hard-hearted and less human – precisely because I've been with humans! By chance I caught a midday performance and was expecting a little fun, humor, and relaxation – a respite from human bloodshed. It was the exact opposite. Battles of past generations look downright compassionate compared to today's: no more trifles – it's murder, pure and simple. The men wear no armor; bodies are exposed to hits on all sides and strikes are always successful.

Most prefer this kind of spectacle to traditional duels and encores. Why? Because there's no helmet or shield to deflect a blade. Why bother with defensive armor or skill? They'll just delay the inevitable: death. In the morning, men are thrown to lions and bears; at noon, to the spectators themselves. They order convicted murderers to face off against soon-to-be murderers, reserving the most recent victor for the next killing. It's always death "to the end," accomplished through fire and sword. And this all happens when the arena's empty. "But he was a thief! And that guy a murderer!" So what? True, his crime fits the punishment; but what was your crime to be condemned to watch this sort of spectacle? "Kill him! Whip him! Burn him! Why does he face the sword so tentatively? Why is he hesitating to kill? Why is he afraid to meet death? Let's see him bleed: give him deep lash wounds! Let's see them fight it out bare-chested, blow by blow!" Then comes intermission. "Let's have something to kill the time – how about a little throat-cutting, shall we?" Come now, can't you understand that bad examples spill over and affect peoples' actions? Thank the gods that you're teaching savagery to a person who isn't even capable of learning it.

The young, malleable, all too easily influenced mind must be rescued from the mob. A crowd so contrary to their sensibilities would have shaken Socrates, Cato, and Laelius to the core. None of us, no matter how much attention s/he devotes to his or her own character, can withstand the onslaught of vices exuding from so great a throng. Only one example of extravagance or greed is all it takes to promote great destruction. A good friend living in the lap of luxury weakens your heart and saps your spirit little by little. A rich neighbor arouses jealousy; a mean-spirited friend corrodes you, even if you're a shining white example of goodness and purity. What do you think happens to good qualities when they're threatened by attacks from the greater population? You must either imitate the public or hate it. Neither is a good option. Don't imitate the wicked just because they comprise the majority, and don't hate the majority just because they're different from you. Turn inward as much as you can. Spend time with those who will improve you, and welcome those you can improve. It's a mutual process: people learn as they teach. It's pointless to let some conceited desire for publicizing your talents lead you into the public eye, just so you can showcase your debating skills or read your composition before an audience. Of course, I've got no problem if you can make your work marketable, but there's no listener who'd really understand you. You might find one or two, but they'd need you to mold and train them so they could comprehend it. "Then what was the point of learning all these things?" Don't worry – it wasn't a waste of time if you learned for your own benefit.

But, to ensure I'm not the only one learning something today, I'll share with you three exceptional sayings expressing the same message. This letter owes you one as payment, and I'll give you the other two as an advance! Democritus says: "To me, one man counts as much as a crowd, and a crowd as much as one man." And this author, whoever he was, when asked what was the point of expending so much energy studying an art few would appreciate, gave this excellent answer: "A few are good enough for me, one is enough, and none is just fine." The third maxim comes from Epicurus' letter to a fellow scholar: "I write not for many, but for you; each of us is a good enough spectator for the other in this 'theater' of studies." Take these sayings to heart, my dear Lucilius, so you'll despise the pleasures that win popular approval. Many sing your praises, but is this something to be proud of if it's the general crowds who appreciate you? Let your talents be "spectators" facing inwards.

89 *Seneca to Lucilius (Ep. 1.8)*

Responding to Lucilius' reply to Seneca's letter on crowds, Seneca writes the following. He asserts that his own withdrawal from public life (and from crowds) is specifically aimed at helping others live a virtuous life.

"You tell me to 'avoid the crowds,' withdraw into myself, and be content with my own conscience. What happened to your philosophical school's precepts ordering one to die while performing some action? What about this?" Why do I seem to be advocating slothfulness? I've shut myself behind closed doors and thrown away the key, so that I may be a greater help to more people. I don't spend a single day in empty leisure. I even devote the night to my studies. I don't plan on sleep but succumb to it. Even when my eyes are straining, drooping from exhaustion, I pry them open, to stay on task.

I've withdrawn not so much from people as from their affairs – especially my own. My work is focused on future generations; it's for them that I record thoughts that might come in handy. I'm putting in writing healthy advice: "useful, medicinal prescriptions," so to speak, things I myself have found to be useful salves for my own wounds – which, though not completely healed, are no longer festering. I illustrate for others the straight path, which I found late in life, exhausted as I was from wandering around. I exclaim: "Avoid what the mob likes, what pure chance allots! Freeze at the stroke of good luck: be suspicious and fearful." Wild beasts and fish are duped by alluring hope. You think these are the *gifts* of good fortune? No, they're *traps*. Whoever wants to live safe and sound must avoid the sticky lyme used to trap birds, the so-called "gifts" that deceive us, fools that we are. We think we're the ones in control, when in fact they're the ones ensnaring us. This kind of life path leads us to a precipitous cliff ending with a sheer plummet downwards. When success begins driving us crossways, it's impossible to stay on course; and it's a slow and difficult end. Fortune doesn't just keel us over but plunges us headfirst, hurling us against the rocks.

So maintain a healthy, sound way of life: indulge your body only for good health. Treat it harshly so it won't disobey the mind. Let food satisfy hunger, drink quench thirst; let clothing protect against the cold, and a house against the harsh seasons. It doesn't matter if it's built of sod or multi-colored marble. Remember, straw protects just as effectively as gold: each is a roof over your head. Scorn what wasteful work produces for decoration or embellishment. Only the soul is truly wonderful: "If the soul is great, nothing else is." If I talk to myself this way or share such thoughts with future generations, don't you think I'm doing more good than by walking down to the forum to appear on behalf of someone's bond, by hearing or pressing my signet ring's approval on someone's will, or by offering my help, in word or deed, for the Senate or for a political candidate? Trust me, those who seem to be doing nothing are actually occupied in nobler tasks. They're busy with worldly and divine matters.

I must end and, as usual, pay out a reward for this letter. It won't come from my own account. I'm still robbing Epicurus! I read this saying of his only today: "Be a slave to philosophy, so that you may experience true freedom." When one surrenders to philosophy, one is immediately released; for submitting to philosophy is freedom itself. Maybe you'll ask why I quote Epicurus more than our own Stoics. Why do you consider these sayings as Epicurus' property instead of public property? How many poets say things that philosophers have quoted (or should quote!)? I won't touch on the tragic poets or our own Roman dramatists, for they're somewhat serious and sit halfway between comedy and tragedy. How many incredibly sage verses you'll find scattered in mime! How many of Publilius' verses should be quoted by tragic actors! Here's one of his verses pertaining to philosophy – and especially relevant for what I mentioned above, namely the idea that our possessions don't come from chance: "Everything you obtain from desire is alien." I recall you've expressed the same thing much more effectively: "What fortune has made yours is not really yours." And here's one more from you, an even better one: "Any good that was given can also be taken away." I won't charge for these last two, since they're yours! So long.

90 Seneca to Lucilius (Ep. *1.12*)

Everywhere I turn, I see signs of my advancing old age. When I visited my suburban villa, I complained about the expense of running a dilapidated building, and the caretaker said that the run-down parts weren't the result of negligence – he was taking care of everything – but the villa was simply old. This was the estate that blossomed in the care of my very own hands! What does my future hold, if the stones of my own age are already crumbling? In anger, I grabbed my first opportunity to vent: "It looks like these plane trees have been overlooked: they have no leaves. Look how knotted and warped the branches are, how pathetic and neglected the lopped-off stems! They wouldn't be like this if someone had built a trench around them and gave them some water!" The caretaker swore up and down that he was doing everything as he should and wasn't slowing his efforts, but the trees were old, plain and simple. Between the two of us, *I* was the one who had planted them; *I* first saw their leaf buds sprout. Turning to the door, I asked: "Who's that old fellow, the decrepit man you stationed by the front entrance – and rightly so, since he looks like he's about to take his final exit out the door of life any day now? Where did you acquire him?

Why the heck did you agree to take on someone else's corpse to bury?" But then the man spoke up, "Don't you recognize me? I'm Felicio! You used to give me little toy action figures all the time. I'm your little pet slave, the son of Philositus, the caretaker." "That man has lost his marbles," I said. "Has my darling slave now become a little boy again? It's entirely possible; his teeth are starting to fall out!"

Thanks to my villa, everywhere I looked I was reminded of my old age. Let's embrace and love old age; it offers copious pleasures, provided you know where to find them. Fruits are the most gratifying when they're perfectly ripe; the beauty of boyhood climaxes exactly when that stage is ending. For the man who loves to drink wine, the last sip is the best – the one that immerses him, pushing him over the edge, into intoxication. Every pleasure retains its most delightful aspect right until the end. Life is happiest when it's already beginning to slope downwards but hasn't yet arrived at the steep drop. The time period teetering on the "roof's edge" has its own pleasure. For lack of interest in pleasures replaces the pleasures themselves! How sweet to be done with them and to have left them behind!

"It's troublesome," you say, "to see death right in front of your eyes." First, a young man should keep death in close view just as much as an old one. We aren't summoned to death in the order in which our names are recorded in the births census. Second, no one's so old that s/he's deluded if s/he hopes for one more day. One day marks a stage of life. One's entire lifespan is divided into parts; these consisting of circles, the larger ones surrounding the smaller. One encircles all the others: this is the one representing the period from birth to death. There's another circle demarcating the years of youth, and another encompassing in its circumference our entire childhood. Then, in its own class, there is the year that encloses all the portions of time that, when multiplied, comprise life. The month is organized by a narrower circle; the smallest one represents the day and has its beginning and end – from sunrise to sunset. Heraclitus the Obscure (nicknamed "Obscure" on account of his confusing way of speaking) said: "One day is equal to every day." People interpret this in different ways. For example, one interpretation is that any day is equal to another in its number of hours; this is in fact the case. For, if a "day" is equated to 24 hours, then all days are, by necessity, equal – since night attains what the day loses. Others think Heraclitus means that one day is equal to all others through similarity; for the longest space of time has nothing you won't find in one day, such as day and night [. . .] nothing that makes the day any different when it's shorter from what it is when it's longer. Therefore each day must be ordered to bring up the rear, that is, as if it completed and filled out our whole life.

Pacuvius, who was governor of Syria for so long that it was as if he owned it, used to celebrate his own funeral with wine and the usual feast. After banquet he'd have himself carried to his room, while eunuchs would clap and sing in Greek, to musical accompaniment: "He has lived, he has lived!" And so he had himself buried each and every day. Let's, however, turn his perverse example into a good, applicable one and, when we're lying down to sleep, let's say with joy and lightheartedness: "I have lived and completed the life course fortune granted me." If the supreme god adds one more day, let us happily accept it. The happiest man, who's most secure in his own skin, is the one who anticipates tomorrow calmly; whoever begins each morning by saying "I have lived" gets out of bed and starts the day with a bonus. But it's time to close this letter. "Really?" "It will arrive without even a little pittance?" No worries! It brings something with it, actually not "something" but quite a lot. For what's more notable than the maxim I offer you in this letter? "It's a terrible thing to live in constrained circumstances, but there's nothing forcing you to live in constraint." Naturally, of course. Everywhere you'll find many short and smooth pathways toward freedom; let's thank god that no one can be held fast in life. It's possible to disdain the constraints holding us. "Epicurus," you say, "uttered these words. Why are you quoting them from a foreigner?" When something is a truth, I'll take as my own. I continue heaping Epicurus on you so that those who swear on others' words, devaluing *what* is said instead of *who* says it, may learn that the best thoughts belong to everyone.

91 Seneca to Lucilius (Ep. 2.18)

The feast of the Saturnalia, held in December 17–23, honored the Roman god Saturn and involved a reversal of normal social customs (e.g., slaves assumed the role of their masters, and vice versa). Given its carnivalesque nature, it was an especially popular holiday. Seneca, however, advises Lucilius to practice restraint and moderation.

It's December and the city's in a tizzy. It's carte blanche on all-around partying. Everywhere you can hear the sounds of huge preparations, as if the Saturnalia were different from any other regular workday! In fact the difference is so tiny that I think whoever said "December was once just a month; now it's a whole year!" is spot on. If you were here, I'd happily discuss with you what you think we should do: whether we should maintain our daily routine or, in order not to be overly conspicuous, whether we should dine merrily and hang up our togas, like everyone else. For changing clothes, which used to happen only in times of chaos or serious political upheaval, has now transformed into something we do for the sake of pleasure, on feast days. If I know you, you'd be playing the role of umpire: you'd have wanted us not to be like the mob wearing their Saturnalian party hats, but not to be entirely unlike them either – unless, that is, we should use the holiday as an appropriate time to instruct our souls to abstain from the pleasures into which the whole rest of the population rushes headfirst. Yet here's the clearest proof of a person's inner strength: he doesn't willingly seek the allurements and temptations typically enticing someone into luxury and doesn't allow himself to be led on that path. It takes great strength to remain hungry and sober amid a drunken and puking crowd. It shows much more self-control, *not* to withdraw, but to do everything everyone else is doing... only in a different way, neither flaunting one's flag nor blending in with the mob. It *is* possible to enjoy a festival without going overboard.

However that may be, I'm really eager to test your mental strength, so I'll also offer you a challenge by using precepts from the great masters. Choose a few days when you'll be content with the scantiest, simplest food and with harsh, scratchy clothing. Say to yourself: "Is this what I was fearing?" In times of security the mind should prepare itself beforehand for difficult times, it should strengthen itself by anticipating Fortune's wrath. A soldier practices drills during peacetime, constructs a rampart when no enemy's in sight, and wears himself out with extra work so he'll be ready to go when the time calls for it. If you don't want him to tremble when it counts, then train him beforehand. This is precisely what some people achieved when, once a month, they did a run through of living in poverty, approaching need and want head on – so they'd never fear what they had so often practiced.

Now, don't think that I mean you should have meals like Timon's, or the "poor man's hovel" – or whatever "meager" meal the extravagant millionaire eats to find respite from the tedium of his or her rich lifestyle. The pull-out cot needs to be a real one; and the same goes for your scratchy cloak. Your bread should be hard and moldy. Do this for three or four days, sometimes more, so that it's not just some game but a real trial. Then, Lucilius, trust me, you'll rejoice, satisfied with a penny's worth of food. You'll realize that peace of mind doesn't require riches, for even when she's angry Fortune will provide what's necessary for you to get by. Nevertheless, don't think you're doing something out of the ordinary: you'll be doing exactly what many thousands of slaves, many thousands of poor do every day. But give yourself credit: you're doing this willingly, and it will be as easy for you to live like this permanently as it was to try it for a short while. Let's practice on a dummy; let's get to know poverty, so Fortune won't find us unprepared. We'll feel more secure in our wealth if we know it's not so very horrible to be poor.

That teacher of pleasure, Epicurus, reserved certain days when he'd eat only enough to satisfy hunger: his point was to see whether he fell short of total pleasure, by how much, and whether it was worthwhile to make up for the difference through a good bit of effort. He says as much in his letters to Polyaenus, written during Charinus' archonship: he boasts that *he* lived on less than a penny, while Metrodorus, who hadn't yet made such progress, required a full penny.

Do you think such food can really fill someone up? Yes, and it can fill him up with pleasure too – and it's the type of pleasure that isn't shallow, fleeting, requiring replenishing; it's the steadfast, reliable kind. Water and porridge or a crust of barley bread don't make the tastiest of meals, but it's a supreme pleasure to derive enjoyment even from these sorts of foods and to take it to the point where no unjust blow from Fortune can rip that enjoyment away from you. Even prison food is more liberal, and even those sentenced to death receive more food from their executioner! It takes an extremely enlightened spirit to reduce one's diet to a point that even prisoners awaiting execution don't have to fear! Such a practice truly forestalls Fortune's spear. So, my dear Lucilius, begin to follow the custom of these people, and reserve some days when you can take a break from all your affairs and become accustomed to making do with as little as possible. Become best friends with poverty. As Virgil says: "Dare, dear guest, to condemn riches and make yourself worthy of a god."

No one deserves a relationship with god more than the person who's scorned riches. I'm not forbidding you to possess them, but I want to ensure you own them without trembling in fear. You'll be successful only by one method: by convincing yourself you'll live *without* them as happily as you live *with* them and by treating them as if they might vanish any second. Let me begin to fold this letter up. "First," you say, "settle your account." Okay, I'll pay you with Epicurus: "Out-of-control anger breeds madness." You can't ignore the truth of this saying, since you've possessed both slaves and enemies. This emotion, enflamed by love as much as by hate, rages against all types of people, and it's just as likely to erupt amid serious matters as amid trival and frivolous ones. The source from which this emotion explodes makes no difference: it's the kind of soul it ends up in that matters. The same goes for fire: the *intensity* of the flame isn't as important as *where* the fire catches. The flames won't burn solid things; nevertheless, dry and easily flammable material can turn a single spark into a massive conflagration. So, my dear Lucilius, the end result of intense anger is madness, and you must avoid anger not for the sake of moderation, but for the sake of sanity. Goodbye.

92 *Seneca to Lucilius* (Ep. 2.21)

You think you're experiencing challenges with those men you wrote me about? It's with yourself you've got the greatest challenge: you're your own worst enemy. You have no idea what you want. You're better at outlining the plan than at following it through. You see where happiness lies, but you don't have the guts to reach out and grab it. Let me clue you in as to what's holding you back, since you don't see it yourself: you think the things you're planning to give up are valuable and, even though you resolve to attain a calm state of mind, your current flashy lifestyle (the same one you hope to abandon) is holding you back – it's as if you think you're going to fall into a dark and grimy existence. You're making a mistake, Lucilius. Moving from that old life into this new one involves an ascent, not a descent. The difference between luster and actual light is equivalent to the difference between your old life and the new: the latter possesses its own natural light source, and the former acquires its brightness from another source. Luster is created when an external light hits it, but it becomes a dull shadow when anyone blocks the source; light, on the other hand, shines brightly from an innate source within.

Your own studies will make you bright and illustrious. Take Epicurus, for example. He was writing to Idomeneus and rescuing him from a glitzy lifestyle, replacing it with a true and steady kind of fame;

at that time Idomeneus was a powerful state leader dealing with serious matters: "If renown is what you want," Epicurus said, "then my letters will make you more famous than all your personal treasures, which currently make you feel valued." Was Epicurus exaggerating? Who would know the name of Idomeneus if Epicurus hadn't inscribed it in those letters? All those magistrates and satraps – even the king himself, whose title Idomeneus sought – have sunk into nameless oblivion. Cicero's letters have kept Atticus' name alive. He would have had no advantage with Agrippa as a son-in-law, with Tiberius as his granddaughter's husband, or with a Drusus Caesar as a great-grandson; his name would still have sunk into silence even among such prominent names – if it weren't for his epistolary bond with Cicero.

The deep flood of time will flow over us. A few brilliant minds will stretch their heads above the waters and, while they are fated to pass into eternal silence, they'll resist drowning into oblivion, surviving for a long time to come. Epicurus promised his friend this very thing, and now I promise it to you, Lucilius. I'll attain esteem among future generations, and I'll lead your name into eternal renown with mine. Our Virgil promised unending fame to two heroes, and he delivered: "Two fortunate men! If my verses possess any power, no day will ever erase the recollection of your names from time, so long as Aeneas' home inhabits that immovable rock, the Capitoline hill, and the Roman father holds the reins of power." Whomever Fortune has promoted, whoever has become part and parcel of another's power, his fame flourishes and his house is packed with visitors – provided he maintains his status. But when he loses that he's lost from memory. The fame of the innately brilliant individual increases, however; not only does he attain distinction, but whatever clings to his memory is also passed along to the next generation.

Idomeneus can't make an appearance in my letter for free, so he'll offer payment from his own account. Epicurus wrote him with that famous saying where he urges him to make Pythocles rich, though not in that common, dangerous way. "If you want to make Pythocles rich," he said, "don't increase the size of his bank account, but rather subtract from his desires." The point is clear enough and doesn't require explanation or elaboration. But let me give you a piece of advice. Don't think this maxim applies only to riches. You can use it for just about anything. For example: "If you want to make Pythocles honorable, don't add to his honors but subtract from his desires." "If you want Pythocles to live in endless pleasure, don't add to his pleasures, but subtract from his desires." "If you want Pythocles to live until old age, don't add years but subtract from his desires." Take note: these words don't belong just to Epicurus, but to everyone. When it comes to philosophy, I think we should act the same way we do in the Senate: when someone has made a motion that I only partly approve of, I demand that he divide the motion and I vote for the part I support.

I'll happily reiterate Epicurus' distinguished words in order to offer solid proof for certain followers (who rush to him out of inferior motives) – people who think they'll exploit him to excuse their own vices. In fact, no matter what philosophical school they embrace, they must live their life virtuously. Take a trip to Epicurus' gardens and read the inscription there: "Stranger, you'll benefit to linger awhile. Here you'll find the highest good: pleasure." The house's guardian, a kind host, will be ready and waiting for you. He'll offer you porridge and water – as much as you could want – and he'll ask: "You have been well received, I hope? This garden won't excite your appetite, but it will satisfy it; it won't make you thirstier with every sip, but quenches thirst with a natural remedy that doesn't cost a cent. It's in this type of 'pleasure' I've spent my twilight years." When I speak to you about desires, I'm referring to the kind that reject mitigation and require some inducement in order to cease altogether. For when it comes to extraordinary desires – ones that may be condoned, or criticized and curbed – let me make this one point: *that* kind of desire is natural, but not necessary for life. You owe it nothing, and if you spend something on it, it's your own choice. But the belly doesn't listen to advice: it makes demands. It calls your name over and over. Still, it's not an annoying creditor; for a small price it can be sent away. Just give it only what you owe, not everything you own. Goodbye.

93 *Seneca to Lucilius (*Ep. 3.27)

"Really, *you*'re giving me advice?" you ask. "Have you already followed your own advice, righted your own mistakes? Is that why you've got the free time to work on improving others?" No, come on, I'm not so foolish to think I'm going to cure others when I'm still sick myself. No, what I'm doing is chatting with you about our common ills and sharing remedies, as if we were lying sick in the same hospital ward. So listen to me talking to myself: I'm going to let you into my innermost secret thoughts, and you'll be my excuse for self-reflection. Here's what I'm saying to myself: "How old are you? It's embarrassing to desire and to pursue the same things you did when you were just a kid. When it comes to your dying day, above all, take care of this one thing: be sure your faults die before you do. Throw away those disordered pleasures. They require you to pay a high price, not just for future pleasures, but for past ones that now prove harmful. Consider crimes: even if one gets away with committing them, the accompanying anxiety never goes away. It's the same with depraved pleasures: you regret them long past the time you enjoyed them. They're flimsy, unreliable, and, even if innocuous, temporary. Look around instead for some lasting good. But the only true 'good' is what the soul discovers for itself and from itself. Virtue alone offers endless, carefree joy. Even if some obstacle presents itself, it's just a passing cloud, floating under the sun, never blocking it."

When will you attain this kind of joy? Until now, you haven't exactly been dragging your feet, but you need to step up the pace. There's much work remaining and, if you want to accomplish it, you need to burn the midnight oil and focus your energy. Someone else can't do it for you. Literary studies (not philosophy) provide extra help. For example, a wealthy man from our generation, Calvisius Sabinus, had a freedman's thick wallet – and his brains. I've never laid eyes on a tackier man with all his filthy wealth. His memory was so abominable he couldn't even recall the name of Odysseus, Achilles, or Priam – names we know like the back of our hands! Not even any little old servile announcer, who must invent names because he forgets them, does as pathetic a job calling out the names of his master's relatives, as Sabinus does calling out the names of Homer's Trojan and Greek heroes. Yet he really wanted to *appear* to be well read. So he invented the following short-cut. He bought a bunch of slaves at an exorbitant price: one who knew Homer by heart; another, Hesiod by heart; and one for each of the nine lyric poets. Amazed? Don't be. No price was too high: if he couldn't find one "ready-made," he got one "custom-ordered."

After he collected his expensive entourage, he began putting on some pretty unbelievable dinner parties. He stationed the slaves at the foot of his dining couch. Every now and then he'd ask them for a few verses he could recite, but once he started he'd forget the quotation mid-sentence. Satellius Quadratus, a toady and ridiculer of stupid millionaires (the two go hand in hand), joked that maybe Sabinus should get some philologists to perform the usual slave's duty of "cleaning up the after-meal crumbs." Sabinus confessed he had paid 100,000 sesterces for each slave, to which Satellius quipped: "You could have purchased just as many bookcases for that price!" Nevertheless, Sabinus maintained his claim: *he* knew whatever everyone in his own house knew. So this same Satellius began urging Sabinus to take up wrestling (even though the guy is sickly, pale, and skinny). "How can I possibly do that? I'm barely alive as it is." "Don't say no, I'm begging," Satellius replied. "Don't you see how many perfectly fit slaves you have?" A sound mind can't be borrowed or bought. As I see it, even if one was for sale, you wouldn't find a buyer. Sick minds, however, are bought and sold every day.

But take what I owe and say goodbye. "Riches are poverty adapted to the law of nature." Epicurus often says this in various contexts, but it can't be reiterated enough. Certain people need only the prescription for their cure; others require the medicine to be poured down their throat. Goodbye.

94 Seneca to Lucilius (Ep. 4.40)

Seneca writes to Lucilius about the importance of philosophy and rhetoric: he should avoid listening to philosophers who are more concerned with style than with substance.

Thanks for writing me so often. You're revealing yourself to me in a way only you can. Reading any one of your letters immediately makes me feel you're right here. If the portraits of our absent friends delight us – since they refresh our memory and alleviate our longing (even if it's a false and empty consolation) – then aren't letters all the more delightful, since they bring us the real-life traces, the real-life proof of our absent friend? The thing that's sweetest when we meet face to face is also the same that comes from a friend's hand imprinted on his or her letter: recognition.

You write about a talk you heard from the philosopher Serapio when he stayed at your place: "He has a habit of assembling all his words for one giant outpouring, not letting them flow forth one by one, but crowding them, piling them atop one another; so many words emerge at one time that a single voice doesn't suffice." In a philosopher, I disapprove of this speaking style. A philosopher's discourse, like her life, should be composed. Nothing that races and rushes forward at the speed of light maintains order. That's why Homer assigned to the orator that swift type of speech, which comes suddenly from nowhere, like a sudden snow-shower. But it's from the old man that eloquent speech flows forth, gently, sweeter than honey.

So listen: that forceful type of speaking, fast and verbose, is appropriate for the showman, not for someone discussing an important matter and imparting a serious lesson. At the same time I don't want anyone giving a speech drop by drop any more than by a torrential river. He shouldn't strain or deafen ears. A meager, stripped-down type of speech doesn't hold the audience's attention: it's tedious, slow as molasses, halting. That said, we're more likely to absorb a long-anticipated word than one that flies right past us. Lastly, people are said to "hand over" precepts to their students. Yet how can anything be "handed over" when it takes flight and slips away? Besides, discourse communicating a truth should be straightforward and uncomplicated. The style currently in vogue offers no real truth. It tries to impress the common mob and to seize oblivious ears by swift attack, allowing no room for discussion; it simply flies away. How can speech like that regulate others when it can't even regulate itself? Shouldn't every speech designed to heal minds percolate within us? Remedies offer no help unless they penetrate the body and remain there.

In addition, this type of speech is empty and meaningless – verbal bling more than substance. My fears should be alleviated, my annoyances quieted, my fantasies shattered, my extravagances curbed, my greed censured. How can any of these be accomplished in a rush? What doctor heals sick people on the fly? Can such a jangle of hurling, grating words bring any pleasure? No, of course not. When you figure out the magician's trick you're generally content; the same goes for hearing a contrived speech: you only need to hear it once. What's worth learning or emulating from these kinds of speakers? If their *speech* is so confused and uncontrollable, what's the listener supposed to think about their *souls*? It's what happens when running down a hill: you never stop where you intended, the momentum forces the body to keep going. A speech with this kind of speed can't keep its own power in check. It's inappropriate for philosophy, which requires meticulously arranged words, not ones haphazardly released; philosophical precepts need to proceed step by step.

"What are you saying? Can't philosophy sometimes take a more forceful approach?" Certainly; but not at the cost of self-respect and decorum, which excessive violence rips away. Philosophy should possess great vigor, but in moderation – a continuous stream, not a rushing torrent. I don't think even the *orator* should use the type of rapid-fire speech that can't be recalled, which races ahead without rhyme or reason. How are jury members, who are sometimes inexperienced and uneducated, supposed to follow? Even when the orator gets carried away, trying to show off, or his emotions get the best of him, he should express his words only as quickly as ears can process them.

It's best, then, if you don't listen to lectures delivered by men who emphasize word count more than word choice. And, if you have to choose between the two types, go for a speaking style like that of Publius Vinicius. When asked in what manner Vinicius spoke, Asellius answered: "Gradually!" Or, as Geminus Varius commented, "I don't know how you can call that man 'eloquent.' He can't even string three words together." But why shouldn't you prefer to speak the way Vinicius does? Some insulting heckler may butt in, like when Vinicius' words were crawling along one by one (as if he were dictating, not speaking), and some guy interrupted: "Hey, aren't you going to say something?" I prefer a wise man to avoid the rushing pace of Quintus Haterius, a very famous orator in his day. Haterius never took a breath, never paused; once he got started, he stopped only when he was done.

Still, I think certain speaking styles are suitable for certain nations. One can endure this kind of unrestrained style in the Greeks. But when we write, we Romans have become used even to punctuation. The father of Roman eloquence, our famous Cicero, took his time speaking. The Latin language is naturally prone to looking around, weighing the possibilities, and providing something worth considering. Fabianus, a man of particular distinction in life, in knowledge, and, less importantly, in eloquence, used to debate expediently rather than hurriedly: you'd consider it effortlessness, not rapidity. I permit this to a wise man, though I don't demand it. His speech should proceed unhindered, though it should flow forth naturally rather than erupting forcefully.

Here's another reason why I strongly discourage you from this "sickness": the only way to excel at talking fast is by sacrificing your dignity. You'd need to obliterate every mark of modesty from your face and to turn deaf ears upon yourself. That's because this type of careless wording produces phrases you'd rather not hear. To repeat: it's impossible to succeed at this speaking style and keep your modesty intact. Besides, it requires daily practice and it redirects your focus from substance to mere fluff. And even if these words were ready at hand, able to pour forth with little effort, they'd still need to be tempered. Just as an unassuming gait suits a philosopher, so, too, does a speaking style that's moderate and not too intrepid. So, here's my point: I urge you, be a slow talker.

95 *Seneca to Lucilius* (*Ep.* 5.47)

I'm happy to hear from recent visitors to your place that you're on friendly terms with your slaves: this bodes well for your prudence and knowledge. "They're just slaves," people say. Actually, they're human beings. "They're slaves!" No, they're not; they're comrades. "But they're *slaves*!" "No, they're just lower ranked friends." "Slaves, I say." "Okay, fine, they're slaves, I'll concede; but only if you realize that Fortune has the same amount of power over slaves as over freeborn." This is why I can't help smiling bemusedly at people who think it's somehow humiliating to dine with their own slaves. Why? Is it all due to some snotty tradition demanding that a master be surrounded by a crowd of standing slaves while he dines? The master scarfs down more than he can chew, and eagerly and greedily stuffs his belly to the point where it's so stretched out it can no longer do its job. Thus it takes him more work to digest than to ingest. Meanwhile the poor slaves aren't allowed to move their lips – even to utter a word. The whipping rod stifles any murmur, and not even accidental sounds – be they a cough, a sneeze, or a hiccup – can avoid the lash. There's a huge price to pay for breaking the silence. Throughout the whole night the slaves stand around with empty stomachs and silent, empty mouths.

As a result, then, slaves who aren't allowed to talk in front of their master wind up talking *about* him. In the good old days, slaves could not only speak in front of their master, but even have a conversation with him; their mouths weren't "sewn up," and they were ready to stick their neck out for their masters, to incur danger. They opened their mouths at dinner parties, but when it came to torture – they kept them shut. There's a similarly snobby maxim tossed around today: "You have as many enemies as you have slaves." We don't buy them already enemies: we *make* them so. I won't mention the other cruel, inhumane acts. We exploit them not as humans, but as beasts of burden. While we recline enjoying the dinner, one slave mops up vomit while another's on his hands and knees, under the table, collecting the drunken partiers' spills. Another slave carves up some pricey fowl: going along the breast and butt with a skilled hand and confident knife he cuts out choice bits. Poor guy. He lives his life for this one sole purpose: to carve fattened hens expertly. (He does have it better, though, than the other wretch who teaches this "art" for the pleasure of it: that one's far more pathetic than the guy who's forced to learn it.) Another slave, the wine-pourer, is decked out in drag and wrestles with his age: he can't escape his boyhood and is dragged back to it, and, although he's got a soldier's physique, he's hairless: all his hair has either been waxed or plucked out from the root. He stays awake all night long, dividing his time between serving his master's drunkenness and serving his lust: he must be a man in the bedroom but a boy in the dining room.

There's another slave whose title is guest appraiser; this poor guy must stand still and watch the diners, determining whose flattery or whose excess – in the form of gluttony or talk – gets a repeated invitation tomorrow. Then there are the caterers, who possess a nuanced sense of their master's palate, who know what excites his mouth, what tempts his eyes, what novel food inspires his already nauseous tummy, what will bring him to the point of loathing food out of sheer fullness, and what he'll be hungry to eat on which particular day. This master can't stomach the idea of dining with these kinds of slaves; he thinks it's an insult to his "majesty" to sit at the same table with his own slave! God forbid! But how many future masters is he creating? I've seen Callistus' former master waiting outside Callistus' door for a handout! I've seen the door slammed in his face while others were let in – he's the same master who once slapped a "for sale" tag on Callistus and put him on the forum's auction block. But that slave, long ago thrown into the first group of those who allowed the auctioneer to practice his voice, has returned the favor: he's turned him away, deeming his former master unworthy of stepping foot in *his* own house! The master once sold Callistus: but now look how much Callistus is making him pay!

Remember, the man you call "slave" arose from the same seeds of mankind, delights in the same sky, breathes the same air, and, like you, lives and dies. You could just as easily view him as freeborn as he could view you a slave. Thanks to the massacres during Marius and Sulla's day, Fortune brought down many who had been born into the most distinguished families and were destined for a senatorial career: she made one a shepherd, another – caretaker of a little farmhouse. So go ahead, despise the man whose humble fortune you yourself might descend into; but do it at your own risk. I don't want to delve too deeply into such a big debate – about the treatment of slaves, whom we, Romans tend to treat arrogantly, cruelly, and disparagingly. Still, here's my advice: live with your inferiors in the same way you'd want your superiors to live with you. Each time you think about all the authority you wield over your slave, don't forget: your master has just as much power over you. "What? I have no master," you say. Well, you're still a babe: maybe one day you will. Don't you know how old Hecuba was when she became a slave? Or Croesus? Or Darius' mother? Or Plato? Or Diogenes?

Live with your slave on kind, even close terms; share conversation with him and let him take part in your plans and in your life. Right about now, an entire band of snobs is shouting at me: "There's nothing more shameful, nothing more despicable." Yet these men are the same ones I've caught in the act of kissing the hands of other people's slaves. Don't you see how our ancestors eliminated every ounce of ill will from masters and every insult from slaves? They called the master the "father of the household" and the slaves "people of the family" [*familiares*], a word still used today. They established a festival in which masters not only ate with their slaves, but even associated with them closely. They allowed their slaves to acquire honors within the house, to administer justice: they treated the household like a mini-republic.

"So, are you saying I should invite all my slaves to my table?" No, no more than I'm suggesting you invite all freeborn men to it. You're mistaken if you think I'm turning away certain slaves because they have dirtier job than others, like the mule-driver or ploughman. I'll evaluate them not according to job title, but according to character: each man gives himself his own character, but his duties are assigned to him. Let certain slaves dine with you because they deserve it, as some in fact do. If they have any servile qualities due to their humble associations, these qualities will be shaken off through interaction with people of higher status. There's no need to seek friends just in the forum or in the Senate house: if you're attentive and diligent, you'll find them at home, too. Good material often goes wasted without an artist; try it out and you'll see. Someone who's planning on buying a horse and only inspects the saddle and the reins, but not the horse itself, is an idiot. The same goes for the person who judges another only on the basis of what the latter is wearing, or on the basis of his or her rank – and rank is nothing but a piece of clothing covering us.

"He's a slave." His soul might be that of a freeborn man. "She's a slave." Is this a liability? Show me who isn't a slave. One individual is a slave to lust, another to greed; one, to ambition, another to hope. All humans are slaves to fear. I can tell you the name of a former consul who's a slave to an old shrew, a millionaire who's a slave to a maid; I'll show you noble, high-ranking youths who act like the slaves of mimes: and there's no kind of slavery more disgusting than self-imposed slavery. So don't let those awful, fastidious people discourage you from presenting yourself to your slaves as somebody openly cheerful, not snobby and superior. Let them esteem you, not fear you. Someone will argue that I'm making a case for freeing slaves and overthrowing masters from their high pedestal, all because I've said: "Let them esteem you, not fear you." "Doesn't he really mean," they ask, "that slaves should esteem their 'masters' like clients or early morning callers?" Whoever says this forgets that what's sufficient for a god isn't too meager for masters. The man who's "esteemed" is "loved." And love cannot be mixed up with fear. Hence I'll think you are right if you don't want your slaves to fear you and if you only administer *verbal* whippings: whips are for animals who don't speak. Things that irritate us aren't harmful; but a hedonistic lifestyle makes us prone to rage. If we don't get what we want right when we want it, we're incensed. We put on the costumes of kings, they're the ones who forget their own power and others' frailty and boil up with rage – as if they've been physically injured, even though the majesty of their own high position keeps them safe from dangers like this. They aren't stupid or ignorant, but they seize the opportunity for doing harm by searching it out. They let themselves be injured just so they can inflict injury.

I don't want to delay you further; you don't need an exhortation. Here's one definition of goodness: it designs its own guidelines for pleasure and sticks to them. Badness is fickle, freqently changing not into something better, but just into something different. Goodbye.

Paul the Apostle

Paul the Apostle, also known as Paul of Tarsus (5–67 CE), was named Saul before converting to Christianity. Paul was a Roman citizen and a prominent Christian missionary, who supported himself with the help of his family's tent-making business.

Figure 4.1 Detail of St. Paul from the cupola mosaic. Location: Baptistery of the Arians, Ravenna, Italy. Source: Scala / Art Resource, NY

Fourteen New Testament letters are ascribed to him; scholars have challenged the authenticity of several. According to the Book of Acts, Paul made three missions. At the end of the third he was arrested after a dispute with a group of Jews. After two years of imprisonment at Caesarea, Paul traveled to Rome in 59 CE, where he preached while awaiting his trial (a right afforded to him on account of his Roman citizenship). According to Christian tradition, Paul was martyred – beheaded under Nero in the mid-60s CE.

96 *Paul to Philemon* (Philem.) *Late 50s* CE

The letter to Philemon is thought to be authentic – a letter written by Paul. Scholars dispute its date: they question whether Paul wrote it during his imprisonment at Rome, in Philippi, or in Caesarea. Philemon himself was in Asia Minor, the master of a slave named Onesimus. Onesimus has been serving Paul, who made him convert to Christianity. It seems that Onesimus was a runaway slave and possibly wronged his master in some way; Paul writes to Philemon requesting that Onesimus continue to reside with him, and perhaps even be given his freedom.

Paul, a prisoner of Jesus Christ, and our brother Timothy, to our fellow worker, dearest Philemon, to our sister Apphia, to our fellow soldier Archippus, and to the church in your house: grace and peace to you from God our Father and our Lord, Jesus Christ.

I hear of your love and faith in the Lord Jesus and in all those devoted to God; I always thank God when I mention you in my prayers, so that your sharing of your faith may prove effective toward your realizing all the good we can do for Christ. You love has given me such joy and comfort, brother, because, thanks to you, the hearts of those devoted to God have been renewed. So, even though I could boldly give orders to you in the name of Christ to make you fulfill your duty, I prefer to ask you this favor through love instead: thus I, Paul, now an old man and a prisoner of Christ Jesus, appeal to you for my child, Onesimus, whose father I became while I was bound in chains; he was once useless to you, but now he's useful both to me and to you.

I'm sending him – my own heart – back to you, though I wanted to keep him here so he could help me while I'm imprisoned on behalf of the Good News. I didn't want to do anything without your agreement so that your good deed would be voluntary, not forced. Maybe the reason why he was temporarily separated from you was that you might have him back forever, no longer a slave, but more than a slave – a beloved brother, cherished particularly by me but even more by you, both as a man and as one sharing in the Lord.

So, if you count me as your partner, welcome him like you'd welcome me. If he has wronged you somehow or owes you something, charge it to me. I, Paul, write this in my own very hand: I will repay it! (I won't mention you owe me your very self.) Indeed, brother, grant me this favor in the Lord, renew my heart in Christ. I'm confident about your obedience and I know you'll do what I ask, and even more. One last thing: prepare a room for me, since I hope, through your prayers, to be reunited with you.

Epaphras, my fellow prisoner in Christ Jesus, sends his greetings. So do my co-workers Mark, Aristarchus, Demas, and Luke. The grace of the Lord Jesus Christ be with your spirit.

Jude

The Jude who wrote the following letter from the New Testament is usually identified as Jude the Apostle (distinct from Jude Iscariot), and also identified as the brother of James and possibly the brother of Jesus. If this is the case, the letter dates to c. 67 CE. Some scholars argue, however, that a Christian who wrote under the name of the earlier Jude composed the letter in the late first or second century CE. The author warned Christians against impostors and false teachers; he intended the letter to be circulated among churches in Palestine.

97 *Epistle of Jude*

Jude, servant of Jesus Christ and brother of James, to those beloved in God the Father, and protected and called for Jesus Christ.

May peace and love be multiplied for you! Dearest friends, I was eagerly planning to write you about our mutual salvation, but I felt obliged instead to write, urging you to fight on behalf of the faith that was once bestowed upon God's holy people. For certain people, who were censured and condemned long ago, have secretly sneaked in among you; they're unholy, exploiting God's grace to excuse their immorality. They reject the only master, our Lord, Jesus Christ.

I want to remind you, although you already know it well: the Lord saved the people from Egypt, but later He brought to ruin those who didn't trust in Him. And the angels who didn't rightly preserve their positions but abandoned their dwelling place, God has kept them in darkness, bound in eternal chains until the judgment of the great day. In like fashion, Sodom and Gomorrah and the surrounding cities have practised immorality and sexual licentiousness; they serve as an example and suffer the punishment of eternal fire. Similarly, these men pollute their bodies through their visionary fantasies; they reject authority and they blaspheme God's glory. But the archangel Michael, when he was contending with the devil in the fight over Moses' body, didn't dare charge him with blasphemy, but said instead: "May the Lord punish you!"

But these men slander what they're ignorant of; when it comes to things they know innately, like wild beasts they'll cause their own self-destruction. Woe to them! They've taken the pathway of Cain, and for the sake of personal gain they've rushed into the same mistake as Balaam. They have destroyed themselves through rebellion, just like Korah against Moses long ago. These same men are a stain at your banquets of fellowship when they feast with you, without a second thought, "tending only to themselves." They're like rainless clouds conjured up by winds, like trees of autumn void of fruit – doubly dead, in fact, since they have no roots. They're like the savage waves of the sea, spewing with the foam of their own shame; they're like stars wandering lost, without any course, which the dark of darkness governs forever.

These are the kinds of men Enoch (seventh generation from Adam) predicted, saying: "Look, the Lord has come, along with his thousands of saints, to bring judgment upon all, to condemn the unholy for all the unholy deeds they godlessly committed and for all the harsh words unholy sinners have uttered against Him." These are the men who grumble and complain, conducting themselves according to their own desires; they "talk the talk" when it comes to themselves, but they flatter others if it works to their advantage.

Remember, dearest friends, the words spoken earlier by the messengers of our Lord, Jesus Christ: "In the final days deceivers will come who conduct themselves according to their own unholy desires." These are the men who cause divisions, who live by their gut instincts, not by the spirit. But, beloved, build yourselves up by that most holy faith of yours and, with prayers to the Holy Spirit, take care of yourselves through God's love, waiting for the mercy of our Lord Jesus Christ to lead you to eternal life. Show compassion to those who doubt; save some by "snatching them from the fire," save others with fear, hating even their clothes stained by polluted flesh.

To the one who's able to protect us from falling and stands us face to face before His glory, blameless and with great exultation, to the one God, our Savior, may there be glory and majesty, power and authority through Jesus Christ, our Lord, before all eternity, now and for ever and ever, Amen.

Martial

Marcus Valerius Martialis (40–103 CE) was educated in his hometown, Bibilis, Spain, and later moved to Rome. There he established himself as a prominent poet, financially supported by friends and patrons. He was well connected in Rome and was friends with Pliny the Younger (see Letter 122). Martial's first literary work, the *Book of Spectacles* (81 CE), is a collection of poems celebrating the inauguration of the Flavian Amphitheater (the Colosseum, completed under Emperor Domitian in 81 CE). In 84 CE he produced two more books: the *Xenia* and the *Apophoreta*, which comprise two-line inscriptions accompanying presents. Between 86 and 103 CE Martial published 12 books of *Epigrams* (*Epigrammata*) – short, pithy poems commenting on everyday life at Rome any satirizing many of his contemporaries. The following selections, from the *Epigrams*, include epistolary prefaces in prose as well as epigrams exhibiting epistolary qualities.

98 *Martial to his* Epigrams (Epigr. *1.70*)

Following a typical epistolary tradition (cf. Letters 69, 73), Martial gives directions for delivering the book.

Go in my place, book, and deliver my greetings. You've got your orders, my little, obedient volume: go to Proculus' shining bright house. "How do I get there?" you ask. I'll tell you: pass the temple of Castor, the temple of Vesta nearby, and the House of the Vestal Virgins; from there, go up the sacred hill to the august Palatine, where many statues of our revered leader glitter. Don't be distracted by the sunbeams of the stunning colossus, which happily outshines the statue at Rhodes. Turn at drunken Bacchus' house, where you'll see Cybele's dome with its painted Corybants. Right ahead on your left, you'll come face to face with a brilliant house; the entranceway of a grand house stands waiting: that's your destination. Don't worry about arrogance or a snobby welcome: no door opens up wider, and Apollo and his learned sisters, the Muses, love no house more. If he asks "Why doesn't Martial come himself?" give this excuse: "Because these pages, whatever they're worth, couldn't possibly claim as their author a mere morning visitor."

99 *Martial to Decianus* (Epigr. *2.1*)

Valerius Martial to his friend, Decianus, greetings.

"What's your point in writing a letter?" you ask. "Isn't it enough that I read your epigrams? What will you say in a letter that you can't say in your poems? I understand why tragedy or comedy get their 'letters,' (that is, their prologues): they aren't allowed to speak for themselves. But epigrams don't need a public announcer; they're content being their own mouthpiece – and a wicked one at that! Epigrams turn whatever page they want into a letter. So, come on, don't be an idiot dressing a dancer head to toe in a heavy toga. Seriously, would you be happy holding a stick to fight a net man in the gladiatorial games? I'm sitting with people who immediately throw a fit over this." Holy crap, I swear you're right, Decianus. Maybe you knew what type of letter, and how long, was going to consume all your time? Okay, have it your way. Anyone who happens to come upon this book has *you* to thank for not being completely exhausted by the end of page one!

100 *Martial to Emperor Domitianus* (Epigr. *8, Preface and 1*)

A prose epistolary preface accompanying Book 8 of the *Epigrams*, which is dedicated to the Emperor Domitian.

To Emperor Domitian Caesar Augustus Germanicus Dacicus: Valerius Martial sends his greetings.

All my little books, sir, to which you've given fame – I mean life – supplicate you. And I think they'll be read for this very reason. This particular book, entitled "Book Eight," enjoys more frequent opportunities for displaying its piety. Thus it didn't require too much creative effort, since there was already plenty of subject matter to work with. Still, occasionally I tried to mix it up with various jokes; that way each and every line wouldn't overwhelm your heavenly modesty with praise, something that would more likely exhaust you than satiate us. Besides, although the most serious and highest ranking authors have composed epigrams almost with the verbal freedom of mime, I haven't allowed these epigrams to speak with the kind of licentious abandon they usually do. Since the greater – and better – part of the volume is linked to the dignity of your sacred name, this book needs to remember that it shouldn't approach temples unless it's religiously purified. To let readers know that I'll hold myself to this very rule, I decided to announce it at the very beginning, through a very short epigram:

Book, you're about to enter the laurel-wreathed home of our ruler: learn to speak more modestly and respectfully. Go away, nude Venus: this isn't your little book. Instead, *you*, Pallas Athena, you, Caesar's special favorite, come to me.

101 Martial to his brother Toranius (Epigr. *9, Preface)*

Greetings, my Toranius, dearest brother.

I wrote an epigram out of sequence to the most distinguished Stertinius, who wanted to place my statue bust in his personal library. I decided to write you about him so you'd know whom I'm calling Avitus. Goodbye and prepare for a visit soon.

> Poet of sublime heart, renowned (though not by your own choice), to whom distant death will grant a worthy reward: let this short poem live inscribed beneath my statue, which you, Avitus, place alongside other distinguished images. I'm the one whose little poetic trifles are second to none. You don't marvel at me, reader, but I think you adore me. Greater men can sing greater works; I speak of small themes, and I'm perfectly happy if you pick me up and hold me in your hands again and again.

Statius

Publius Papinius Statius (45 CE–96 CE) was a Roman poet who lived during the reign of Emperor Domitian, being a contemporary of Martial and Pliny. He was originally from Naples and educated by his father, himself a highly successful poet, who may have been Domitian's tutor. In 92 CE, shortly after the release of his epic poem *Tebaïs* (*The Thebaid*), Statius published the first three books of the *Silvae*, a collection of occasional poems celebrating a wide range of individuals living in and around Rome. He published a fourth book in 95 CE and simultaneously began work on a second epic poem, *Achilleïs* (*The Achilleid*), an account of Achilles' early life and education. Statius died before completing this work, and a fifth book of *Silvae* was published posthumously. The selections below comprise epistolary prose prefaces that would have accompanied the books' publication and are likely a version of the letters sent privately to the individual book's dedicatee. These epistolary prose prefaces serve as programmatic statements and tables of contents. In addition, one selection (*Silvae* 4.4) is a verse epistle that follows earlier epistolary traditions.

102 *Statius to Stella* (*Silv. 1, Preface*)

Statius expresses hesitation about publishing poetry that he considers inferior to the epic genre. His reluctance, however, is half-hearted. (This letter has survived incomplete.)

I've really been hesitating for quite some time now, Stella (you, who is so excellent and distinguished in our mutual pursuits), as to whether I should collect and publish these little poems, which flowed from my heart one by one, in the heat of the moment, and with a certain pleasing swiftness. Why should I burden them with the weight of publication right now – the same time I'm still worrying about my *Thebaïs* (though it's out of my hands)? But we read Virgil's *Gnat* and recognize Homer's parodic *Battle of the Frogs and Mice*; not one of the famous and esteemed poets hasn't had a little fun before producing his major opus. Besides, it was too late to withhold the poems since I had already given them to you and the others – whom they honor. But when it comes to a general readership, the pieces automatically lose much of their justified leniency because they've lost their only major source of praise: their extemporaneity. None required more than two days to complete, some just a single day – I'm more than a little afraid that these verses themselves will prove the validity of this statement!

The first poem has a sacred witness: I stuck to the hymnal formula "The beginning commences with Jupiter." I dared to hand over these hundred verses celebrating "The Great Horse" to our very generous emperor, the day after he dedicated the statue. Somebody might claim: "You could have seen it beforehand." You yourself, dearest Stella, will counter him: you know full well I composed "The Wedding Hymn," which you requested, in just two days – quite a bold proclamation! After all, it's 300 lines and maybe you'll stretch the truth for a friend. The extremely learned Manilius Vopiscus, who is rescuing our literature from the brink of decay, frequently cites my name to boast that I finished his descriptive "Tiburtina Villa" in one day. Next comes the poem "Rutilius Gallicus' Recovery." I won't say anything more about him so people don't think I'm taking advantage of my witness' death by fibbing. When it comes to Claudius Etruscus' testimony, that must be waived; he received my "Bath" almost before dinner ended! Lastly, the "Calends of December," which is believable, for that night was the happiest, never before experienced among public pleasures . . .

103 *Statius to Marcellus* (*Silv. 3, Preface*)

In addition to introducing the book, Statius uses this preface to defend himself against critics.

Statius to Marcellus, greetings.

I've found a book, dearest Marcellus, which I can dedicate to your loyalty. I don't think I've ever begun one of my little works without invoking the spirit of our great emperor, but this book begins with three [. . .] than that the forth focuses on honoring you. The "Seventeenth Consulship" is the first poem; it pays tribute to our victor in Germany; the second one, "A Thank You Note," is a thanksgiving for the honor of attending an official banquet at our emperor's palace. The third, "The Domitian Highway," reveals my admiration for the newly constructed road, which has eliminated all the irritating delays we used to experience with the old sandy road. Thanks to this public work, you'll receive my "Letter" (the fourth poem in this volume), which I sent you from Naples! Next is the "Lyric Ode" to Septimius Severus, a young man who, as you know, is also one of the most distinguished equestrians; yes, he's your fellow classmate and, beyond that link, he's also my very dear friend. I can even count the sixth poem, "A Statuette of Hercules," as a gift to you: it honors Novius Vindex, who deserved it because of our mutual friendship and shared literary pursuits (and he's also your friend). I've already declared my regard for Vibius Maximus' eloquence and status sufficiently, by publishing my letter to him regarding the release of my *Thebaïs*. In addition, I'm now publishing this "Ode" demanding his swift return from Dalmatia. Next comes a short poem for my fellow townsman, Julius Menecrates, a brilliant young man and son-in-law to my friend Pollius; my "Congratulations" applauds how he's brought distinction to our Naples through the number of his children. As for Plotius Grypus, a young senatorial man, I'll give him a more deserving piece some other time, but for now I'm including in this volume my "Hendecasyllables," which we laughed over together during the Saturnalia.

Why are there more poems in Book Four than in the previous three? So that my critics – who, I hear, disparaged me for publishing this kind of poetry – won't think they've gotten the best of me. First, it's pointless to argue against a done deal. Second, I had already presented many of them, personally, to our Lord Caesar – and how much more significant is that than just publishing them? Moreover, is it illegal to practice for fun? "In private, no," they say. And yet it's fine for people to watch boxing spars, or to attend gladiatorial practice sessions. Finally, whoever reads my poems with bias can go ahead and immediately proclaim himself my enemy. So why should I follow any of his advice? In sum, I'm the one clearly on display, risking ridicule. So let my critic keep quiet and be glad it's not him! As for this book, you can be the one to defend it and, if you do, that's the end of that. If not, we'll both be the target of criticism! Take care.

*104 Statius to Vitorius Marcellus (*Silv. 4.4*)*

Statius writes to his friend, the senator Vitorius Marcellus, urging him to enjoy a holiday from Rome during the hot summer months. Marcellus was a friend of the famous Roman rhetor Quintilian and the dedicatee of the latter's *Institutio oratoria* (*Education of the Orator*), which was a manual of sorts, tracing the education of an orator from boyhood to adulthood. Marcellus held the post of *curator viae Latinae* (an official in charge of overseeing repairs to the Via Latina, a major road leading southwest from Rome through Latium). In addition, he was an accomplished orator in the centumviral court for civil cases; as Statius notes, this court took a recess in the summer ("the moderating spear of the hundred judges stands idle"), thus giving Marcellus an opportunity to leave Rome for a bit.

Run, my letter, run through the fields near Naples and don't waste any time! Begin where the famous old Appian Way forks off to become the Domitian Highway, that road on which a solid foundation now rests atop the soft sands. Once you've made your swift journey to the hills of Rome, head immediately to the right bank of the gold-colored Tiber, where the Etruscan shore from deep below helps create the Naval Pool, which is used for mock sea battles and surrounded by suburban pleasure gardens. There you'll see a man distinguished in appearance and spirit: this is Marcellus. You'll recognize him by his noticeably tall stature. First, say the usual "Hello!" and, once you're settled inside, give him the following message in verse:

"Already the departure of rainy spring exhausts the land and the sky, which rapidly turns on its axis; the dog days of summer burn the heavens with their heat, and the thickly packed crowds of lofty Rome are thinning out. Some have sought refuge in the shrine at Praeneste or in Diana's wooded grove at Nemi; others in the shivering Mt. Algidus or shady Tusculum. Some have headed toward the woods at Tivoli, others toward the cool waters of the Anio river. What about you? What district draws you, with its milder climate, away from noisy Rome? What change of scenery has allowed you to escape the summer sun? What about Gallus, your chief concern and dearest friend above all others – and my good friend, too? Should I praise him more for his upstanding character or intellect? Is he spending his summer on the shores of Latium, or has he now returned to quarry-filled Luna, his Tuscan home? But if he's near you, I must not be too far away when you two chat, since my ears are burning!"

While the fierce mane of Leo, the constellation, still blazes, strip your heart of cares and sneak away from all that relentless work of yours. After all, the Parthian covers his quiver and unstrings his bow; the charioteer also takes some time to soothe his horses in the cool waters of the Alpheus river after an effort exerted at Olympia. And my lyre grows tired and relaxes its strings. A restful break taken at the right time nourishes and rejuvenates one's strength: a vacation increases productivity. After he had sung of Briseis and put his lyre down, Achilles was much fiercer rushing to the battlefield after Hector. The same will be true of you. Some quiet repose for a little while will enkindle your energy, and you'll spring back to your regular activities, fresh and renewed. Surely right now Rome's laws aren't settling disputes. The slow season enjoys peace, and the harvest's return has dismissed the forum courts. There aren't throngs of defendants or complaining clients in your courtyard, summoning you to come out. The moderating spear of the hundred judges stands idle – that court where your reputation for eloquent speaking is preeminent, surpassing your youthful years; and it is already celebrated far and wide.

Lucky you are when it comes to concerns! Your heart may not reside in poetry's peaceful garlands and laurel wreaths, but your intellect flourishes and your mind is ready and willing to take on great deeds. I, however, console my life of leisure through song and seek the ever changing tides of fame. Look at me: I find rest on Naple's shoreline, where once the Siren Parthenope sought refuge; there, with a listless thumb, I pluck the slender strings of my lyre. Sitting at the edge of Virgil's shrine, I take heart and sing before my great master's tomb. If Fate grants you a long life (I pray for this to happen) and the power of our Latin emperor continues, perhaps you'll be sent to govern Ausonian cohorts, to guard the people living along the Rhine or the dark shores of Iceland, the banks of the Danube or the imposing pass through the Caucasus mountains; you enthusiastically worship him before Jupiter the Thunderer, and he's added another responsibility to your current post as praetor, making you curator of the Latin road and thus charging you to oversee repairs along its long slanting stretch of highway. For eloquence isn't your only powerful attribute: your limbs are prepared for war, your strong arms are able to bear the heavy breastplate. If you train to enter the field as a soldier, your helmet's crest will nod high above everyone else; or, if you'll be a cavalryman controlling the jingling reins, the spirited horse will be your slave. While I'm entering old age singing of other peoples' deeds, you, handsomely decked out in your armor, will be the one performing the deeds worthy of song and preparing great examples for little Geta to model. His grandfather already demands worthy deeds and offers him right here at home examples of triumphs to emulate. Up, rise up and get going, child: overtake your young father, fortunate in your mother's bloodline and in your father's courageous excellence! With an eye to its own interests, the Senate house is already happily raising you within its Tyrian purple fold, glad to promise your placement in every high office.

These are the words I'm singing to you, Marcellus, from the Bay of Naples, where the Vesuvius still spews up evidence of its devestating wrath, pouring out flames that rival Sicily's Mt. Etna. Unbelievable, but true! When crops grow again and these scorched lands become green, will future generations believe that whole cities and peoples lie flattened below; that family farms have disappeared at one fell swoop? The summit still hasn't ceased its lethal threats. May a similar fate stay far away from your hometown, and may nature's madness skip over the Marrucinian mountains. If you're wondering what my Muses are up to, my *Thebaïs* has now completed her journey and furled her sails: she's reached that long-awaited harbor. On Mt. Parnassus' ridges in the woods of Helicon, she's made an offering of incense and of the innards of a virgin heifer upon the festal flames, and she's hung up my hair ribbons from a votive tree. Now a different headband comes to rest atop my empty locks: Troy, yes, Troy and great Achilles are my theme, but the father who wields the bow and arrow calls me away, pointing out the even greater wars of Rome's emperor. For a long time I've felt that inclination, but fear has always held me back. Will my shoulders stand firm under such a mass, or will my neck bend from its great weight? Tell me, Marcellus, can I tolerate it? Or is my ship, accustomed as it is to smaller waves, not ready to face the dangers of the Ionian sea?

Goodbye for now and keep your love for this deeply devoted poet close to your heart. For Tirynthian Hercules is no more generous than you when it comes to nourishing friendship. Faithful Theseus' fame yields to you, along with that of the hero who dragged the torn body of Hector round and round the walls of Troy, to console himself over the loss of his slain friend.

*105 Statius to Abascantus (*Silv. 5, *Preface)*

Book 5 of the *Silvae* was published posthumously. Thus the following preface does not ennumerate the contents of the book, as do the other epistolary prefaces. Instead it is addressed to Abascantus and concerns only the book's first poem, a lament following the death of Abascantus' wife Priscilla. This preface, then, likely corresponds to the original letter Statius would have sent to Abascantus to accompany the poem. It was customary in the ancient Rome for an author to send a copy of his work to its dedicatee, along with a prefatory letter such as the one we see here.

Statius to his friend Abascantus, greetings.

Good examples need to be honored with unabashed enthusiasm, since they benefit the public interest. Your loyalty to your wife, Priscilla, is an innate part of your character and evokes everyone's empathy, especially a husband's. Loving a wife who's still alive is a joy; loving one who's dead is a duty. But I'm not just any old person from the crowd, and it's not just a sense of obligation that spurs me into accepting this opportunity: Priscilla loved my wife and, by loving her, increased her own esteem in my eyes – so I'm an ingrate if I overlook your tears. Moreover, I always try to oblige anyone connected to the imperial court, even with my modest talent. For anyone who worships the gods in good faith loves their priests as well. Still, even though it's been a long time since I wanted us to become closer friends, I would have preferred a different occasion to make this happen.

Pliny the Younger

Gaius Plinius Caecilius Secundus (61–112 CE) was the nephew of Pliny the Elder, who in 79 CE died while trying to rescue victims of Mt. Vesuvius' eruption. In his will he adopted Pliny the Younger, who was 17 at the time. Pliny was born in Comum (Como) in northern Italy and received his advanced education at Rome, where he studied under the famous rhetorician Quintilian. He rose from equestrian to senatorial rank and witnessed the succession of several emperors, including Domitian and Trajan. He was active as a lawyer, both defending and prosecuting high-profile cases in the centumviral court. In 103 CE he was elected augur and in 110 CE the Emperor Trajan specially appointed Pliny to assess the financial troubles of the province Bithynia and Pontus; Book 10 of Pliny's *Letters* comprises the correspondence with Trajan during this time. Pliny was a well-known orator of his day, but only one speech survives: his *Panegyic* of Trajan, presented before the Roman Senate in 100 CE. In addition to poetry (much of it now lost), Pliny produced a collection of letters: the first nine books he carefully arranged and published, but scholars debate about the formal arrangement and publication date of Book 10, some believing that it was published posthumously. Pliny was well connected to other prominent writers of the time, including Martial, Statius, Tacitus, and Suetonius. Additional letters of Pliny are available on www.wiley.com/go/romanletters.

*106 Pliny to Septicius Clarus (*Ep. *1.1)*

You've often urged me to collect and publish my letters, which I wrote with a good deal of care. I've assembled them not in their original chronological order (I wasn't composing a history), but just as I happened to come upon them. Now it's up to you not to regret your advice – and up to me not to regret following it! So I'll be sure to recover any other letters still lying around overlooked, and I won't withhold those I write later on.

*107 Pliny to Arrianus Maturus (*Ep. *1.2)*

Because I see you'll be arriving later than I thought, I'm now presenting you with the speech I promised you in earlier letters. Please read and edit it as you normally do, in fact even more so, because I don't think I've ever written with this kind of "panache," as the Greeks say. When it comes to Attic style I've always tried following your Demosthenes, and more recently Calvus, but only in figures of speech, since only a "few favored by Jupiter" can reproduce the force of such great men. Not to be presumptuous, but the subject matter particularly recommended emulating them. Nearly the entire speech, in fact, involved a vigorous intensity that woke me up from my slumber of inactivity – well, inasmuch as I'm one who can be woken up! Nonetheless, I haven't altogether abandoned the tropes of our pal Marcus Tully when appropriate embellishments called for veering off-track a little; we don't necessarily want a sharp tenor to be abrasive.

Please don't think I'm asking for leniency from you: I particularly want to benefit from your critical eye. I'll admit my friends and I are considering publishing – well, at least if you "vote the white pebble" and approve the plan, even if it proves a mistake! Obviously I must publish something, and I might as well publish something that's ready to go. There's laziness for you! I really must publish for several reasons, but especially because they say the books I've already released still find their way into readers' hands even though they've lost their novelty as new releases. Of course, the booksellers may just be flattering me. But they're smart to do so, as long as their lies motivate my literary activities! Ciao!

108 Pliny to Cornelius Tacitus (Ep. *1.6*)

Laugh, go ahead, laugh: I, yes, yours truly, have captured three boars, very good-looking ones at that. "*You*?" Yes, *me*! Really! And I didn't even totally retreat from my current slothfulness. I was sitting by my nets – not with a spear or javelin next to me, but with stilus and tablets. I was contemplating and taking some notes, so that, even if I came home empty-handed, my notebooks would still be jam-packed. Don't censure this type of study. It's amazing how exercising the body stimulates the mind. Further, the forest's all-encompassing emptiness and silence facilitate hunting and are persuasive stimuli for mental fitness. So the next time you go hunting, follow my example and, along with your lunch box and water bottle, bring your notebooks: you'll find that Minerva roams the hillside no less than the woodland goddess Diana. So long.

109 Pliny to Minucius Fundanus (Ep. *1.9*)

It's amazing how, when it comes to specific days, one can generally recount one's day-to-day activities in the city, but not when one's lumping them all together. If you ask someone "What did you do today?" he'll respond that he attended a coming-of-age ceremony, an engagement party, or a wedding; or that he was asked to witness a will, support someone in court, or serve as an assessor. All these activities seem vitally important on the actual day you do them, but completely inane when you recall how you've done them day after day. They seem even more pointless once you're outside the city in the countryside. Then you ask yourself: "How many days did I waste doing such-and-such mind-numbing activity?"

This is what happens to me once I'm at my seaside villa in Laurentum, where I'm either reading or writing, or squeezing in some exercise, which keeps my mind in tip-top shape. I hear and say nothing that I'll later regret; I don't have to listen to nasty rumors slandering anyone, and I've only myself to blame if I don't write as much as I should. Hopes and fears don't vex me; no idle gossip disturbs me. I have conversations only with myself and my books. Oh, what an honest, genuine life! What a sincere, lovely kind of repose, far better than any business dealings! The sea and the shore serve perfectly as the truest, most solitary library! How many different ways they inspire me and guide my pen! You too, Fundanus, as soon as you can, abandon that noisy hubbub, that useless running around, and the countless silly tasks, and devote yourself to literature or leisure. As our very wise and witty Atilius once said: "Better to be busy at leisure than to be busy at nothing."

Figure 4.2 Imaginary architectural landscape. Ancient Roman fresco from the Villa of Arianna in Stabiae. Location: Museo Archeologico Nazionale, Naples, Italy. Source: Vanni / Art Resource, NY

*110 Pliny to Fabius Justus (*Ep. *1.11)*

It's been a long time since you sent me a letter. "I have nothing to write," you say. Well, write that: "I have nothing to write." Or at least write the salutation our elders began a letter with: "If you're well, excellent: I'm well, too." This suffices for me – just knowing you're okay. You think I'm joking? I'm serious. Let me know what you're up to, because otherwise I can't help worrying.

*111 Pliny to Calestrius Tiro (*Ep. *1.12)*

Pliny describes his sadness following Corellius Rufus' suicide.

I've suffered a severe loss, well, if one can use the word "loss" to describe the death of such a great man. Corellius Rufus has died. What's more, it was by his own doing, which only added acid to my wound. This type of death is the most sorrowful type. When people consciously take their own life, grief is insurmountable because we know they could have lived longer. It was, above all, reason (which, for philosophers, is the same as inevitability) that compelled Rufus to do what he did, even though he had many reasons for living: the clearest conscience, the best reputation, the greatest influence – and even more: a daughter, a wife, a grandson, a sister, and true friends. But such a long, severe illness tormented him that these prizes of life, great as they are, couldn't compete with his reason for dying. I heard him say that at the age of 32 he developed hereditary gout in his foot, just like his father; it's not uncommon for diseases to be passed down through the generations, like anything else. While still young, he mastered the pain through his temperate and pure lifestyle. More recently, even with advancing age and the disease becoming more burdensome, he kept going through sheer mental strength, even when suffering immeasurable torment – torture such as he never deserved. The pain had worked its way beyond his feet and deep inside, throughout every limb and joint.

During Domitian's reign I visited him lying in his house in Rome's suburbs. His slaves left the room – the usual practice when one of his particularly loyal friends entered; but this time even his wife left, although she could be trusted with any secret. He scanned the whole room before speaking. "Why do you think I've outlasted such pain for so long? It's so that I can outlive that despicable thief, our emperor, even if by one day." Had his body equaled the strength of his mind, he would have done so; nonetheless, the god heard his wish; and, confident in this thought, he felt free to die, cutting the ropes of life, which could no longer bind him to this world.

The illness became more severe, though he tried assuaging it through self-control. Then he became determined to escape the pain. One day, then another, then a third and a fourth passed, and he still refused to eat. His wife Hispulla sent a mutual friend, C. Geminius, to me with the grimmest message: Corellius was determined to die and neither his wife's nor daughter's entreaties could sway him to do otherwise. I was the only one left who might convince him and call him back to life. I took off. I wasn't far from his house when Julius Atticus brought another message, again from Hispulla: nothing, not even my entreaties, would change his mind. He had become thoroughly fixated in his resolve. To the doctor who was trying to get him to eat, he simply said "I've made up my mind" – an expression I've never forgotten, in my admiration and longing for him. I think what a friend, what a man I've lost. He lived 67 years, an impressive age even for the healthiest men – I realize this. He escaped an unrelenting illness – I know this. He left behind a legacy of survivors, a flourishing empire, which was dearer to him than anything else – I know all this too. But I'm grieving as if over the death of a young and healthy man; I grieve for myself, as silly as this may seem to you. But I truly lost my life's guardian, guide, and teacher.

Let me end by saying what I recently told my pal Calvisius in the first stage of my grief: "I fear I'll now live less conscientiously." So write and send me some consolation, but not the usual "He was old, he was sick." I know this. Send me something new, but compelling, something I've never heard or read before. The consoling sentiments I've heard and read long ago come to mind naturally, but are worthless at a time of such profound heartache.

112 Pliny to Sosius Senecius (Ep. 1.13)

Authors frequently organized readings of their compositions; these "*recitationes*" offered an opportunity for an author to receive feedback before publication, as well as to promote his literary expertise. Pliny complains that audiences aren't engaged enough.

The year has yielded a great crop of poets. Throughout the whole month of April there was a public reading nearly every day. I'm happy literature is alive and flourishing and talent is making a comeback, but, even still, audiences are slow to form. Most people stay put, wasting their time listening to gossip; from time to time they demand to be notified when the reader has entered, whether he's gone through the preface, or whether he's near the end of the book. Then, and only then, they finally come crawling in at a snail's pace. They don't stay long but leave before the end, some slinking out sneakily, others blatantly and unabashedly.

Good god, what a state! In our parents' day they say Emperor Claudius was strolling on the Palatine when he heard applause and inquired about its source. After learning that Nonianus was giving a reading, the emperor surprised everyone by unexpectedly stopping to listen. Nowadays anyone who has oodles of time on his hands and is invited to a reading way in advance (and given a friendly reminder more than once) either doesn't go or, if he does, complains he's wasted a day – precisely because he has not wasted it! So, thanks to these apathetic and arrogant audiences, we should all the more praise and applaud those who aren't discouraged from writing and giving readings of their work.

I've supported nearly everyone, mostly friends. And there's hardly anyone who loves literature and doesn't love me, too. Thus I've stayed in the city longer than I originally intended. Now I can return to my country retreat and write something. But it won't be intended for a formal reading: I don't want to seem I've been attending all my friends' readings just so they'd return the favor.

113 *Pliny to Junius Mauricus* (Ep. *1.14*)

You asked me to keep a lookout for a husband for your brother's daughter. Well, you've certainly chosen the best person for the job! You know how much I respect and esteem your brother, a man of such caliber. When I was just starting out, he provided such heartening encouragement – and even praise – on purpose, to ensure I lived up to my potential. You couldn't commission a greater, more satisfying task, and I couldn't undertake anything more important than selecting a young man suitable for giving grandsons to Arulenus Rusticus. It might have been a long search, but, as fate would have it, I've got the perfect bachelor: Minucius Acilianus. He loves me as one of his peers (he's a few years younger), but respects me as his senior. He wants to be molded and shaped by me just like I was by you and your relatives.

He's from Brixia, one of our Italian towns, which still preserves much of its scrupulous frugality and ancient rusticity. His father is Minucius Macrinus, a leading equestrian perfectly satisfied with his rank: Vespasian selected him for promotion to preaetorian rank, but he resolutely chose a life of virtuous quiet over our status (or, should I say, our desire for it?). His maternal grandmother is Serrana Procula from Padua. You know well Padua's reputation as the pinnacle of morality; nevertheless, even for Paduans, Serrana is a paragon of austerity. Publius Acilius is Minucius' uncle, a man of outstanding dignity, discretion, and loyalty. In sum, everyone and everything in the entire extended household will please you as if they were your own.

As for Acilianus, you'll find he's full of energy and industry and exceedingly modest. He's already served honorably as quaestor, tribune, and praetor, so you won't feel obliged to canvass for votes on his behalf. He's got a handsome face and a ruddy complexion, imbued with vigor and humility. His whole body possesses a natural beauty and a certain senatorial refinement. I don't think I should skip over these details: they're almost like a reward for a bride who has kept her virginity intact. I'm not sure if I should mention his father's abundant financial resources. When I think about you and your brother, and his future son-in-law, I don't think I need to mention financial matters; but when I consider public attitudes, and even our city's laws (which actually regard personal estates as being of paramount importance), I don't think I should ignore finances. When it comes to practical matters – their future children and *their* future children – there's no doubt that this "voting pebble," so to speak, must be a factor in electing the perfect son-in-law.

You might think I'm swayed by affection, and thus embellishing beyond what the situation demands. But, on my honor, I promise you'll discover the future surpasses all expectations. I love this young man as he deserves; but the fact that I love him doesn't mean I'm going to exaggerate.

114 Pliny to Septicius Clarus (Ep. *1.15*)

The letter contains passages in a mock legal tone, because Septicius was a prominent lawyer and jurist.

Wait a minute, you there! You accepted my dinner invitation and now you're not coming? The law has spoken: you'll pay me back every last penny, no small sum. Everything was ready: for each guest, one lettuce, three snails, two eggs, barley water, and wine mixed with honey and chilled with snow (yes, that's right, you'll also have to calculate this in your reimbursement, an expensive ingredient that melts away on the tray) – oh, and don't forget the olives, beetroot, cucumbers and onions, and a thousand other items no less splendid. You would have heard comics, a reader, a singer – or, knowing my generosity, all of them! But, nooo, you preferred the oysters, pig uterus, sea urchins, and Spanish dancing girls at so-and-so's house. You'll pay the price – I'm not saying how! You've behaved like a boor: you've begrudged maybe yourself, definitely me, and, well, perhaps us both, a good time. We would have had such a blast, laughing and learning! Maybe you can eat more magnificently at other peoples' homes, but you won't find a more cheerful, candid, and carefree time than at Chez Pliny. In short, give me a try: if afterwards you're not declining other peoples' dinner invitations, you can always turn down mine!

115 Pliny to Erucius (Ep. *1.16*)

I've always loved our friend Pompeius Saturninus and, even before I knew him, I was always extolling his talents: so diverse, adaptable, and versatile! He completely grabs, captivates, and enthralls me. I've heard him in the lawcourts pleading forcefully and fervently, and, whether it was a thoughtfully prepared speech or an impromptu one, it had equal polish and embellishment. His speeches frequently display strategically placed maxims, have a thoughtful and impressive organization, and incorporate words both novel and archaic. I find all of these qualities remarkably appealing whether I hear them in person – as they gush forth with a certain vigorous torrent – or later, when I go over them again in my head. You'll feel the same way, too, when you get the chance to hold his speeches in your hands and compare them to those of any of our bygone orators, whom he rivals. Nonetheless, you'll be even more impressed with his histories on account of their conciseness and clarity, their charm and brilliance, and especially their sublime narratives. For the same brilliance he displays in private courtroom speeches is all the more crisp, periodic, and compelling in his public speeches.

And there's more: he composes poetry like Catullus or Calvus – he's almost the real thing! How much of their charm, sweetness, and bitterness he captures! Some of the phrases he uses are a bit harsher, but context necessitates them, and he does intersperse softer and gentler words, just like Catullus and Calvus did. Recently he read to me some letters that, he said, his wife wrote. I thought I was listening to prose versions of Plautus or Terence! Whether his wife wrote them, as he asserts, or he did (which he denies), he deserves equal credit – either for being their author or for being the one who shaped such a learned, polished wife (a woman he married when she was just a girl). So I spend the whole day with him: I read him before I start writing; I read him when I'm finished; I read him when I'm just relaxing – he's always a new experience. I strongly recommend you, even urge you to read him. We shouldn't ignore his work just because he's still alive. If he had flourished in a previous generation, we'd be hunting down not only every one of his books, but also portrait busts of him. So why should his present-day status and fame shrink as if we've had our fill of him? It's a real shame and disgrace not to admire a man who so much deserves it just because it's possible for us to see him, touch him, and not only praise him but also love him. Goodbye.

116 *Pliny to Tacitus (*Ep. *1.20)*

Pliny comments on a current stylistic debate of the time: compositions written in a terser, more concise style versus ones written in a longer, fuller style.

I often debate with a certain man, educated and experienced, who in courtroom speeches prefers brevity above all. Sure, I think brevity is essential, if it suits the case. But, when you omit things that really should be addressed and give only a cursory and terse treatment to elements that should be driven into, impressed upon, and poured over your listeners' ears, it's like colluding with your opponent. In most cases a longer treatment imparts a certain force and weight to your words; like a sword penetrating the body, a speech impresses the mind not through a prick, but through a full thrust.

At this point the same man goes through some examples with me; from the Greeks he cites Lysias' speeches; and, from our Romans, the speeches of the Gracchi and of Cato – most of which, admittedly, are concise and short. I counter his Lysias with Demosthenes, Aeschines, and Hyperides (and many others); and his Cato and the Gracchi with Pollio, Caesar, Calius, and, above all, Marcus Tullius, whose longest speech is also considered his best. No kidding: like all the good things, a good book is even better the bigger it is! Notice how statues, drawings, paintings – in short, representations of people, many animals, and even trees – are far more impressive when the objects they represent are reproduced on a grand scale, as long as they're proportionate. The same goes for speeches; and even when it comes to the actual scrolls, size adds a certain authority and beauty.

This guy cites many other examples I usually employ to support my own position; he's slick and cunning when he argues, so he dodges my punch, throws another, and contends that the authors I model had said fewer things than they published. I disagree. There are numerous speeches I can call on to testify, like Cicero's *In Defense of Murena* or *In Defense of Varenus*, in which the enumeration of the specific crimes only by name embodies brevity and straightforwardness. It's clear, then, that many parts of the delivered speech never made it into the written version. Cicero also said that, in defending Cluentius, he followed traditional custom and pleaded the entire case himself, from beginning to end. He took four days to defend Cornelius, proof that the speech he delivered over so many days was quite extensive. Later, after cutting it down and revising it, he compressed it into one volume – a big one, but nonetheless only one.

A good courtroom speech is one thing, a good *written* one is something else. I realize that this is obvious to most, but, unless I'm mistaken, I'm convinced it's possible for a delivered speech to be successful even if the written one is not; but the reverse is not true. That's because the written version serves as the draft, that is, the archetype for the oral one. So the countless rhetorical figures we find in the best courtroom speeches appear even in orations that we have only in written form. For example, in Cicero's *Against Verres*, there's a part that reads: "What artist? What's his name? Oh, that's right, thanks for reminding me. It was Polyclitus." Clearly the most polished courtroom speech is the one that most closely resembles the written version, but only if the orator is allowed the entire block of time that is due to him. If the allotted time is denied, that's a serious infraction on the part of the judge, not the orator.

Many laws support my position; such is the one granting speakers an open-ended time limit, which advises not brevity, but fullness: this involves attentiveness. Brevity has no place in the courtroom except in the most restricted cases. I'll add what experience, the best teacher of all, has taught me. I've continually worked as an attorney; time after time I've sat as a judge; and I've repeatedly served as an assessor. In all these positions I've learned that something might move one group of listeners, something else another group, and generally it's the smallest details that have the biggest effect. Everyone has different opinions and different inclinations. As a result, people who simultaneously hear the same speech often reach a different conclusion. When they do agree, it's been through different emotional responses. Moreover, each person prefers his or her own way of discovering the facts and accepts as the most convincing, forceful conclusion the one he or she independently predicted (even if someone else says it). Therefore something must be given to everyone – something that each can grasp, each can recognize.

Once, when Regulus and I were both pleading in the same case, he said: "You think you need to explain every point, but I go straight for the jugular." True enough, he grabs whatever he can get his hands on, but usually it's the wrong thing. "It's possible that, when you think you've got the jugular, in reality you're clenching the knee or the ankle," I responded. "I, however, can't locate the jugular, so I test everything, try everything out, leave no stone unturned." I go the same way about my farms: I tend and cultivate my grapes as attentively as my orchards, and my orchards as carefully as my fields; there I sow not just farro and wheat, but barley, beans, and all the other legumes. Likewise, when I'm delivering a speech, I scatter my "seeds" far and wide, so that I may "harvest" whatever happens to sprout.

A judge's temperament is no less predictable, uncertain, and treacherous than storms and droughts. I won't skip what Eupolis the comic poet said when praising that supreme orator, Pericles: "Besides acuteness, persuasion sat upon his lips. He thus charmed his listeners and, of all the orators, he alone pierced the minds of his audience." But Pericles wouldn't have achieved his "persuasion" or "charm" through brevity or speed – or both (for, they are, in fact, different) if he hadn't also possessed superior skill. Being able to delight and persuade requires plenty of talking – and the time to do so. The orator who leaves the point in his listeners' mind isn't the one who uses it just to puncture, but to plunge it in. Another comic poet said this about Pericles: "He thundered and flashed lightning, upturning Greece on its head." A pruned speech that abruptly cuts short doesn't "thunder" and "flash." Only one that is full, grand, and lofty does. Besides, the thundering, flashing type only confounds and alarms.

"Still, the middle path is the best." Sure, who denies it? But the orator who says too little about his subject doesn't maintain this golden mean any more than the one who says too much. The same goes both for the orator who's too concise and for the one who's too garrulous; people frequently label the latter "excessive and redundant" and the former "measly and weak." The first overshoots the mark, the second misses it. Both are equally flawed; but, while the terse orator falls short because of feebleness, for the garrolous power is the cause. This is surely a fault involving lack of refinement, but at least it's the result of a bigger talent. I'm not saying I approve of Homer's Thyestes with his "torrential tongue," but rather of someone more like Odysseus, with his "words that fall like winter snowflakes." I also very much like Menelaus, "a man of few words, but always to the point." Given a choice, I prefer the speech that's like a winter snowstorm: thick, continuous, abundant – and, lastly, divine and heavenly. "But audiences prefer a short speech." True, but you are, after all, talking about lazy listeners – it's ridiculous to consider their whims and wishes judicious and astute. If you keep these people in mind, you'd be giving not just a short speech, but no speech at all.

That's my opinion so far, which I'll modify if yours differs; but, if so, you must clearly explain your thinking. Although I should bow to your authority, in such a serious matter as this, I think it's more appropriate to be persuaded through reason than through authority. So, if you think I'm correct, write back and tell me, but do it in a brief letter – then you'll really be confirming your approval! If you think I'm wrong, then you better begin writing a long, fulsome letter. I haven't corrupted you, have I, by demanding a short letter if you agree and a long letter if you disagree? Ciao!

117 Pliny to Valerius Paulinus (Ep. 2.2)

I'm pissed at you; whether for good reason or not, I'm still pissed. You know love is sometimes unfair, often vicious, and always "petty," as the Greeks say. I've got good reason to be angry (whether or not that's fair), and I'm as furious as if my cause were just. Why? Because it's been an eternity since you sent me a letter. There's one way to appease me: write me many letters – really long ones. This is the only acceptable atonement: anything else will seem phony. I don't want to hear you say "I wasn't at Rome" or "I was busy." And, for gods' sake, please don't let me hear "I was sick." Here at my villa I'm enjoying equal time writing and resting, two activities naturally suited for a holiday.

118 Pliny to Junius Avitus (Ep. 2.6)

It'd take too long to explain (and it doesn't really matter) how I happened to be dining with an acquaintance who called himself "elegant" and "economical" but was what I'd term "vulgar" and "extravagant." He served only the best for himself and a select few; all the other guests got just some skimpy leftovers. He even divided the wine into three teeny-tiny flasks according to type, not so that each guest may have a choice, but so as to force them to drink whatever they were served: one kind for himself and us, another for his inferior friends (he classifies them, too), and yet another for all the freedmen. The guest reclining next to me noticed this and asked if I approved. "No," I said. "Well, what's your normal practice?" he asked. "I give everyone the same thing. It's a dinner party, not a pecking-order contest. I consider them equals in everything else, and it's no different at the dining table." "Even your freedmen?" "Certainly. For at a banquet they're my fellow diners, not my freedmen." Then he said: "That must be really expensive." "No, not at all." "How so?" "Because I don't serve them the wine I drink, but rather I drink their wine."

It's true. If you temper your greed, it's no burden to share with others what you yourself enjoy. So, if you want to lessen expenses, greed must be kept in check and brought to order. This can be done much more effectively by restraining yourself and not insulting others. What's the point of all this? That you, a young man of exceptional character, won't be impressed by luxury disguised as frugality, which you see at some people's tables. Moreover, because I care about you, it's sensible for you to take advantage of my experiences as examples of what you should avoid. So remember: above all, spurn this horrible new alliance between extravagance and vulgarity, which are bad enough on their own, but even more disgraceful when combined.

119 Pliny to Annius Severus (Ep. 3.6)

Corinthian bronze was a particularly valuable and famous type of bronze from Corinth and a favorite material among art collectors.

I inherited some money and I recently used it to purchase a Corinthian bronze statue: just small, but a cheerful, realistic one (at least as far as I can tell). In many things I'm no expert – and I'm definitely not one when it comes to art. Still, even I can judge the quality of this piece. It's a nude, so it doesn't hide any faults or qualities. It re-creates an old man standing. His bones, muscles, nerves, and veins are plainly visible – even the wrinkles are lifelike. He has a receding hairline and is going bald; he has a broad forehead, a narrow face, and slender neck; his shoulders sag, the chest lies flat, and his stomach appears hollow. The back gives the same veristic impression of age.

The bronze itself reflects the sheen of a true, genuine antique; in fact all the features are of such high quality that they captivate an artist's eye and delight the lay person, which is exactly why I purchased it, even though I am just an amateur. But I didn't buy the bronze for my house (I still don't own any there), but for public display in my hometown, specifically in the temple of Jupiter. It's a gift worthy of a temple and of a god. Therefore, since you often undertake commissions for me, would you please take care of this one? Will you immediately order a base for the statue? Select any marble you like. Just make sure it's inscribed with my name, my titles, and anything else you think appropriate.

I'll get the statue to you as soon as I find someone who won't mind bringing it your way; otherwise I'll just do it myself. You'll prefer the latter, and, if I can get away from my official duties, I'm determined to visit. You may be happy to hear I'm promising to make a trip to see you, but less so when I add that the visit can only last a few days, since all the obligations currently keeping me here also prevent me from being gone for too long.

120 Pliny to Vestricius Spurinna and Cottia (Ep. 3.10)

Pliny explains why he didn't send a written version of a consolation he gave a reading of.

The last time we met I never mentioned I had composed something on your son. Why not? First of all, I was motivated to write the piece not just so that I could say I had written it, but to satisfy my own affection for your son and to soothe my grief over his death. Second, Spurinna, since you told me you heard I had given a reading, I was assuming you also heard what the subject was. Further, I was worried that, by mentioning your son, I'd renew your grief over his heartbreaking death and thus upset you on a day meant for festivities. I've also been debating whether I should send you only the version I read at the reading, as you requested, or whether I should include the additions I was planning to incorporate for a published version.

One little piece doesn't come anywhere close to fully expressing my feelings and cherished memories of someone so dear to my heart, someone whose fame will travel far, dispersing widely in all directions. In fact, while I was deliberating whether to show you everything I've written so far or reserve some of it for later, it dawned on me that your friendship and candidness made me want to send you everything, especially since you promise you won't publish any of the additions until I say the word.

It's certainly difficult for you to deal with this in the mid of your grief; nonetheless, just as you'd advise a sculptor or painter commissioned to create a portrait of your son about what to include and what to leave out, please provide suggestions for me: guide me while I try to produce an effigy – not one easily broken or destroyed, but one you'll believe to last forever. And the more accurate, the more beautiful, the more perfect I make it, the longer it will survive.

121 Pliny to Publius Acilius (Ep. 3.14)

There's been an event so heinous that a letter doesn't do it justice: the ex-praetor, Larcius Macedo, was attacked by his own slaves. True, he was an arrogant and cruel master, who forgot that his own father had been a slave (or perhaps he remembered it too personally). He was bathing at his villa in Formiae. Suddenly his slaves surrounded him: one grabbed him by the throat, another struck his face, another punched his chest and belly, and even – I can barely say it – crushed his genitals. When they thought he was dead, they tossed him onto the hot floor to check. As he was – or pretended to be – unconscious, he lay there, stretched out and still, making them think he was dead.

Then, finally, his remaining loyal slaves took him away as if he had passed out from the heat, while all his concubines came running out shrieking and crying. Roused by their voices and revived by the coolness, he opened his eyes, moved his body, and confirmed that he was still alive (as it was now safe to do so). The treacherous slaves fled; many were caught and the rest are being hunted down. For a few days Macedo seemed to recover a bit. He later died, but not without the satisfaction of revenge: before he passed away he got to see these slaves punished as murderers. You see how many dangers, how many outrages and insults we're faced with; you may be a gentle, easy-going master, but that doesn't mean you're safe. They killed not out of hatred for their master, but out of evil.

That's the current situation. What else is new? Nothing, otherwise I'd tell you. I'm still holding the letter, and the feast day allows time to add things. Oh, I just remembered one more thing about this same Macedo. While he was at the public baths at Rome, something noteworthy, and perhaps, as events now prove, even prophetic occurred: one of his slaves lightly touched a Roman knight so he could pass by. This knight turned around and punched not the slave who touched him, but Macedo himself. The blow was so hard it nearly knocked him out. So it looks like the baths were the location for the first insult to Macedo, and his last. Ciao.

122 Pliny to Cornelius Priscus (Ep. 3.21)

I just received the terribly sad news that Valerius Martial has died. He was naturally gifted and sharp-witted: his writing was full of bite, humor, and bluntness. When he retired from Rome, I covered his travel expenses as a gift, in return for his friendship and poems about me. This was common practice among our ancestors: to reward with monetary gifts or offices the writers who had sung the praise of individuals or cities. Nowadays, alongside other splendid and distinguished customs, this practice has been one of the first to die out. Once we stopped doing anything worthy of literary praise, we think it's silly to receive it. Want to know what little verses of his won my gratitude? I'd direct you to the volume, but I know some by heart. If you like these, you can find the rest in his published books. This one addresses the Muses, demanding that when they seek my home on the Esquiline Hill they come with due reverence:

> Don't come knocking on this learned door, drunk
> and in the middle of the day.
>
> He devotes every waking hour to stern Minerva, busily writing for the ears of the hundred
> speeches, which later generations will compare to

Arpinum's son. Go more safely when lamplight burns late at night; this is the best hour, when Bacchus is raving mad, when rose-entwined crowns reign, and hair drips perfume. Then, only then, let those straight-laced Catos read my poems.

Was I right back then to part with this man so affably? And now am I right to grieve the death of one of my closest friends? He gave me as much as he could and, given the chance, he would have given more. But what greater gift is there, other than securing someone glory, fame, and an immortal name? You say his poems may not survive forever and ever; true, maybe they won't, but he wrote them with this goal in mind.

*123 Pliny to Fabatus (*Ep. 4.1*)*

We're so happy to hear you're eager to see your granddaughter and me after so long. The feeling is mutual. In fact we can't wait, so no further delays! We're packing our bags as I speak, and we'll get there as quickly as possible, depending on what the road is like. There will be one brief delay: we're making a detour through Tuscany – not to check on my land (that can be postponed), but to fulfill a crucial obligation. There's a town called Tifernum, on the Tiber, near my estate; the town adopted me as its patron when I was practically still a boy (a decision involving enthusiasm more than sound judgment!). My arrivals are met with celebration, my departures with disappointment, and the inhabitants express delight for my public offices.

To thank them (for it's hugely embarrassing to be surpassed in displays of affection), I personally paid for a temple to be built there. Now that it's done, it would be irreligious to postpone its dedication any longer. Therefore we'll be in Tifernum on the dedication day, which I've decided to commemorate with a feast, and we'll probably stay there until the following day; but, if so, we'll speed up our pace even more. My main concern is to find you and your daughter in good health, and we look forward to seeing the smile on your face when you receive us safe and sound.

*124 Pliny to Attius Clementius (*Ep. 4.2*)*

Regulus has lost his son – the one tragedy he didn't deserve, though I doubt *he* thinks it's a tragedy. The boy had a sharp, albeit undependable mind: he had the potential to pursue the right path – too bad he followed in his father's footsteps. Regulus had released him from his paternal control, so that he could inherit his mother's estate; once "sold" (as those who really knew what Regulus was like called it), he started buying his son's affection with a despicable display of indulgence, unnatural in a parent. It's unbelievable, but we *are* talking about Regulus, after all. Still, he grieves for his dead son like a madman. The boy enjoyed many ponies for riding and driving, along with large and small dogs, nightingales, parrots, and blackbirds. Regulus had them all slaughtered round the boy's funeral pyre. That wasn't grief, but a parade of grief.

An unfathomable crowd swarms around him, and, although they despise and hate him, they put on a show as if they loved and admired him. To put it briefly, in the act of wooing Regulus, they imitate him. He confines himself to his gardens in Trastevere, where he's covered a huge stretch of land with massive colonnades, spoiling the shore with his statues. As a result, he's extravagant despite his extreme avarice and celebrated despite his extreme infamy.

So he is Rome's buzzing mosquito at the most unhealthy, malaria-ridden time of the year, and he finds solace in being such a nuisance. He says he's going to get married, another of his questionable actions, like all his other perversities. You'll soon hear about the mourner's wedding, the old man's wedding; one is too early, the other too late. How can I predict this? Not because he himself confirms it (nobody is better at lying), but because undoubtedly Regulus will always do exactly what he should *not* do.

125 *Pliny to Catius Lepidus* (Ep. 4.7)

I've often told you about Regulus' inner drive. It's remarkable the way he acheives what he sets out to do. He was resolved to mourn his son: and so he does, like no one else you've ever seen. He was determined to have as many statues and portraits of his son as possible: he commissions every workshop to carry it out. One workshop re-creates Regulus Jr. in color, another in wax; one in bronze, another in silver, yet another in gold; one in ivory, another in marble. Recently he amassed a huge audience to listen to a public reading of a memoir about his son. Yes, it's about the life of a boy, but he read it anyway. He also distributed thousands of copies of the memoir throughout Italy and all the provinces. He sent along a public letter asking municipal leaders to choose someone with the best voice to read the book to the public. It was done. Can you imagine – if Regulus had directed this "drive" of his (or whatever we might call this "resolve" to get what you want) toward better endeavors? What good he could have accomplished! Still, this drive is the lot of bad people more than good ones. As the Greek saying goes: "Ignorance breeds boldness, logic breeds reluctance." That's because a good conscience can weaken the impulsiveness of an upright person and impudence can strengthen that of a crooked one. Regulus is the perfect example. His lungs are weak, his speech muddled; he stammers; he can't think on his feet, doesn't remember a thing, and possesses nothing except an irrational resourcefulness, a shamelessness that, in all its madness, has earned him the name "orator." Herennius Senecio inverted Cato's famous quotation about the orator precisely so as to make it fit Regulus: "An orator is a bad man unskilled in speaking." By god, Senecio's characterization of Regulus surpasses even Cato's original definition! Do you have a letter you can send to compete with this one? You do if you can write me whether any of my friends in your town, maybe even yourself, publicly read Regulus' pathetic memoir, barking like a common street hawker, with an "artificial high-pitched voice," as Demosthenes says. The work is so gauche that it's more likely to incite laughter than tears: you'd think it was written *by* a boy, not *about* one.

126 *Pliny to Pliny Paternus* (Ep. 4.14)

Perhaps you were anticipating one of my usual speeches. Instead I'm sending you some less serious, lighter works from my "stockroom" of foreign, luxury "merchandise." Enclosed with this letter are my hendecasyllables: I had a blast composing them in my spare time: in my carriage, at the bath, and during dinner. You'll see me joking and playing around; you'll read my passions, my sorrows, my grumbling, and my rage. Sometimes I write concisely, other times more ornately. With this variety I try to ensure everyone will find something they like. If some seem rather racy to you, remember from your own literary training that the most distinguished and austere authors who covered such themes not only wrote on licentious subjects, but did it in blunt, straightforward language. I've refrained from doing so not because I'm more straight-laced (why should I be?), but because I'm more tentative. I'm well aware of Catullus' rule of thumb for such little works: "The true poet should be virtuous, not necessarily his verses: they'll possess wit and charm, but only if they're delicate and coarse."

How much do I value your opinion? You can tell from the fact that I prefer you not simply to praise some chosen selections, but to provide feedback on the entire work, which admittedly can be less gratifying once the parts start becoming monotonous. Moreover, a gifted, perceptive reader shouldn't compare totally different excerpts but assess the value of each on its own merit. One last thing: notice that I've entitled these little poetic nuggets *Hendecasyllables*, a title entirely based on their poetic meter. Call them what you like: epigrams, idylls, eclogues – or, as others do, mini-poems. I'm going to stick to my original name: *Hendecasyllables*.

Please be completely honest and tell me what you'd tell someone else if I were out of the room – this isn't a tough request. For, if this were my only publication or my great opus, you might seem a bit harsh if you were saying: "You need to find a career." But there's nothing unkind in advising: "Don't give up your day job." Ciao.

127 *Pliny to Calpurnia Hispulla* (Ep. 4.19)

Pliny writes to his new wife's aunt.

You are a paragon of loyalty, loving your excellent, affectionate brother as equally as he loved you. You love his daughter as if she were your own, filling the role of aunt and even taking the place of her deceased father. So I'm sure you'll be particularly happy to hear she's proven herself worthy of her father, of you, and of her grandfather. She is the epitome of good judgment and frugality, and she loves me – clear proof of her devotion. In addition, she keenly appreciates literature, an interest stemming from her love for me. She has copies of my little books, reads them over and over again, even memorizes them by heart. How anxious she gets when I'm about to plead in court, and how ecstatic for me when I'm done! She organizes messengers to report back on any shouts of approval I elicit from my audience along with the final verdict. Whenever I give a reading, she sits nearby, hidden behind a curtain, listening fervently and absorbing all the praise I receive. She even composes musical arrangements for my verses and sings them to accompany her lyre; she has no teacher except love, the best instructor of all.

So I'm fully confident that our conjugal harmony will grow day by day, lasting forever. It is not my age or my body she adores (they grow old and perish), but my fame. What else would one expect from a woman raised at your hands, instilled with your lessons, who, under your care, has seen only what's virtuous and honorable, and, lastly, who's grown to love me just as you predicted? You respected my mother as if she were your own; from boyhood on you shaped and encouraged me to become the man you always said I'd become in her eyes. Therefore *we* thank you all the more: *I* because you gave her to me, and *she* because you gave me to her – a perfectly matched couple.

128 *Pliny to Sempronius Rufus* (Ep. 4.22)

Pliny writes about an inquiry into games held at Vienna (ancient Roman Vindobona).

I've just taken part, as a consultant to our noble emperor, in an inquiry regarding the gymnastic contests among the Viennese – which are celebrated according to the will of a certain individual. The local magistrate, Trebonius Rufinus, a distinguished friend of mine, had the games eliminated and abolished; but he was then accused of not having the authority to do so. He pleaded his own case skillfully and effectively, and his speech won favor because he spoke efficiently and with the dignity that befits a Roman man and upstanding citizen. When the time for the verdict came, Junius Mauricus, the most staunchly just and righteous man, announced that the games would not be restored. He added: "I only wish we could also terminate them at Rome." Your response will be that he acted steadily and bravely: is this a surprise? One expects nothing less from Mauricus. He behaved no less courageously years ago, in the presence of Emperor Nerva, when he was dining with a few people; Veiento (I only have to mention his name and it says it all) was next to him – even leaning on Nerva's side. A discussion began about the blind Catullus Messalinus, whose unfortunate blindness only agmented his cruel nature. He possessed no fear, shame, or pity (it was for this reason that Emperor Domitian frequently used him like a whirling weapon aimed blindly and randomly at honest men). Everyone was deploring Messalinus' depravity and bloodthirsty tendencies, when Nerva himself said: "I wonder what would have happened to him if he were alive today." Without missing a beat, Mauricus responded: "He'd be dining with us."

I've gotten away from the point, but intentionally. They decided to eliminate the games, which had infected the morals of the Viennese people just as the games here have infected everything. The vices of Vienna stay among their people, but ours wander far and wide: the most acute disease, whether it's occupying a body or an empire, is the one that originates in the head. Goodbye.

129 Pliny to Domitius Apollinaris (Ep. *5.6*)

Thanks for your concern regarding my plans to spend the summer at my Tuscan villa, and for trying to dissuade me from going. You consider it unhealthy. It's true, the areas near the coast are oppressive and malaria-ridden; but my villa is inland, quite a distance from the shore. It lies at the foot of the Appennines, mountains especially beneficial for one's health. So, to dispel your fears, here's a description of the villa's temperate climate and pleasant locale – which you'll enjoy hearing about as much as I'll enjoy telling you.

The winter climate is cold and icy, completely halting the growth of the myrtles, olive trees, and all the other plants that require consistent warmth to flourish. Laurel, on the other hand, tolerates the winter and even develops a nice glossy shine in it. Occasionally the winter kills it, but no more frequently than at Rome. The summer is mercifully temperate: a light breeze is always blowing; rarely a strong wind. This accounts for the fact that many senior citizens are living here: you'd see the grandfathers and great-grandfathers of young men, and you'd get to listen to all their old fables and stories from the past: a visit here is like a trip back in time to a bygone age.

The countryside is stunning. Picture this: a vast amphitheater, but one that only nature herself could construct. You see a broad stretch of flat plains surrounded by mountains, with ancient groves of tall trees covering the mountaintops. There's plenty of varied hunting. Further down the mountain slopes are forests with trees mature enough for felling. Rolling between the forests are small hills with rich organic soil: you'd be hard-pressed to find a rock anywhere. The soil here is just as fertile as in the plains, and these hills produce just as many crops, only they're harvested later in the season.

On the lower slopes grapevines extend everywhere, their rows intertwining to weave one continuous view. At the lower edge, bushes emerge like a hedge. Then come the meadows and the farmland, where only huge oxen and the strongest plow can break up the soil. When the plow makes a first go around, it turns up big clods of solid earth; and you have to go at least nine times to thoroughly break up the soil into workable furrows. The blossoming meadows sparkle like gemstones, abounding with clover and all kinds of tender plants, so green and soft they always look like fresh new growth. Ever flowing streams nurture these meadows, but wherever there's runoff, the downward slope of the land prevents it from pooling into a swampy bog, since any water that isn't absorbed just empties into the Tiber. The Tiber cuts through the middle of the fields and can be navigated in winter and spring for the transport of produce to Rome. In the summer its water level drops and the dry bed forces it to relinquish its reputation as a formidable river, but autumn restores it.

It's a great pleasure to stand atop a mountain looking down at the surrounding countryside; you'll feel like you're viewing not real scenery, but a painting of exceptional beauty, and one of a kind: wherever your eyes roam, they're refreshed by the varied and perfect composition.

My villa sits at the bottom of the hill, but its view is as if from the top. The ascent is so gentle and gradual you don't even realize you've been climbing until you reach the summit. Behind the villa lie the Apennines, a distance away. Even on a calm, peaceful day I get a mountain breeze – never harsh or excessive, but mild: by the time the wind reaches me, it's considerably weaker. Most of the house faces south; in the summer it enjoys sunshine beginning at midday and in the winter much earlier, as if it were inviting the sun into the portico. The portico's length is proportionate to its width. Here you'll find many rooms, along with a traditional atrium. In front is a terrace, separated into different areas and edged with boxwood. From there a raised border slopes downward, and on either side there are boxwood topiaries, cut and shaped into different animals. This leads to level ground, where you'll see the softest acanthus growing – it's almost as soft as silk. Then there's a walkway bordered by bushes, cut and trained to grow into various shapes. Beyond these you'll find an exercise area like a circular racetrack, with variously shaped boxwood surrounding the perimeter and dwarf shrubs purposefully trimmed to be permanently small. A wall confines them all, and tiered boxwood grows over the wall and conceals it. Outside the wall there's a meadow: its natural beauty is just as worth looking at as the formal garden's carefully manicured beauty. Beyond it lie fields, and also many meadows and trees.

A dining room extends downwards from the top of the portico; through its doors you can look out to the end of the terrace and beyond, to the meadows and much of the surrounding countryside. The windows on one side of the dining room face an area of the terrace and the villa's overhang; the windows on the other side offer a view of the adjacent riding track's tree foliage. Opposite almost the middle of the portico is an annex of rooms set back a bit, with a small courtyard shaded by four plane trees. In the middle, a marble fountain with gurgling water sprays the surrounding trees, refreshing the ground beneath with a light sprinkling. One of the rooms is a bedroom, which shuts out all daytime noise, and next to it is a casual everyday dining room for close friends. It looks out onto the small courtyard and part of the portico. There's another bedroom, green-hued from the nearby plane tree's shade and decorated with marble from the baseboard all the way up to the top, and it has an equally impressive fresco depicting birds perched on tree branches. Here' you'll find a small fountain with a bowl; and the water spraying from small jets around the bowl creates a wonderfully soothing gurgling sound. The corner of the portico hosts a very large room facing the dining room. From some of its windows you can see the terrace, and from others the meadow. Below the dining room windows in front is a small pool, delightful in sight and sound, since water leaps down from above and produces white bubbles as it hits the marble. This same room enjoys copious sunshine and is quite warm in the winter. It also contains a hypocaustic heating system, so on cloudy days the steam generated from the furnace below makes up for the lack of sunlight. From there you go into the baths' spacious, cheerful dressing room, which then leads to the cooling room, where there's a large, shady plunge-bath. If you want space to swim in warmer water, there's a swimming pool in the forecourt and, next to it, a well serving as a skin tonic when you've had your fill of warm water. Next to the cooling room is another one, where the sun's kindly rays are ever present. It's not as warm, however, as the hot room, since it projects outwards. Inside are three plunge-baths: two fully placed in the sun and the third in the shade – although it's still well lit.

Above the changing room is a ballcourt with plenty of room for other types of exercise: it has several circular zones. Not too far away from the bath is a staircase leading to a three-room suite and a covered portico. One room overlooks the small court with its four plane trees; the second overlooks the meadow; and the third gives a sweeping view of the vineyards and sky. The upper end of the crypto-porticus forms its own room looking out to the hippodrome, the vineyards, and the mountains; next to it is a room that enjoys the sun, especially during winter. Adjacent is another room, which connects the hippodrome to the villa. This is the villa's layout from the front.

On the side of the villa is a summer crypto-porticus situated higher up, which seems not just to look into the vineyards from above, but actually to touch them. Halfway down the crypto-porticus there's a dining room that receives the most refreshing breeze from the Apennine valleys. It has wide windows at the back and these look upon the vines, which you can see just as well from the doors, even though you're looking through the porticus. On the windowless side of the dining room there's a discrete, private staircase used for serving food at dinner parties. At the end there's a room looking out to the crypto-porticus, and that's no less enjoyable than the view of the vineyard. Beneath is a similar crypto-porticus, partially underground, which retains a consistently icy temperature and, because of its own airflow, neither requires nor admits any breeze. Behind both of them, a winter porticus begins where the dining room ends. This one is cool in the morning hours, but in the afternoon it gets quite hot. Off it are two suites: one comprises four rooms, the other three, and all these rooms enjoy sun or shade depending on the position of the sun during the day.

The hippodrome far surpasses the charm and layout of the villa buildings. The middle of it is wide open and visible as soon as one enters; it's surrounded by plane trees covered in ivy, so the trees are green up top from their own foliage and green all the way to the bottom from the vines. Ivy creeps along all the trunks and branches, connecting neighboring trees with its intertwining growth. Boxwood is planted between the trees, and laurel surrounds the boxwood in an outer ring, offering additional shade. At this point, the straight part of the hippodrome begins to round into a semi-circle and changes appearance; for cypress trees overhang all around, making this part darker and shadier. The interior rings – and there are many of them – have plenty of sun. There you'll find even roses; and cool shade alternates with soothing warm sunshine. At the end of these meandering pathways, back along the straight part, there are many more paths divided by intervening boxwood; and there are small grass lawns in some parts, boxwood in others, shaped into a thousand different forms – even letters spelling the gardener's name, or his master's. Small obelisks of boxwood and fruit trees are variously scattered around. Then, suddenly, a re-creation of the rural countryside appears in the midst of this very cultivated garden, with short plane trees adorning the middle space. Beyond this you'll find glossy smooth acanthus here and there and more boxwood fashioned into names and shapes.

At the top of the hippodrome is a semi-circular dining couch made of white marble and shaded by four columns of Carystian marble with overhanging grapevines. Jetted water flows out of the couch, almost as if peoples' weight were causing it to do so, and a hollowed-out rock catches the water, which is then contained in a simple marble basin; there the water is regulated by a secret mechanism, so that the basin is always full without spilling over. The dinner's appetizers and main dishes are set on the basin's surrounding ledge, while the lighter morsels "swim around" in containers shaped like little boats or birds. There's another fountain opposite, which shoots water up and catches it as it falls down; this is repeated over and over. A room faces the dining couch, and each contributes to the beauty of the other. The room is in gleaming marble and its doors lead you into trees and bushes, while the upper and lower windows overlook all the plants above and below. Next comes a little alcove, which is both part of the room and separate from it. Here lies a bed and there are windows everywhere, but the light only just percolates through the shade thrown by a luxuriant vine crawling all the way up to the roof. When you recline there it feels like you're in a grove, minus any risk of getting wet from a rain shower! Here, too, a fountain leaps up and falls back down, and in many different places you'll find marble seats, just as pleasing as the room itself – to anyone tired from walking. Next to every chair there is a little fountain. Purposely designed babbling streams resound throughout the hippodrome; their direction can be hand-adjusted to water this or that part of the garden, or all of it at once.

I would have tried not to blather on and on, but I already explained: my goal was to let my letter be your guide and lead you into every nook and cranny. I was confident you wouldn't find it tedious to *read* about a place that certainly wouldn't be tedious to *visit*. Besides, you can sit and take a rest whenever you like (just put down the letter for a bit)! Moreover, I've indulged my own passion: I'm greatly attached to the places I've designed myself, or to those I'm trying to refine. In a nutshell – and why shouldn't I be clear about my opinions, right or wrong? – I think a writer's first and foremost obligation is to re-read the title of his work, asking himself repeatedly what it is he's decided to write about. As long as he sticks to the topic at hand, he's not over-writing. If he inserts unrelated material, he'll be overdoing it. Look at how many lines Homer uses to describe the shield of Achilles, or Vergil to describe Aeneas' armor; nevertheless, both depictions are of appropriate lengths, because each author sticks to his point. You know how Aratus researches and collects everything he can on the tiniest stars but still preserves the proper length, simply because that subject isn't a digression but the work's main focus. Let me "compare small with great": I'm trying to recreate my entire villa right in front of your eyes (as if I were escorting you around the property), so, as long as I stick to the point, it's not the *letter* describing the villa that's sizeable, but the *villa* the letter describes. But let me get back on course (otherwise, if I continue going off-track with this digression, I'll be justly chastised for breaking my own rule). So here you have my reasons why I prefer my Tuscan villa to all my others, including those at Tusculum, Tibur, and Praeneste. I'll add one more reason: this is where I enjoy deeper peace and quiet, where I'm more relaxed and restful. I don't have to dress up in a toga, nobody is fetching me; everything is calm and serene – all factors contributing to the healthy atmosphere of the place as much as the pure-blue sky and clean air. Here I'm at my healthiest, both in mind and in body. For my studies exercise my mind, while hunting exercises my body. And my healthiest slaves reside here: so far, I haven't lost a single one I brought with me (knock on wood). Now only let the gods continue to protect this place – my pride and joy!

130 Pliny to Titinius Capito (Ep. 5.8)

You suggest that I write a history, and you're not the only one. Many have often advised me to do this very thing. I really want to: not because I'm confident I'll do it well (a rather rash statement if one's not experienced at it), but because I think that securing immortality for those who deserve it and ensuring that the fame of those who deserve immortality lives on are especially noble endeavors. Moreover, by publicizing the fame of others, one disseminates his own. Nothing excites me more than the idea of achieving eternal fame, a human being's most worthy enterprise – especially for someone who has a clear conscience and has no reason to fear being written into history books. So day and night I think about whether "I too will one day arise from the earth," as Virgil says. If so, that would be an answer to my prayers, since "to fly a victor throughout the lips of men" (to quote Virgil again) exceeds my wish. "Yet, if only I could ..." but enough: I'll be content with what history seems to promise. Oratory and poetry, unless one is exceptionally eloquent, earn small esteem; history, on the other hand, wins great praise whatever one's style. People are naturally curious, so even a plain and simple style will make narrated events captivating to anyone who enjoys gossip and a good story. I also have my own special example urging me on: my uncle, who's also my adopted father, wrote histories – and he did so with the greatest scruple. I agree with the philosophers: it's especially honorable to follow in our predecessors' footsteps – provided they haven't strayed from the straight and narrow.

So why am I stalling? I've been involved in several rather significant court cases, and although I'm only modestly hopeful of them, I do plan on revising them; that way all the hard work I invested won't die when I do, just because I didn't complete the final polishing. When it comes to one's posthumous legacy, anything that's incomplete might as well have never been started. I know what you're going to say: "Why not revise your speeches and write a history concomitantly?" If only! But each is such a significant enterprise on its own. I have plenty on my plate just finishing the speeches. I began speaking in the forum when I was 18, and only just now am I beginning to realize what it really means to be a superior orator (and my understanding is still a bit foggy). What would happen if I doubled or tripled my current workload?

It's true, oratory and history share many overlaps, but they're actually quite different in those aspects, which seem alike. For example, both narrate events, but oratory does it differently: it describes the more low and gritty stories from everyday life, while history deals with all the elevated and brilliant ones. When it comes to style, consider the body of a horse: oratory is the bones, the little muscles and tendons, while history comprises the bulging muscles and long, flowing mane. Oratory succeeds by its force, sharpness, and intensity; history, by its drawn-out style, eloquence, and even charm. Finally, each relies upon different words, a different tone, and different sentence construction. As Thucydides says, there's quite a difference between a "possession" and a "prize essay," history being the former, oratory the latter. I don't think I should confuse and mix up the two genres by working on them simultaneously, since they are in fact so intrinsically dissimilar in their respective claims to fame. Otherwise I might jumble myself all up, turning history into oratory and oratory into history. Meanwhile, to use language near and dear to me, the "defense" asks the "court" to grant indulgence.

No doubt you're already wondering what historical period I want most of all to pursue. Ancient history, which other authors have already covered? I've got all the evidence, but pulling it together into a cohesive whole would be quite taxing. Or should I embark on more recent events, which still need a historian to record them? But then I face the possibility of receiving little thanks and of offending my readers greatly. For, in addition to the fact that people's vices nowadays offer more to criticize than to extol, if you give even just a little praise, you'll be blamed for giving too much, and if you criticize anything, however lightly, you'll be blamed for not being critical enough. You can't win. But this won't deter me. I'm abundantly confident about fulfilling my desire to write history. But I have one request: throw out an idea. What topic do you think I should focus on? If you don't suggest something, I may hesitate and, despite my readiness, find another excuse to postpone my goal. Take care.

131 Pliny to Aefulanus Marcellinus (Ep. 5.16)

I write with the most crushing news: our friend Fundanus has lost his younger daughter. I've never seen a girl so cheerful and lovable, or more deserving of a longer life – and even of immortality. She was barely 14 years old and already possessed the discretion of a woman five times her age. She had the dignity of a Roman matron, even in her girlish sweetness and respect for her own virginal purity. Remember how she used to wrap her arms around her dad's neck and hold onto him! And how modestly and affectionately she used to embrace her father's friends, including us. Oh, how she loved her nurses, the slaves who used to watch over her, her teachers – everyone who was involved in her upbringing! She was so enthusiastic and perceptive when she read – which was quite frequently. She used to play with reserve, and only occasionally. She dealt with this latest illness with such self-control, patience, and strength! She obeyed her doctors, encouraged her sister and father, and, even when her body gave out, she could still hang on, through her own sheer determination. And she preserved this mindset to the very end; neither the persistence of her illness nor the fear of death could break it. We feel her loss and our grief all the more deeply this way.

Oh, what a grim, utterly bitter funeral! The fact that she died at such a young age makes her death that much more grievous. She was engaged to marry the perfect groom. The wedding day was set, the invitations sent out. Joy turns now to grief. I can't fully express (there are too many sorrowful examples to count) how painful it was to hear Fundanus giving the orders to take all the money earmarked for clothes, pearls, and gemstones and use it instead to buy incense, ointments, and other funeral aromatics. Fundanus, we know, is a well-educated man, a philosopher, a man who's devoted himself since youth to advanced studies and arts. Now he rejects everything he's learned, all the things he's heard and often spoken about; he has banished all his other virtues and is completely and totally focused on devotion to his daughter. You'll forgive him, even praise him, if you consider what he has lost: a daughter, one who resembled him in character as much as in physical appearance and expression. She was a carbon copy of her father, his mirror image.

So, if you're planning on sending him a letter addressing his grief – a grief fully warranted – just be sure to offer him some comforting words: nothing stern, like a scolding, but something gentle and kind. He'll be more receptive to your suggestions as time passes. A fresh, raw wound refuses a physician's hand; but after a while it can bear it, and later it even welcomes it. Grief is the same: when someone has experienced a recent loss, s/he initially rejects and avoids words of consolation. But soon s/he's willing to accept them and, when the solace is offered gently, finds comfort.

132 *Pliny to Tiro* (Ep. 6.1)

As long as I was staying north of the Po River and you were down in Picenum, I didn't miss you so much. Now that I'm back in Rome and you're still in Picenum, I miss you much more. I'm not sure if it's because the places where we're usually together remind me of you more acutely, or because nothing sharpens one's desire for absent friends like being in their vicinity but not in their company. This is especially the case when, the closer you are to enjoying their company, the more impatient you feel when you're unable to do so. Whatever the reason, rescue me from this torture! Come back, or I'll return to the very place I just stupidly hurried away from, just to test out whether you'll send me letters like this when you're back at Rome without me.

133 *Pliny to Fundanus* (Ep. 6.6)

If ever I've really needed you here, it's now. Please come. I need an ally to share in my promise, my toil, and my anxiety. Here's why: Julius Naso is seeking election amid many other candidates, good ones at that. The challenge of winning is as great as the triumph he'll enjoy if he does. So I'm on tenterhooks, balancing between hope and fear, feeling as if I've never even been a consul myself! It's like I've returned to my old canvassing days. Naso deserves my attention because he's long esteemed me. I can't say that I was friends with his father, since our difference in age didn't allow it. Still, when I was a young boy, people pointed out Naso's father as a model to follow. He was an ardent lover of learning and very fond of those eager to learn; he used to go almost daily to hear the lectures of Quintilian and Nicetes Sacerdos, whom I was studying under. He was a man of such brilliance and gravitas that his reputation alone should be an advantage to his son. But now there are many in the Senate who have no idea who Naso Sr. was, and many who, although they did know him, only show respect for people still living. So, since his father's reputation – although a source of pride – has been disregarded and his popularity is weak, Naso will have to rely chiefly on himself and his own hard work. Fortunately this is something he's always zealously done (it's almost as if he foresaw this situation): he's made friends and connections and cultivated them; he singled me out as a close friend and someone to emulate as soon as he felt confident about making his own decisions. When I'm speaking in the courts, he anxiously stands next to me; when I'm giving a reading of my work, he's at my side. He shows interest in my little compositions as soon as they come out. His brother used to accompany him, but he recently died. Naso is now alone. So I'm the one who must try to take his brother's place. I mourn over such an untimely, undeserved death, and that Naso, now without the support of his excellent brother, is left with only his friends.

For these reasons I urge you: come and join your vote with mine. I'm very eager to show you off, making the rounds with you by my side. It is this influence, your visible presence, I think, that will make me more successful in winning votes, even from my friends. Put down whatever you're doing: my circumstances, loyalty, even my honor demand it. It's a well-known fact that I've undertaken the role of supporting a candidate. I'm the one canvassing, the one taking a risk. If Naso wins the office he is seeking, the honor belongs to him but, should he lose, the defeat is all mine. Goodbye.

134 *Pliny to his wife Calpurnia* (Ep. 6.7)

You write that my absence seriously affects you and that your one solace are my little books, which you hold instead of my hand, often lying down beside them in the same spot I'd normally be. It's nice to hear you miss me and can find comfort in these kinds of antidotes. I, in turn, read your letters over and over again, repeatedly taking them in my hands, as if reading them for the first time. But then this just enflames my desire to see you: your letters echo all the sweetness and charm of your voice when you talk to me in person! Still, write as often as you can, even though your letters bring me as much torture as happiness. Goodbye.

135 *Pliny to Tacitus* (Ep. 6.20)

You say the letter I wrote at your request, describing the death of my uncle, inspired you to learn more about the terrors and misfortunes I suffered at Misenum (I had started on the topic and then stopped). Well, as Virgil says, "although my mind shrinks in horror to remember it all, I will begin."

After my uncle left, I devoted the rest of my time to my studies (which is why I had stayed behind at Misenum). Then I took a bath, had dinner, and slept, albeit restlessly and only briefly. For many days we had been experiencing earthquakes; this wasn't too alarming, since earthquakes are a usual occurrence for the Campania region. But that night the shaking got so strong, everything seemed like it was – not just moving, but being overturned. My mother rushed into my room; at that moment I was also out of bed to go wake her up in case she was still asleep. We sat in the outdoor courtyard, which divides the buildings from the nearby sea. It may have been courage or just stupidity (I was only 17 at the time), but I demanded a book of Livy and, as if having nothing better to do, I read and continued writing down the excerpts I had already started. Then, suddenly, a friend of my uncle appeared who had recently come from Spain to visit. When he saw my mother and me sitting there, with me (unbelievably) still reading, he chastised my irresponsibility and my mother's tolerance of it. Regardless, I continued, focused no less on my book.

It was dawn, and the light had been faint and muted until then. The surrounding buildings had already been wobbling; and although we were in an open space, it was a small one. There was a realistic, serious fear of some major destruction. In the end it seemed best to leave town. A shocked mob followed us, as they preferred following someone else's lead rather than their own (fear looks then a lot like prudence). In a thick column they pushed and pressed us forward. Past the houses we stopped, and we experienced many unbelievable, frightening scenes. We had ordered carriages to be brought, and, although it was a very flat, level ground, they were running in opposite directions and wouldn't stay still even after we wedged stones behind the wheels. Meanwhile we saw the sea being sucked back from shore by the earthquake; many sea creatures were left behind, stranded on dry sand. Behind us a black ominous cloud, broken up by twisted zigzag fiery flashes, gaped open, showing long tongues of flames that were just like larger versions of sheet lightning.

Then the same friend from Spain spoke more urgently and insistently to my mother and me: "If *your* brother and *your* uncle is alive, he'll want you both to live; if he's dead, he'd want you both to survive him. So what are you waiting for? Why aren't you escaping?" We answered we couldn't allow ourselves to think about our own safety when we were uncertain about his. My uncle's friend didn't bother sticking around and sped away to flee the danger. Not long afterwards, the cloud started moving down from the sky and toward the lands, covering the sea; it had already surrounded and concealed Capri and hid Pt. Misenum from view. At that point my mother was begging, urging, commanding me to escape however I could: "You're young – save yourself! Age and weakness slow me down. I'd die with peace of mind if I knew I wasn't the cause of your death." But I was unwilling to escape without her, too, so I grabbed her hand and forced her to pick up her pace. She grudgingly obeyed, blaming herself for slowing me down. Ash was falling around us, though gently. I looked around: a thick darkness was coming up behind us like a flood, stretching over the lands. "Let's turn off the road," I said, "while we can still see, so the mob doesn't throw us to the ground and trample us in the dark."

We had barely sat down and it became night: not a moonless or cloudy night, but the kind when it feels like you're locked up in a closet with no lamp. You could hear the shrieks of women, the cries of infants, the shouts of men. Some were calling for their parents, others for their children, some for their wives, trying to identify them by their voices. Some were lamenting their own downfall, others the fate of their relatives. There were some who, fearing death, prayed for its arrival. Many lifted their hands up to the heavens; more believed that the gods no longer existed and determined that what they were experiencing was eternal, never ending darkness for the whole universe. There were plenty of people aggravating the real dangers through fabricated ones: some said that this part of Misenum had fallen or that part was burning, lying to people who bought into their stories.

A little later light returned, but not daylight. Rather it seemed to indicate the advancing flames, though in fact the fire kept a good way off. Darkness returned, as did the ash, now thick and heavy. From time to time we stood up and shook it off, or it would have covered us, crushing us under its weight. I'd boast that I didn't once groan or cry in fear, if, even in the sad, significant consolation of my own mortality, I hadn't believed everything was perishing with me and I with it. At last the darkness thinned out, as if it had dissipated into smoke or a cloud. Soon real daylight returned, but it was dim, like when there's an eclipse. How scary to witness before our very eyes everything changed, buried in deep ash, like snow. We returned to Misenum, somehow attended to our bodily needs, and spent a fearful, anxious night wavering between hope and fear. Fear prevailed, for the earthquakes persisted, and many crazy people with their hyperbolic, terrifying predictions turned their own and others' maladies into jokes by comparison. Nevertheless, not even at that point, despite all the dangers we had experienced and were still expecting, did we have any intention of leaving – not until we received news of my uncle.

You'll read this not with any plan to commit it to history – it's not at all worthy of that. And besides, if these details don't even seem to deserve a letter, you've got only yourself to blame, since you're the one who requested it!

136 Pliny to Quintilianus (Ep. 6.32)

You live quite moderately within your means and have raised your daughter to be the kind of girl everyone expects of you and her grandfather, Tutilius. Still, since she's going to marry the very distinguished Nonius Celer, whose public position calls for fashionable elegance, your daughter should have clothing and an entourage that complement her future husband's position. These things certainly won't increase her worth, but they will enhance it. I know you're rich when it comes to your intellect, but less so when it comes to your wallet. So I'm assuming some of your burden and, like a second father to "our" girl, I'm giving you 50,000 sesterces for her expenses. I'd give you more, except I know that the modest amount of this gift is the only thing to convince you to accept it. Goodbye.

137 Pliny to Maximus (Ep. 6.34)

You were right to host a gladiatorial show for the people of Verona, who have loved you, respected you, and given you many honors for quite some time now. Verona was also the hometown of your wife, a very respectable woman who loved you dearly and whose memory should be honored through some public work or spectacle: this type of show fulfilled perfectly such an act of exemplary homage. Further, such a large number of people joined in the request that, if you had refused, you would have gained a reputation for being rude rather than principled. Your exceptional flexiblity and generousity in hosting the show are also to be commended, since such behavior is indicative of a charitable heart. I wish the African panthers you purchased had arrived in time; but you still get credit, even though the weather delayed them. After all, it's not your fault that you weren't able to show them off! Ciao.

138 Pliny to Fuscus Salinator (Ep. 7.9)

You ask how I think you should spend your vacation. First, the most useful thing, as many suggest, is to translate Greek into Latin and Latin into Greek. This activity enhances one's breadth and richness in vocabulary, figures of speech, and power of explication. Moreover, by imitating the best examples you'll develop a similar capacity for writing your own original works. At the same time, the translator cannot possibly overlook certain details missed by the reader: translation demands a sharp eye and critical thinking. After you've read something closely enough to remember the topic and its contents, it's perfectly fine to attempt to write something of equal weight and then to compare your version with the original, thoroughly considering how one is more satisfying than the other. Congratulate yourself if yours is the better one; if it's the original, you should feel humbled. It's also a good idea on occasion to choose a particularly well-known passage and compete with it by trying to improve it. This is a bold exercise, but not an arrogant one if you do it privately. We've witnessed many people undertaking endeavors of this sort and earning great praise; thanks to self-confidence, they've surpassed the authors whom they only meant to emulate. You can also return to revising old speeches, retaining much, eliminating more, adding in some sections, and revising others. This is time-consuming and tedious, but the benefits outweigh the challenge, since the process will rekindle a flame and revive your interest when it's been broken and and its object is forgotten. It's like attaching brand new "limbs," so to speak, to an intact "body," but doing so without spoiling the original.

I know right now that your primary interest is in forensic oratory, but that's not a good enough reason for recommending that you always employ this contentious and controversial style of writing.

Soil rejuvenates when you rotate your crops; likewise, our minds are reinvigorated when we focus on different intellectual activities, now and again. I'd like to see you sometimes concentrate on a passage from history, or carefully compose some epistles. For frequently even a speech requires historical narrative or a poetic description, and letter-writing encourages a straightforward, concise writing style. It's also a good idea to take a break by writing poetry, not a long, continuous poem (which can only be completed when you have abundant free time), but that type of succinct, lively poem, which provides a break from your other duties and obligations, however essential these may be. This is called "light-hearted" poetry and occasionally offers as much fame as serious poetry. So: how about I encourage you to write a poem with some inspiration from a few of my own verses? Here you go:

> Glory to wax, which fashions and forms at the will of skilled fingers, and on command creates Mars, or now chaste Minvera, sculpting Venus, and now her son. Sacred springs snuff out flames of fire and likewise delight field and flower; so, too, is the mind of man: duly bent and shaped, through gentle arts, to accept change.

This is exactly what all the best orators (and the greatest people, too) used to do to train or to amuse themselves – or rather, to train *and* amuse themselves. It's amazing how the mind and the spirit are exercised and relaxed through the act of composing these little poems. They comprise our loves and hates, our anger, sadness, and sarcasm – in fact all the areas of life, and everything that involves our public careers and interests. These little pieces offer the same advantage as other forms of poetry: once we've fully experienced the confines of writing in poetic meter, we rejoice in the freedom of prose and are more than happy to return to a genre that has clearly shown, by comparison, to be of the easier type.

You have perhaps more than you asked for, but I forgot – one more thing. I haven't mentioned what I think you should be reading, although I implied it when I explained what I thought you should be writing. Remember to be diligent and pick authors from each genre. They say it's better to be deeply read than broadly read. The standard, approved authors are familiar enough, so I don't need to elaborate. Besides, I've let this letter go on for long enough; so all this time when I'm advising you what you should read and write, I'm robbing you of the time to actually do so! So: why don't you pick up your tablets and compose something like what I've suggested, or continue something you've already begun? So long.

*139 Pliny to Tacitus (*Ep. *7.33)*

I predict your histories will be immortal, and I'm sure my prophecy will prove correct! All the more reason for me to want to be included in them. For, if we normally go out of our way to ensure the best artist portrays our image, shouldn't we also want the best – for instance an author and eulogist such as yourself – to be the one recording our deeds? Below is a description of an event you surely know about already (given your diligence), since it was listed in the public records. Still, I'm including it here, so you'll know how pleased I'd be if you were to give my now famous deed (thanks to the danger involved) the distinction of your brilliant testimony.

The Senate had appointed me, along with Herennius Senecio, as attorney for the province of Baetica, against Baebius Massa. After his conviction, the Senate formally resolved that his estate be confiscated. When Senecio found out that the consuls were going to consider Massa's request for his property to be returned to him, he approached me and said: "Let us use the same cooperation we employed in carrying out our previous prosecution, so we can demand the consuls not to allow Massa's property to be dispersed, since they're required to keep it in their custody." I responded: "Think about it – don't you believe we've already fulfilled our role, now that the case is closed?" "*You* can feel that way if you like: you have no other connection with the province," Senecio replied. "I, on the other hand, was born there and served as quaestor there." So I said: "If you've made up your mind, I'll follow your lead. That way, if there is any negative outcome, you won't have to shoulder the burden alone."

So we went to the consuls; Senecio did the talking, and I added just a few words. We had barely closed our mouths when Massa complained that Senecio was motivated not by professional responsibility, but by personal animosity. He then demanded that Senecio be prosecuted on grounds of treason. There was a collective gasping in horror. I, however, spoke up: "I fear, most distinguished consuls, that Bassa's silence regarding me – I mean, his leaving me out of his accusation against Senecio – has in fact made me *his* defender." My statement earned approval all around and was later the subject of much buzz and praise. Even Emperor Nerva – who, when he was just a private citizen, was fully aware of everything done for the public good – sent me a very remarkable letter: in it he congratulated me, and also our age, for providing a "model" (to use his words) for future generations to emulate.

No matter how this anecdote presents itself, you'll make it better known, and even more illustrious and renowned; but I'm not asking you to stretch the facts. For history should aim for truth, and truth suffices for actions honorably performed.

140 *Pliny to Fabatus* (Ep. 8.10)

Since you so very much want to see a great-grandchild come from us, you'll be especially devastated to hear that your granddaughter has suffered a miscarriage. She's young and thus had no idea she was pregnant; so she didn't take proper care of herself and did several things she shouldn't have. She has paid a heavy price for her mistake, greatly endangering her own life. You're surely disappointed that, in your advanced age, you've been deprived of a namesake – a child who would obviously have been viable. But thank the gods that, although they deprived you of a great-grandchild – for now anyway – they didn't also deprive you of your granddaughter. They'll grant us children: clearly she's able to get pregnant and, despite the unfortunate outcome, this offers positive hope for the future.

I'm using the same words through which I encourage, advise, and cheer up myself, for you're just as impatient for great-grandchildren as I am for children: you and I will smooth their path toward offices, turning things in their favor. I'll leave them a famous name and a deeply rooted family tree. Only let them be born, I pray, and exchange our grief for joy. Goodbye.

141 *Pliny to Calpurnia Hispulla* (Ep. 8.11)

I know you love your niece more affectionately than even a mother could, so I think I should reverse my news, announcing first what should really be second. That way you'll first feel joy, which leaves no room for worry. Still, I'm concerned that your gratitude will then turn into fear and, just as you're rejoicing at the news of her escape from danger, you'll shudder at just how close it was. She's upbeat and beginning to return to her old self – and to me. Only now, in her recovery, she's realizing just how seriously her life was threatened.

She *was* indeed in critical danger (I think we're safely out of the woods, so we can say now "was"): not through her fault, but through her youth. And that's why she suffered a miscarriage – the sad proof of an unsuspected pregnancy. Therefore, although there's now no grandson or granddaughter as a consolation for the loss of your brother, remember, this has only been delayed, not denied. She's safe and healthy, and we have hope in this. All the same, explain the misfortune to your father, since he'll take it better if it comes from a woman's mouth.

142 Pliny to Plinius Paternus (Ep. 8.16)

Lately I've been consumed with worry: many of my slaves have suffered illnesses and, in the case of younger ones, even death. Two things, though insufficient, offer consolation in such grief. First, my readiness to offer freedom: that way I don't feel their deaths are premature if they die as free men rather than slaves. Second, I allow my slaves to write up a kind of will, which I treat as legal and binding. They enumerate their orders and requests, and I fulfill them as if I've been legally authorized to do so. They divide up their possessions, arranging for gifts and inheritances within the confines of the household. A house plays the role of a kind of government and republic for slaves. And yet, although I find peace in these two comforts, I'm still broken-hearted and distraught at the same aspect of humanity that's led me to provide these favors in the first place. Naturally, I wouldn't want to be someone who's heartless; I'm fully aware that some people judge misfortunes like these ones to be little more than a "financial loss," and still consider themselves great and wise human beings. I really don't know whether they're great or wise, but they're most definitely not "human." To be a human being, one must be affected by grief. A human being should have feelings: s/he may try resisting them, but s/he accepts words of consolation and recognizes their necessity. I could go on, but maybe I've said more than I should. Even in grief one can experience pleasure; this is certainly true if you have a friend to hold you tight when you cry – a friend who's ready to comfort your tears with sympathy and support.

143 Pliny to Sabinus (Ep. 9.2)

You're thoughtful to request not only frequent letters, but very long ones. I've hesitated, partly because of your hectic life and partly because I've been very busy, mostly with boring business matters that distract me and impair my concentration. Besides, there's not much worth writing about. Our current environment's not like it was during the time of Cicero, whom you point at as a model for me. Not only was he intellectually brilliant, but he had a plethora of varied, significant topics worthy of his genius. I, on the other hand, don't have to tell you how narrowly I'm limited. I could perhaps send you a literary letter just for fun, but nothing seems more inappropriate when I imagine you amid all your weapons, military camps, horns, and trumpets – and all the sweat and dust beneath a blazing sun. That's my excuse: a reasonable one, I think, though I'm uncertain whether I really want you to accept it. For the greatest affection involves refusing to pardon friends for their short letters even though you know their reason to be justified!

144 Pliny to Paulinus (Ep. 9.3)

Everyone has a personal opinion on this, but when it comes to the quintessentially happy man, I think that's someone who delights in the thought of a splendid, lasting name, who's confident in posterity's assessment of him, and who lives envisioning his own unending fame. If I didn't have my eyes on the prize of immortality, maybe I'd be content with a lazy, idle retirement. Everyone, I think, must plan on two possibilities: an immortal name or a mortal end. Those who aim for the former will work hard, sweating and straining; those who accept the latter allow themselves peaceful relaxation and don't waste their short lives with merely ephemeral work, as I see many doing; their "seemingly" *hard* work – miserable and thankless as it is – leads them to self-loathing. I'm telling you exactly what I tell myself every day; if you disagree, I can stop it. But likely you won't, since you're always considering some endeavor, something memorable and immortal.

145 Pliny to Calvisius Rufus (Ep. *9.6)*

I've been spending my time enjoyably, relaxing among my books and my writing tablets. "How's that possible? Aren't you in Rome?" I am, but the chariot races were on, which I find completely unappealing. I never find anything new or unique about them, nothing requiring a second visit: once is plenty. So I'm all the more astonished that so many people have a childish desire to watch over and over again those galloping horses and drivers standing in chariots. If it were the horses' speed or the charioteer's skill they found so appealing, then I'd get it. But these days it's all about the factions – the particular colors the teams sport, which spectators enjoy so much. Imagine, right in the middle of a race, one color is reassigned here and another there: accordingly, the audience's zeal and cheering shift accordingly. Spectators immediately ditch their support for the drivers and horses they had originally picked, along with the names they had already started cheering for. That's how much value and weight they assign to one measly jersey. I'm not talking about the general crowd (they're more worthless than the jersey), but about certain prominent individuals. When I envision how they sit glued to their seats, "participating" in such pointless, mind-numbing, endless inactivity, I delight in the fact that their idea of "entertainment" doesn't at all entice me. So for the last few days I've been happily utilizing my free time for productive literary activities, while everyone else wastes theirs on the laziest of the fruitless pastimes.

146 Pliny to Julius Genitor (Ep. *9.17)*

I got your letter complaining about a really sumptuous dinner party; you found it distasteful because it involved mimes, promiscuous male dancers, and clowns making the rounds at the tables. Can you stop scowling for a second? It's true, I don't have anything like that at *my* parties, but I can tolerate those who do. Why don't I have them? Because I've never found anything pleasurable about them, nothing novel or festive – I find nothing attractive in the dancer's effeminate moves, the mime's impertinence, or the clown's idiocy. But this isn't my personal philosophy, just my taste. Yet many people judge the things *we* find captivating and amusing to be absolutely repulsive, pointless, and tedious! When a reader, a musician, or an actor is brought into the dining room, how many get up and leave? Or how many recline with a frown on their face, just as you did when, until the very end, you forced yourself to endure those "horrible horrors," as you call them! So let's be generous toward others' "entertainment," so we can demand the same generosity toward ourselves.

147 Pliny to Maximus (Ep. *9.23)*

Frequently, when I've been pleading cases in court, the one hundred men of the jury have upheld the authority and weight of their judgments and then, all of a sudden, they stand up together and extol me, as if they're overcome and somehow compelled. From the Senate, too, I've won as many accolades as I could hope for. But I've never ever experienced greater pleasure than from a recent conversation I had with Tacitus. He described how, at the recent chariot races, he was sitting next to a Roman knight. They were chatting about various intellectual topics, and then the man asked him: "Are you Italian or from one of the provinces?" "You know me," Tacitus replied, "from your studies." "Are you Tacitus or Pliny?" the man then asked. There are no words to express my joy – our two names, not merely attached to bodies, but attached to "studies." It's as if "Tacitus" and "Pliny" are synonymous with "literature," and people recognize us, above all, because of our literary works.

Something similar occurred a couple of days ago: I was dining at my house, reclining in the spot above the distinguished Fadius Rufinus and a man from his hometown, who had just come to Rome for the very first time. Rufinus pointed at me, saying: "See this man here?" He then spoke at length about my literary works, at which point the man said: "Ohhh, it's Pliny!" I admit it: I'm happy to be rewarded for all my efforts. If Demosthenes' pleasure was warranted after an old Attic lady recognized him by saying "Look, there's Demosthenes!" – then don't I have a right to celebrate when my name is famous? It's true: I *am* happy, and I'm happy to admit it! I'm not afraid of seeming big-headed if I can refer to others' assessments of me and not just my own, especially when I'm writing to you. You're never jealous over others peoples' fame and you always support mine. Ciao.

*148 Pliny to Mustius (*Ep. *9.39)*

On the soothsayers' advice, I must rebuild the temple to Ceres at my villa. Since it's pretty old and small, I need to make it bigger and better, particularly considering how crowded it gets on its annual festival. Every September 13 a huge crowd gathers from all over; they carry out ceremonies, making and fulfilling many vows. But, there's no shelter nearby offering protection from rain or sun. So I think I'd be providing a useful, pious gift if I commissioned the construction of an exceptionally nice temple to serve the goddess, and if I added on some shaded porticoes to serve the visitors. I'd like you to buy four columns of whatever type of marble you think best, and also enough marble to cover the floors and walls. I'll also need a new cult statue, since the current wooden one is so old that parts have broken off. As for the portico, I don't think I need anything unless you're willing to draft a plan that suits the temple's site. I can't have the porticoes surround the temple because on one side there's a river with very steep banks, and on the other side a road. Past the road is a large meadow where the porticoes might go nicely, facing the temple itself. This would work – unless you have a better idea: with your skillful expertise you're used to overcoming the challenges of tricky terrain.

*149 Pliny to Trajan (*Ep. *10.11)*

This letter exemplifies many in Book 10 in which Pliny asks Emperor Trajan for a favor.

My recent illness, sir, makes me indebted to my doctor, Potumius Marinus. If you'd fulfill a request of mine with your usual kindness, I'd like to repay my thanks to Marinus with a favor from you. So I'm asking that you grant citizenship to his relatives – Chrysippus son of Mithridates; Chrisippus' wife Stratonica, daughter of Epigonus; and Chrysippus' two sons Epigonus and Mirthridates – and that they remain under the power of their father and the rights of patrons toward freedmen be preserved for them. At the request of their patron, I also ask that you to grant Roman citizenship to Lucius Satrius Abascantus, Publius Caesius Phosphorus, and Pancharia Soteris.

*150 Pliny to Trajan (*Ep. *10.13)*

Pliny requests a favor for himself. The prestigious priesthood of augur involved interpreting the will of the gods; the Seven Men (Septemviri) were priests charged with overseeing public religious feasts.

I know, sir, that proof of your esteem will greatly enhance my own reputation, especially when it comes from you, such an excellent ruler. Thus I'm asking you to confer upon me another honor, in addition to those that, through your kindness, have already helped advance my career. Would you appoint me either as augur or as one of the Seven Men, since both have vacancies? If so, as an augur and with all its associated rights, I could officially offer you in public the prayers I now devotedly offer you in private.

*151 Pliny to Trajan (*Ep. *10.17)*

In Letters 151–154 Pliny updates Trajan on his journey to Bythinia–Pontus and informs him of some of the problems he finds there. Trajan replies accordingly.

I enjoyed a very safe and healthy sailing journey all the way to Ephesus, sir, but, once I began my road trip from there, I began suffering from the intense sun and a touch of fever, so I stopped at Pergamum. Later, when I continued along the coast by boat, unfavorable winds further postponed me; so I entered Bithynia on September 17, much later than I had hoped. Still, I can't complain about the delay since I was able to celebrate your birthday in my province – a very auspicious stroke of luck! Right now I'm investigating the finances of Prusa (its spending, revenue, and debts), and the deeper I dig, the more obvious it becomes how necessary this inquiry really is. Certain private individuals possess large amounts of money for various reasons, expending certain amounts for rather illegal purposes. I'm writing to you, sir, shortly after my arrival.

It's now September 17, sir, and I'm writing this just after entering my province; I found it loyal and respectful toward you, as you deserve all humankind to be. Please consider, sir, whether you think it might be necessary to send a land surveyor this way. I think quite a nice monetary sum could be recuperated from the public works managers, if we conduct accurate surveys. This is certainly my sense after attentively investigating Prusa's finances.

*152 Trajan to Pliny (*Ep. *10.18)*

I wish you and your companions could have made it to Bithynia without any physical discomfort and that your travels *from* Ephesus had been just as easy as those *to* Ephesus. I noticed your arrival, my dearest Pliny, from the date of your letter. The locals, I believe, understand I'm looking out for their best interests; ensure they know you were deliberately and purposefully appointed to represent me. First and foremost: scrutinize the towns' financial states, for it's obvious they're in disarray. When it comes to land surveyors, I barely have enough to cover Rome and her environs. You can find reliable surveyors in every province, so you won't be without them if you'll only willingly and scrupulously search them out.

*153 Pliny to Trajan (*Ep. *10.23)*

The people of Prusa, sir, have a bath, but it's old and dingy. They're very eager for a new one, and I think it's possible for you to fulfill their wish. Funds will be available.

First of all, I've already begun recuperating money from private individuals; second, the Prusians are prepared to shift the income from their olive oil trade to the bath project. This construction request is something the city's distinguished status calls for, as does the brilliance of your rule.

154 Trajan to Pliny (Ep. 10.24)

If the establishment of a new public bath will not overburden Prusa's finances, we can honor their request, provided that no new taxes are levied to pay for it, or that money isn't taken from other sources already earmarked for necessary expenditures.

155 Pliny to Trajan (Ep. 10.31)

Pliny communicates concerns about former criminals in Nicomedia and Nicaea.

Since you've given me authority to refer to you when I'm in doubt, there's no shame on your great nobility in stooping down to my level to consider my concerns. In many of the cities, especially Nicomedia and Nicaea, certain criminals formerly punished through work in the mines or something similar are in fact enjoying the jobs and duties of public slaves, and even receiving their annual salary. When I found this out I thought long and hard about what to do. It seemed too harsh to restore them to their original sentences, especially when so much time has passed and most of them are already old and, as far as one can tell, living upright and frugal lives. At the same time, it didn't seem quite moral to retain in civic positions individuals previously sentenced to criminal punishments. Again, it seemed disadvantageous to support them at public expense when they were working; but, even worse, it seemed dangerous not to. Therefore I decided to put the whole matter on the back burner until I could consult you. Perhaps you're wondering how these individuals happened to be released from their assigned punishments; I asked the same question, but couldn't discover the answer. I reviewed the paperwork recording their sentences, but I found no evidence to document their release. Nevertheless, some, interceding in their defense, said it was a proconsul's or a legate's order that freed the criminals. This is plausible, since it's likely that no one would dare do this without the proper official authority.

156 Trajan to Pliny (Ep. 10.32)

Let's not forget the reason you were sent to that province was that it was obvious that many things required changing. This situation will definitely need correcting: as you wrote, criminals not only have been released without authority, but even given the status of prominent officials. Therefore the men who were sentenced and freed without authority within the last ten years must be sent back to serve out their punishments. If, however, you discover elderly ones sentenced more than ten years ago, let's distribute them among public works, which are still somewhat punitive in nature – for instance working at the public baths, cleaning sewers, or repairing highways and streets.

*157 Pliny to Trajan (*Ep. *10.33)*

When I was visiting a different part of the province, a widespread fire at Nicomedia destroyed many private homes and two public buildings, the temple of Isis, and the senior citizens' club (even though a road separates the two). The fire was particularly extensive – first, because of strong winds and, second, because of peoples' apathy. The general consensus is that they simply stood around like spectators twiddling their thumbs. And there's not even one fire engine to be found anywhere, not one bucket, not one apparatus for fighting the flames. These will now be available per my instructions. Please consider, sir, whether you think we can establish a firemen's fraternity comprising no more than 150 men. I'll make sure that no one is admitted unless he is a fireman and that they won't abuse the privileges accompanying membership. It will be relatively easy to oversee such a small group.

*158 Trajan to Pliny (*Ep. *10.34)*

I imagine you got the idea for a fraternity at Nicomedia, from the example of many other towns. But let's remember that this province, and especially towns of this type, have been especially prone to form factions. Whatever name we give the fraternities and for whatever reason they're formed, once people have assembled for the same collective purpose, soon enough these fraternities will evolve into secret societies. Better, then, just to ensure the necessary equipment is available to fight fires, educate homeowners so they can employ it, and, if the situation demands, put a crowd of onlookers to work.

*159 Pliny to Trajan (*Ep. *10.90)*

The people of Sinope, sir, need a water supply; I believe there's plenty of good water 16 miles away that could be led into the city. There is, however, a questionable, soggy marshland extending more than a mile from the water source. I've ordered an inexpensive land survey, to determine if the bog can support the building project. There's enough money to cover this project, if you will endorse it, sir. It's really necessary for the good health and pleasantness of this exceedingly thirsty city.

*160 Trajan to Pliny (*Ep. *10.91)*

Make sure, my dearest Pliny, you're scrupulous in the land survey you've commenced, seeing if the location you're worried about can withstand an aqueduct's weight. For sure, a water supply must be brought into Sinope as long as the city can independently cover the cost; such a resource will bring the people health and enjoyment.

*161 Pliny to Trajan (*Ep. *10.94)*

Pliny asks a favor for Suetonius. This is the same Suetonius in whose *Twelve Caesars* the letters of Augustus appear (Chapter 3). The "rights of parents of three children" (*ius trium liberorum*), begun under Augustus, offered special privileges and rewards to upper-class Romans with more than three children. Over time it became a much coveted honor, even for the childless.

Suetonius Tranquillus is an extremely upright, distinguished, and learned man; for a long time I've admired his integrity and literary works. Now that we're good friends and I've really gotten to know him, I esteem him all the more. There are two reasons why he should have the rights given to parents of three children: (1) his friends could then promote their good judgment of him; and (2) his marriage has been unlucky in producing children, and so it's left to your goodness (at my suggestion) that he acquire the reward cruel fortune has denied him. I know, sir, I'm asking for quite a big favor, but recall all the previous kindnesses you've granted me; so, please, seriously consider the one I ask for now. The fact that I wouldn't make such a request while I'm away from Rome unless I felt strongly about it proves my earnestness.

162 *Trajan to Pliny* (Ep. *10.95*)

You know well, my dear Pliny, how rarely I grant such favors as these, since even before our most distinguished senators I consistently affirm I haven't exceeded the number I professed I'd uphold. Nonetheless, I've fulfilled your request. I've ordered that it be officially recorded that I have granted to Suetonius Tranquillus the right of three children, with all the regular privileges accompanying this honor.

163 *Pliny to Trajan* (Ep. *10.96*)

Pliny requests Trajan's advice (after the fact) regarding Christians in his province.

It's my habit, sir, to refer to you when I'm uncertain. Who better to guide my hesitation and to enlighten my ignorance? I've never witnessed an interrogation of the Christians – thus I don't know what punishment is normally given, how severe, or how an examination is conducted. I've got no idea if young and old are treated differently; whether pardon is granted for a retraction of belief; or whether someone who professed being a Christian and then retracted deserves special treatment; I don't know whether just being called "Christian," when no crime was committed, deserves punishment – whether just the crimes attached to the name are punishable. For now, I've dealt in the following manner with those who have been relinquished to me: I ask them if they're Christian. If they answer in the affirmative, I ask them a second time and a third, warning them about the punishment. Those who persist in their affirmation, I order to be executed. Whatever the reason for their confession, their persistence and unyielding stubbornness deserve retribution. As for other similarly fanatical insubordinates who are also Roman citizens, I've added them to the list of those being returned to Rome for trial.

Now that I've started, as often happens, charges are coming out of the woodwork: greater numbers and types are emerging. An anonymous pamphlet containing names of many individuals charged with the crime is being passed around. Those denying they're Christians (or ever were), I've decided to let go, that is, once they've repeated an oath to the gods and offered incense and wine to your cult statue (which I had ordered brought in, along with the other gods' cult statues, precisely for this reason). I also order them to swear against the name "Christ." It's my understanding that those who are true Christians can't be compelled to do any of these things.

Thanks to an informer, I received names of others, who first confirmed they were Christians and then later denied it; they asserted it had been been two years or more since they practiced – which some had done for as long as 20 years. All gave devotion to your statue and the other deities' images and denied the name of Christ. They also explained that their guilt, or error, involved only this: they regularly met before dawn on a set date, taking turns to sing verses to Christ as if to a god and swearing an oath – not for any illegal purpose, but to promise they wouldn't commit theft, robbery, adultery, falsehood, or loan defaults. Afterwards they leave, later reconvening to enjoy an everyday harmless meal. They had stopped these practices following my edict (abiding your mandate), which outlawed secret societies. It seemed to me all the more necessary to employ torture to get the truth from two slave women called "attendants": I discovered nothing but an excessive and depraved fanaticism.

So I've postponed additional investigations and rushed immediately to consult you. The matter deserves your attention, particularly given the number of people at stake. Individuals of every age, every rank, and each sex have been and will continue to be called to trial. This zealous contagion has spread and infected not only towns, but also villages and the countryside. Yet it seems the disease can be halted and cured. It's true: temples, which until now were nearly deserted, have begun receiving devotees again, and the sacred rites previously gone by the wayside are once again performed. You can now readily find meat from sacrificed animals to buy: until now you'd be hard-pressed to find consumers. It's easy to surmise, then, that, given a chance at repentance, many can be convinced of the error of their ways.

*164 Trajan to Pliny (*Ep. *10.97)*

My dear Pliny, regarding the Christians, you've acted just as you should. It's impossible to apply a universal policy as a set formula. Regardless, they must not be hunted down; if they're brought to you and found guilty, then punish them. Pardon those who deny they're Christians and manifestly prove this through supplication to our gods. Above all, the anonymous pamphlets being circulated should have absolutely no role whatsoever in prosecutions: they're horrendous examples to follow and have no place in an age such as ours.

John the Elder

John the Elder (first–second century CE), the author of the following two letters, is usually identified with John the Apostle, author of the Gospel of John; more recently, however, stylistic differences between the epistles and the Gospel challenge this association. The author of the epistles is now often identified as John the Elder (John the Presbyter), probably an elder of the church at Ephesus. These two letters may have been written around 95–100 CE and are primarily concerned with the still developing church and its authentic followers.

165 John 2

J. Muir (2009: 171) suggests that John 2 may have been written in response to an ongoing conflict among some early Christians, who asserted that the human Jesus differed from Christ. Here John urges his readers to avoid such disbelievers, even denying them hospitality (lodging, food, drink), which was a deeply embedded cultural institution of the time and an integral part of evangelization. He addresses his letter to a Christian congregation which he calls his "chosen lady."

John the Elder sends greetings to his chosen lady and her children, whom I truly love – and not only I, but everyone else who knows the truth.

Thanks to the truth among us and forever with us, we will receive the grace, mercy and peace from God the Father and Jesus Christ, son of the Father in truth and love.

I was exceedingly happy to learn that some of your children are living in truth, as the Father commanded. And now I ask, lady, that we continue to love one another; I'm not presenting new instructions, but the command we have followed from the very beginning. Indeed *this* is true love: living according to His commands. And His command, as you've heard from the beginning, is to live in love. I'm writing because many impostors have gone out into the world, disavowing that Jesus Christ really was human. Such people are the epitome of deception: they're the antichrist. Look to yourselves. Ensure you don't destroy all we have accomplished, so we receive our full reward. Anyone who goes forth without remaining true to Christ's teachings does not have God. Whoever adheres to Christ's teachings has both the Father and his Son. If anyone comes knocking at your door who doesn't embrace these teachings, don't let him into your home; don't even say "Hello," otherwise you'll be participating in his wicked deeds.

I have many other things to write, but I don't wish to do so with paper and pen; rather, I hope to see you soon and chat face to face – what a joy that will be! The children of your chosen sister send you their greetings.

166 John 3

The author of John 3 is likely the same as that of John 2, so this letter was probably composed contemporaneously (c. 95–100 CE). John addresses a Gaius (otherwise unknown) praising him for his loyalty to the truth (namely the recognition that the human Jesus and Christ are the same). He commends Gaius for showing proper hospitality toward past missionaries and requests him to do so again. According to Rensberger (2001: 123), the epistle represents a type of letter of recommendation; the "brothers" would have carried it with them as an introduction from John, who vouches for their legitimacy and their need for travel assistance. These sorts of recommendation letters were an important tool for Christian missionaries in acquiring shelter, food, and supplies during their travels, and the act of hospitality was, in turn, "vitally important to the maintenance and progress of the Christian mission" (Rensberger 2001: 123–4). John also criticizes a man named Diotrephes, who not only refused to receive a letter of introduction from John's messengers (and thus to give them hospitality), but also expelled from the church others, who had provided hospitality. The exact nature of John's dispute with Diotrephes is not entirely clear, but Rensberger (2001: 124) suggests it may have involved a struggle for authority over a local congregation.

The Elder John to his beloved Gaius, whom I love in truth.

Dearest friend, I pray you're prospering in every way and are in good health, just like your soul. I was so very happy when your friends came and testified to your sincerity; you clearly walk in truth. There's nothing that makes me happier than hearing my children live the truth.

Beloved, you act faithfully in whatever you do for the brothers, even though they're strangers; they've testified to your love before the church. You're acting just as you should when you send them on their way in a manner worthy of God. For they embark upon their journey for the sake of the Name, and they refuse help from non-believing gentiles. Thus we should wholeheartedly help these individuals, showing we're fellow partners in the truth.

I wrote a letter to the church, but Diotrephes, who wants to be the esteemed leader in everything, doesn't accept our words! Thus, if I do come, I won't forget about his behavior, or all the wicked things he's said to disparage us. And he's not satisfied with that: he doesn't welcome the brothers and forbids those who are willing to do so, even kicking them out of the church!

Dearest friend, don't imitate evil but only good. The man who acts virtuously is a man of God; the man who acts unscrupulously doesn't see Him. As for Demetrius, everyone speaks of him highly and the truth confirms it. We confirm it as well, and you know that our testimony is trustworthy.

I have many things to write you, but I don't want to communicate them on paper; I hope instead to see you soon, when we can chat face to face. Peace be with you. All our friends send their hello. Please give love to our friends personally in your neck of the woods.

Fronto

Marcus Cornelius Fronto (c. 100–c. 167 CE) was a Roman citizen born in the Roman colony Cirta (Constantine) in Numidia. Most of our biographical knowledge comes from his correspondence; he was educated at Rome and earned renown for his oratorical and rhetorical skill, often being equated to Cicero. He held various high-randing political positions in Rome, including that of governor of Asia. He was closely associated with the Roman imperial court, serving as tutor to Emperor Antoninus Pius' adopted sons Marcus Aurelius and Lucius Verus, who became co-emperors in 161 CE. In addition to various treatises, Fronto wrote letters, which were only discovered in 1815. They largely include his correspondence with Pius, Marcus Aurelius, and Lucius Verus; and they cover a wide range of topics. Many are didactic in nature (reminiscent of Seneca), and those to Marcus Aurelius are notably affectionate. Some scholars (e.g., Richlin 2006) suggest their relationship may have been sexual. The manuscript contains many corruptions and missing portions.

*167 Fronto to Marcus Aurelius (*Ad Caes. *3.11) 139* CE

Fronto praises Marcus Aurelius for his skillful translation of aphorisms (concise sayings typically ethical or moralizing in nature, also called maxims; a modern example would be, for example, Gandhi's "We must become the change we want to see").

To my lord.

My wife Gratia came home last night. But just as wonderful as having her home is how wonderfully you've translated your aphorisms; the one I just received today is nearly perfect, so much so it could be seamlessly inserted into one of Sallust's books, without straying from Sallust's style. When you make such excellent strides I'm happy, upbeat, healthy – I'm young again! What I'm demanding of you is not easy, but I remember how beneficial it was to me, so I must require it of you too: translate the same aphorism two or three times in the same way you've done with that short little one. Also translate longer ones two or three times. Do it enthusiastically and don't be afraid to take risks. Whatever you dare to accomplish through your brilliance you'll be successful at. True, it's laborious work and takes effort, but it's a distinguished, honorable goal and only a few attain it. [. . .] you have perfectly finished it. This activity will prove exceptionally beneficial to you when you come to compose speeches. So, too, will excerpting some key aphorisms from Sallust's *Jugurtha* or *Catiline*. When you return to Rome, gods willing, I'll ask you again for your daily lines of poetry. Say hello to your mother, my lady, for me.

*168 Marcus Aurelius to Fronto (*Ad Caes. *3.12) 139* CE

Marcus replies to Fronto's previous letter(s) regarding aphorisms.

Dear teacher, I simultaneously received two letters from you. In one you rebuked me for composing a sloppy sentence; in the other, however, you purposefully encouraged me by praising my work. I swear on my life, and that of my mother's and yours, it was your first that made me the happier. In the midst of reading I repeatedly exclaimed, "I'm so lucky!" Someone will say: "Really, you call yourself fortunate because someone teaches you how to express a thought more skillfully, more lucidly, more concisely, more eloquently?" No, that's not the reason. What is it, then? I'm learning from you to speak the truth, the absolutely toughest task for gods and men alike: in fact, even oracles never convey the truth. Rather they're always ambiguous, oblique, or complex. If you're careless, you may be ensnared and, confirming the oracle to fit your wish, recognize the mistake only well after the fact, once the deed is done. Still, oracles offer useful advantages, and such mistakes can be forgiven: they're merely the fault of being duped by piety. But, whether you reproach or guide, your remarks candidly and plainly reveal the right path. So thank you for teaching me to speak the truth *and* concomitantly to hear it. Thus I doubly owe you, but I'm sure you'll try your best to guarantee that I can't repay you! If you won't let me reciprocate, how can I reimburse you other than through my deference? Nevertheless, disloyal to myself, I preferred that you, who have too much care [. . .]. Study hard and quote many textual excerpts [. . .]. Goodbye, my good, best teacher. I'm so happy, best of orators, that you've become such a good friend to me. My lady sends her hello.

169 Marcus Aurelius to Fronto (Ad Caes. *3.2) 140–3* CE

Letters 169–173 deal with a court case in which Fronto is one of the prosecutors. The accused is Herodes Atticus, a famous Greek rhetorician who has been indicted by the Athenians for various crimes. One involves financial corruption: Herodes' father had bequeathed an annual monetary payment to each Athenian citizen, but Herodes Atticus arranged it as a one-time lump sum, deducting from it money the Athenians previously owed his father. In so doing, Herodes' ignored the instructions of his father's will. Herodes was also Marcus Aurelius' good friend and teacher. Marcus writes Fronto, advising him on how he might proceed with the case. Herodes was later elected consul in 143, so it seems he may have been acquitted. These letters illustrate an ongoing correspondence in which the complex nature of Roman friendship is put to the test.

Aurelius Caesar to his Fronto, greetings.

You've often asked what you could do to make me really happy. I've now got an answer. Now you have the chance to boost my affection for you, if that's even possible! The trial is approaching: people will listen closely to your eloquent speeches. They'll also be spiteful toward your rhetorical indignation. I don't know anyone else who would dare advise you in this situation. Those who aren't really your friends prefer to see you hang yourself by behaving uncharacteristically. Your real friends, however, fear seeming too generous toward your opponent if they try to distract you from indicting him – which is, of course, your prerogative. At the same time, if you've been planning on using a particularly elegant phrase or two, they don't have the heart to demand that you keep quiet, and thus to prevent you from delivering them. So, whether you call me an impulsive advisor or a bold little boy, or you deem me too generous toward your opponent, I won't beat around the bush: I'll give you my two cents for what I think is the proper course of action. Why have I said "two cents?" In fact, it's a "request" I'm making, one I make it seriously and promise to repay – just grant me this favor.

"Wait just a minute!" you'll say. "If I'm provoked, I'm not to reciprocate the favor with the same kind of speech?" No, in fact you'll attain greater praise if, even when provoked, you keep silent. Although, if he initiates an attack, it's perfectly acceptable to respond any way you can; but I've asked him not to do this (and I think I've gotten my wish). I love you both, each for your own particular merits. I'm well aware he was raised in the household of my grandfather, Publius Valvisius; I'm equally aware that I've been educated under your tutelage. Thus I'm especially anxious that this awful, hateful business be resolved as respectably as possible. I hope you'll fully accept my advice. At least you'll agree that my heart is in the right place. I'd write and reveal my foolishness rather than not – rather than fall short of being a good friend. Goodbye, my Fronto, dearest and most affectionate.

170 *Fronto to Marcus Aurelius* (Ad Caes. *3.3*) *140–3* CE

Fronto to my lord Caesar.

I've rightly devoted myself to you and applied to you and your father every advantage I've gained during my lifetime. What could be friendlier, more pleasing, more honest? But come on now, I beg of you, throw away the "bold little boy" or "impulsive advisor" names you call yourself. Obviously there's danger in advice if it's advertised as boyish and rash! But trust me (or I'll trust myself): your sensibility far surpasses your seniors'. Moreover, in this matter your advice is valuable – it might as well be coming from a gray-haired old man. Mine, in fact, is the boyish one! What's the point of putting on a rhetorical spectacle for friends and enemies? If that Herodes is a man of substance and morals, I'll find no honor in reproaching and attacking a man like him. If he's a good-for-nothing, worthless man, our battle isn't on level fighting ground and we don't risk losing the same things. Any contact with a pollutant is contaminating, even if you come out on top. But it's more likely that he's a virtuous man, a man you judge worthy of your tutelage. If I know what's good for me, may the gods punish me if I dare abuse verbally any friend of yours. Now, through your great love (which I'm so fortunate to enjoy), I'd like your help and advice as well. I fully recognize I shouldn't mention any details that are irrelevant to the case in order to damage Herodes, but those that do pertain – they appear quite appalling – how do I deal with them? That's precisely my question, and I'm asking for your input. I must address free men who've been savagely beaten and robbed – one was even murdered. I must mention Herodes' disloyality as a son, discounting his father's wishes and legal will. I must condemn brutality and greed, and a certain person must be established as a murderer.

If you think I should do everything I can to oppress and squash my opponent for the charges upon which the case actually rests, be straight with me, my best and sweetest lord; let me know if that's your viewpoint. But if you think I need to give him a break on these issues, I'll seriously consider your thoughts. As I said, rest assured I'll say nothing about his character or give any other irrelevant details of his life. But if you think I should do everything I can to help my case, I'm letting you know here and now: I'll be consistent, and I'll exploit opportunities when they crop up in the case. The charges are appalling and must be spoken of as such. When it comes to particular details about beating and robbing men, I won't mince words: I'll flavor them with bile and venom. But, if I happen to address him as a "little Greek man" and an "idiot," it doesn't mean I'm also calling him a "murderer."

Goodbye, Caesar; continue to love me the most. I, to be sure, deeply love each and every letter and word you write: so, whenever you write, do so in your own hand.

171 *Fronto to Marcus Aurelius* (Ad Caes. *3.4*) *140–3* CE

Greetings, my lord.

I had already closed and sealed the earlier letter when it occurred to me that the other prosecutors – it seems there will be quite a few – may speak rather harshly against Herodes. Carefully consider my unique and specific role. Take care, lord, and live so I may be happy. It looks as if Careolus (who's out of town right now) and our friends Marcianus and Villianus will be pleading the case.

172 Marcus Aurelius to Fronto (Ad Caes. *3.5) 140–3* CE

Hail, dearest Fronto.

Right away let me thank you, beloved Fronto, not only for not rejecting my advice, but even for approving it. Regarding your very friendly letter, here's what I think: everything concerning the case should be presented. But you must not mention anything involving your own personal feelings, even if they're justified and provoked. That way, you won't damage either your credibility or your self-respect in all this tiresome business [. . .]. Let others say whatever they want – my chief concern is that *you* don't say anything that may seemingly contradict your good character, or appear irrelevant, and thus offensive to your audience. Goodbye my dearest, most delightful Fronto.

173 Fronto to Marcus Aurelius (Ad Caes. *3.6) 140–3* CE

To my lord.

Regarding these considerations and my life, I'll proceed according to your wishes. I pray and ask that you never hold back your opinions, but that you advise me – as you're now properly doing – if I ever undertake anything contrary to your will. I'd prefer all the count [. . .] which are in the case to be dealt with one by one, so we may follow Cicero's modus operandi. For, when they condense that decision so tightly, I desire [. . .] but a fight simply cannot be handled this way. Yet, if we're in court pleading through continuous, uninterrupted speeches, even if I don't overstep the boundaries, I still must employ a sharp look, a passionate voice, and harsh words, communicating ire with a nod here, a finger there: your Herodes should bear it calmly. But it's challenging to secure this assurance from him, for people say he's passionate about pleading court cases. I don't necessarily fault him for this per se, but make sure he doesn't appear too aggressive when presenting the facts of his case. Nevertheless, you yourself advise honesty above all, and if someone plays around with verbal weapons and gymnastics, these sportive exercises can't conclude without conflict [. . .].

174 Marcus Aurelius to Fronto (Ad Caes. *1.2) Baiae 143* CE

Marcus responds to a letter in which Fronto complained about an attack of gout; he regrets not being able to visit.

To my teacher Fronto.

What words can adequately express my bad luck? Or how can I sufficiently complain about the obligations forcing me to stay here, imprisoned, shackled by anxiety and worry, forbidden from immediately running to my Fronto, my loveliest of souls, to be next to him during an illness so serious, to hold his hand, to slowly rub that foot – as much as he can tolerate – to soak it in the healing bath and offer a supporting hand when he steps into the water? You call me a friend? I, who's not dropping everything to fly at full speed to your side? Surely I'm more crippled than you with my horrible diffidence, or rather my slothfulness. You ask about me – oh, what should I say? I'm afraid I'll say something you don't want to hear. For you've always striven to encourage me in every way, to distract me from worries with your jokes and elegant words, and to demonstrate how you endure all your troubles with a level head and courageous heart. But where my mind is, I have no idea, unless it's disappeared off to you somewhere. Have pity. With every ounce of self-control and temperance, drive out this illness, which is requiring your courage. I beg you, write back immediately. Tell me what healing springs you're heading to, when you're leaving, how you're feeling now: ease my mind. Meantime, I'll carry your letter all around with me, distressing though it is. Be well, my most delightful Fronto. Though let me be more precise – for indeed you're always well. So instead I pray to you, kind omnipresent gods: ensure good health for my Fronto, my dearest and most delightful. Let him always be healthy, strong, unhindered, and vigorous: give him good health and allow him to be with me. Farewell, most pleasant of men.

*175 Marcus Aurelius to Fronto (*Ad Caes. *4.6) 144–145*

Greetings, my sweetest teacher.

We're doing well. I have a little cold and slept in, but the cold seems better now. From five until nine in the morning, I read a bit of Cato's *Agriculture* or wrote – although, thank god, it was less pathetic than yesterday's junk. After I gave my father his morning greeting, I tended to my throat by swallowing honey water, all the way to my gullet, and then forcing it back up and out; I won't call this "gargling," although I believe the word is used in Novius and elsewhere. After that, I helped my father complete a sacrifice. Next we went out and had a bite to eat. What do you suppose I had? A tiny bit of bread, while I watched others scarfing down beans, onions, and roe-filled fish. Then I worked up a sweat picking grapes; it was a good old time and, as the author says, "we left some clusters hanging high up as a living witness to the vintage." Some time after six in the evening we came home. I only did a little work, and it was a waste of time. After that I chatted a long time with my dear little mother while she sat on the bed. It went something like this: Me: "What do you think my Fronto is doing right this second?" Mom: "What do you think my Gratia is up to?" Me: "What do you think the little sparrow, our little cutie-pie Gratia is doing?" So while we were enjoying this tête-à-tête, debating which of us loved our favorite more, the bell sounded, signaling that my father had gone for his bath. Having bathed, we then had dinner in the oil-press room. Well, I don't mean that we bathed in the oil-press room, but that *first* we bathed and then went to dinner in the press room. We happily listened to the locals joking around. Now I've returned and, before I roll over and start snoring away, I'm completing my task, giving my sweetest teacher a rundown of the day. If it were possible for me to miss him more, I'd be happy to waste even more time! Be well, my Fronto, wherever you are, sweetest honey-bunny, my love, my delight. How do I explain it? I love you but, alas, you're not here.

*176 Marcus Aurelius to Fronto (*Ad Caes. *4.7) 144–5* CE

Greetings, sweetest teacher.

Finally! The mailman has set out so I've finally sent you three days' worth of news. But I can't "say" anything, since I've used up all my breath dictating nearly thirty letters.

About your most recent question regarding letters: I haven't yet mentioned the issue to my father. But when we come to Rome, god willing, remind me and I'll tell you something then. But wait, we're both so absent-minded, you'll forget to remind me, and thus I won't fill you in. But seriously, the issue really does deserve attention. Goodbye my – what should I call you? It's always insufficient. Goodbye my desire, my light, my joy.

177 Fronto to Marcus Aurelius (Ad Caes. 4.9) 145–5 CE

To my lord.

I received your very elegantly written letter. You say the intervening time between my letters inspires a longing for them. So it's true, what Socrates asserted: "Pleasures are linked closely to pain." This is what he declared in prison, when he determined that the pain from the tight shackles was balanced out by the pleasure he experienced when they were removed. Same goes for us: the amount of annoyance we experience in being absent from each other is proportionate to the amount of joy we experience in longing for each other. For desire derives from loving. Absence makes the heart grow fonder, and this, by far, is the best thing about friendship. You asked about my health: I wrote to you previously that my shoulder pain was so bad I couldn't even complete the letter in which I mentioned it and had to have someone else finish it, contrary to my normal practice [. . .].

178 Fronto to Marcus Aurelius (Ad Caes. 5.22) 145–7 CE

This letter and its reply (179) involve a writing exercise for Marcus Aurelius. It was typical in Roman education for the pupil to present a legal or historical question for debate and to develop it into a written paper. Fronto's theme involves the inappropriate behavior of a Roman consul.

To my lord.

I've slept in. I'm sending a writing prompt with a serious theme: A Roman consul has hung up his toga and dressed in protective armor, covering his hands and arms; among the young men at the feast of Minerva he's slain a lion in front of a big Roman audience. He's brought before the censors. Develop and elaborate. Goodbye, sweetest lord. Say hi to your lady.

179 Marcus Aurelius to Fronto (Ad Caes. 5.23) 145–7 CE

Answer.

When did this event happen – and was it at Rome? Are you saying it occurred during Domitian's reign at his Alban villa? Moreover, this kind of prompt requires additional (that is, time-consuming) work to develop the topic into something that's actually believable rather than into a piece that inspires outrage over the event. The topic seems improbable. I definitely would have preferred something along the lines I originally requested. Write back immediately about the event's date.

*180 Fronto to Marcus Aurelius (*Ad Caes. *3.13) 145–7* CE

Fronto writes to Marcus Aurelius about their correspondence; he's sensitive to the many obligations Marcus faces. In ancient Greek, the word *onomatopoeia* refers to the creation of new words (*onoma*, word + *poiein*, to make) – and not, as in English, to the association between the word and the natural sound it imitates.

Inventing new words, "onomatopoeia," is something allowed to poets so they can express their thoughts more accurately, but it's also something I need in order to adequately articulate my joy. The usual, everyday words just won't do: I'm so utterly elated that you wrote me so many letters in such a short time, I simply can't use regular language to express my heart's happiness. Your letters were so eloquent, composed with so much friendliness, caressing, effusiveness, and passion; and you wrote so frequently, despite being saddled with many other business matters and obligations, including to write replies to the numerous letters arriving from throughout the provinces. I had intended – it's not right for me to disguise or keep anything hidden from you – I had intended, I was saying, to make you accuse me of apathy, since I've been writing less frequently: I didn't want to burden you, when you've got so many other concerns, by making you feel obligated to respond to my many letters – yet you're the one writing me daily! But why do I say "daily?" Here's where I need "onomatopoeia." For it would be "daily" if you had written one letter for each day; but, since there are in fact more letters than days, the word "daily" isn't very accurate. Don't be annoyed, lord, that I feared weighing you down with my overly frequent letters; for the more you love me, the more vigilent I should be in not increasing your workload, and the more restrained I should be when it comes to your busy life.

What do I find sweeter than your kiss? For me, that sweet scent, that enjoyment rests in your neck and in your mouth. Yet the last time you were leaving, when your father had already settled into the carriage and the crowds of people waving goodbye and blowing kisses delayed you, it was out of consideration for you that I was the only one who didn't embrace or kiss you. The same goes for everything else: I'll never prioritize my interests over yours. If I could, I'd buy you peace of mind and the lightest load for the price of concerted effort and care on my part.

So, considering how much time and work you put into writing replies, I decided to write you letters more sparingly, even though you were writing me everyday. When I received your letters I experienced something like what a lover experiences seeing his beloved running toward him along a rough and bumpy road: he exults to see his sweetheart approaching, but at the same time fears the potential of him tripping and falling. That's why I dislike that story favored by actors, where a beloved girl, standing in a tower at night holding a lit candle, awaits her lover swimming across the sea to her. For, although I burn with love for you, I'd rather be without you than watch you swimming late at night in the bottomless sea, being afraid of the moon setting, of the wind blowing out your candlelight, of the cold disorienting you, or of some large wave, shallows, or sea creature hurting you. This kind of talk is more appropriate for a lover. And it's far more sensible not to pursue pleasure that's brief and regrettable, especially at the risk of the other person's life.

But turning from fiction to fact: I was particularly intent on not imposing an additional annoyance and burden, beyond the obligations you already must face, by adding even more letters for you to answer – on top of all the ones you already must write daily. For I'd prefer to go without every enjoyment that stems from your love than see you inconvenienced the tiniest bit just for the sake of my happiness.

181 Fronto to Marcus Aurelius (Ad Caes. *5.18) 148–9* CE

To my lord.

I'm enduring the most severe groin pain; all the pain from my back and loins has migrated and settled there. Goodbye, my lord. Greetings to your lady.

182 Marcus Aurelius to Fronto (Ad Caes. *5.19) 148–9* CE

To my teacher, greetings.

I hear you're suffering with groin pain, my teacher, and, since I remember how much irritation this malady usually brings you, I'm very worried. But I'm comforted in the hope that, by the time news reach here, poultices and remedies have successfully alleviated the pain. We still have the summer heat, but, since our little girls are doing well, it feels like we're enjoying nothing but healthy weather and springtime temperatures. Goodbye, my best teacher.

183 Fronto to Marcus Aurelius (Ad Caes. *5.50) 148–9* CE

I'm suffering most severely again, this time with pain on the other side of the groin.

184 Marcus Aurelius to Fronto (Ad Caes. *5.36) 153–154* CE

At this time Fronto was serving as Asia's governor.

To my teacher.

While in Asia, my teacher, if a certain Themistocles comes your way who says he knows my philosophy teacher Apollonius, just know that he came to Rome this winter and was introduced to Apollonius' son at his request. Please, if you will, my teacher, befriend him and offer him as much advice as you can. You're always prepared to act justly and rightly to all Asians; but please willingly impart to Themistocles the counsel, kindness, and courtesies that exist between friends (without inconveniencing anyone) – gifts that a proconsul's loyalty and conscientiousness permit. Goodbye, my most delightful teacher.

*185 Fronto to Marcus Aurelius (*Ad Caes.*5.37) 153–4* CE

To my lord.

This Aridelus who's delivering my letter has taken care of my needs since my youth, everything from fulfilling my love of partridges to more serious duties. He's your freedman; he'll be a diligent steward for you as he's useful, sensible, sharp-minded, and hard-working. He's currently seeking candidacy as a procurator, since he's now legally of the right age and position. Show him your favor, lord, as you can. If you don't recognize his face, just remember when you come across the name Aridelus that I've recommended him to you. Goodbye, my sweetest lord. Say hello to your lady.

*186 Fronto to Marcus Aurelius (*Ad Caes.*5.52) 154–6* CE

To my lord.

I love you ten times over – I've seen your daughter! I think I was seeing you and Faustina as infants when I looked at your baby girl: she has the best features of each of you. I love you ten times more! Goodbye, sweetest lord. Say hello to your lady.

*187 Marcus Aurelius to Fronto (*Ad Caes.*5.53) 154–6* CE

Likewise, we love Gratia all the more because she so closely resembles you! So we completely understand how our little girl's similarity to both of us makes her all the more charming to you; I'm so very pleased you got to see her. Goodbye, my best teacher of all.

*188 Fronto to Marcus (*Ad Ant.*1.3) 163* CE

To my lord Antoninus Augustus.

I've seen your little chickadees, the happiest sight in my life; it's absolutely uncanny how much they look like you! I've taken a shortcut to get to Lorium, a slippery road full of steep hills. Nonetheless I've seen "you," not only right in front of me, but in many places – whether turning left or right! Thank god, they have a healthy color, a strong cry. One was holding a piece of plain white bread, like a little prince; the other, a piece of black bread, just like you'd expect from a philosopher's son! I beg the gods to keep you, the "farmer," safe and sound, along with your "seeds" and the "soil" that produces a crop so like its originator. For even their little voices were so sweet, so charming, that

I recognized in their little chirps – I don't know how – the charming, clear sound of your voice. Now, be careful or you'll find me a bit more boastful, since now I've got little ones to love instead of you, to love not only with my eyes, but with my ears too!

189 Marcus to Fronto (Ad Ant. *1.4) 163* CE

After reading Fronto's letter and his description of Marcus' own children, Marcus feels like he's seen his own children in person, despite their physical separation. The letter serves as a tangible, visual replacement for face-to-face contact.

To my teacher, greetings.

Thanks to your letter, I saw my little boys when you saw them – I saw you, too, when I read your letter. I beg you, my teacher, love me as you do; love me also in the way you love those little ones of ours. But I'm not done: love me as you have been doing. Your letter brought me such exceptional joy that it has inspired me to write this response. For when it comes your elegant letter-writing, what can I say? Nothing, except that you speak Latin while the rest of us speak neither Greek nor Latin. Please write frequently to my lord, my brother; he especially asked me to obtain this promise from you. (His request, however, makes me appear immoderate and overly demanding.) Goodbye, my most delightful teacher. Say hello to your grandson for me.

190 Marcus Antoninus to Fronto (Ad Ant. *2.4) 163* CE

To my teacher, greetings.

Although I'm enjoying the healthy clean air of the country, I feel one important thing is missing, namely knowing that you're in good health, my teacher. I pray to the gods you fill in this gap! This country jaunt of mine is encumbered with official business and is no different from the busy life you lead back in the city. What do I mean, you ask? Pressing concerns won't allow me to expand this letter even a little, and I'll only get a short break some time late tonight. Goodbye, my most delightful teacher.

Oh, if by chance you've got any especially exemplary letters of Cicero, either complete or in excerpt, please share them with me, or let me know which ones you think I should read to hone my writing skills.

191 Fronto to Marcus Antoninus (Ad Ant. *2.5) 163* CE

To my lord.

It's now the fifth day I've been suffering pain throughout my limbs, especially in my neck and groin. I recall I've made excerpts only of those letters of Cicero that debate about eloquence, or involve philosophy, or the republic; I've also made notes of any choice phrase or striking word. I've sent along the excerpts I've found useful for my own purposes. If you think it's a good idea, you may want to have the three books, two to Brutus and one to Axius, copied and then returned to me, for I haven't made any copies of these excerpts. In my opinion, however, all of Cicero's letters should be read, even more so than his speeches. Nothing is more perfect than the letters of Cicero.

192 *Fronto to Aufidius Victorinus (*Ad amicos *1.12) 164* CE

In this letter Fronto endearingly describes his interactions with his grandson.

Fronto to Aufidius Victorinus, son-in-law, greetings.

The letter, dear son, which [. . .]. If we're deserving, the gods will look favorably upon Gratia, my daughter and your wife, so that things turn out well, so that our family will increase with children and grandchildren and that those already born to you will be just like you, along with any future children. Every day brings a quarrel or tiff with that little Victorinus or bitty Fronto. You never demand a reward from anyone for doing or saying something, but your little Fronto babbles no other word more eagerly or frequently than "Give!" I do what I can, offering him a bit of paper or small tablets – things *I* want him to want! He does show affinities, however, with his grandfather: he loves grapes. This was the first food he gobbled down, and for days on end he didn't stop licking grapes with his tongue, or kissing them with his lips, or gumming them, or playing around with them. He also adores little birds, especially baby chicks, doves, and sparrows, a love that (according to my teachers) I also held from my early years of toddlerhood. As I am an old man now, everyone who's even just a little acquainted with me knows my passion for partridges. For there's no deed or word I want to keep hidden from other people. In fact, I'd want everyone else to know, along with me, anything I myself am cognizant of [. . .].

193 *Marcus Antoninus to Fronto (*Nep. am. *1) 165* CE

Marcus Aurelius writes to Fronto expressing his condolences on the death of Fronto's grandson, who died in Germany at the age of 3. Fronto never had the chance to meet him in person. Two other grandsons survived.

To my teacher, greetings.

I have just heard about your loss. Since I'm usually tormented when I hear about just one of your joints being in pain, my teacher, imagine what I endure when it's heartache you're suffering. I'm in shock, and nothing comes to mind other than asking you to take care of yourself, sweetest teacher. The comfort I find in life because of you is even greater than the comfort you find for your sorrows. I haven't written this letter myself, because after my evening bath my hand was shaking. Goodbye, my most delightful teacher.

194 Fronto to Marcus Antoninus (Nep. am. *2) 165* CE

Fronto describes his own grief; this letter can be seen as a twist on the traditional epistolary consolation, in some ways functioning as a self-consolation. Here Fronto touches upon conventional themes, but his grief and anger are palpable.

Fronto to Antoninus Augustus.

Fortune has harassed me my whole life with so many sorrowful losses like this. Besides my other bitter troubles, I've lost five children in the worst way. I lost all, one by one, at separate times, enduring a series of misfortunes: each child was born just after another had died. Thus I always lost a child without having the solace that a surviving one would have brought, since I always fathered others in the midst of fresh grief. To be sure, I bravely endured this heartache, heartache I alone have suffered. My heart faced grief as if in single combat, equal against equal; and it put up a good fight. But it's not just a single opponent I stare down at: grief is multiplied by bitter grief, and I can no longer bear the mound of piled-up sorrows. I even complain to the gods frequently and accost the Fates with admonishments.

Is it at all fair or just that Victorinus, who exhibits the greatest loyalty, gentleness, truthfulness, and innocence, who's further distinguished by his exceptional skills, has suffered the harshest affliction – the death of his son? If Providence does govern affairs, does this seem just? If all human events are determined by fate, should this one have been determined by it? Are no differences made between good men and bad? Can the gods and the Fates make no distinction when it comes to what sort of man will have his son ripped away from him? Some wicked, accursed human, who would have been better off dead, gets to raise his children safe and sound, leaving them behind as heirs at his own death. Victorinus, a virtuous man, has lost his sweetest child – and what a boon to the state if as many children as possible were born in his likeness! What about Providence – oh, what evil – that exercises "foresight" so unfairly? The Fates are called the "Fates" from the Latin verb "to fate." Is this an example of fating justly? The poets assign to the Fates a distaff and threads: no wool-spinner is so unskilled and savage that she weaves a heavy, knotty toga for her master, and then weaves one that's refined and elegant for a slave.

There's no rhyme or reason in the fact that good men are fated the lot of sorrow and bad men enjoy a family life free from distress. Unless perhaps another mistake deceives us: in our ignorance, we're desiring bad things as if they were good for us and, at the opposite end, we ignore what's good as if it were something bad. Death itself, which universally causes grief, brings respite from work, worries, and misfortunes; in freeing us from the horrible chains of the body, it carries us to that peaceful and pleasant assembly of souls where all good things are restored. I'd be more likely to believe this than the notion that all human affairs are directed either by no Providence or by an unfair one.

But if death is something that mortals should welcome rather than dread, the sooner one reconciles himself to it, the happier s/he'll be and the more the gods will smile upon him or her; the sooner s/he'll be released from the body's maladies and the sooner s/he'll go on to enjoy the benefits of a freed soul. Still, no matter how true this may be, it means little to those of us who long for our lost loved ones: the immortality of soul offers us little comfort, since, as long as we're still alive, we're missing those dearest to us. We long for the way they stand, their voice, their features, their free breath; we weep over their lifeless face, their locked lips, their rolled-back eyes, their ghostly white complexion. Even if the soul's immortality were confirmed: the philosophers can discuss it all they like, but this will never soothe a parent's longing for her deceased children.

No matter how these events are divinely determined, they never present long-lasting anxiety, at least for me; my death isn't far off. Whether we are forever dead, something I once desired [. . .]. It's my sweetest grandson, whom I'm raising by my own hand, *he*'s the one who tears at my heart, ripping it apart. For, when I look into his face, I'm seeing the other grandson I've lost – I think I'm envisioning a copy of his face and hearing the echo of his voice. This is the mental image my grief incites. Still, not knowing how he really looked, I go crazy imagining his face.

My daughter is rational. Her husband, best of men, will keep her calm. He'll console her, crying and sighing right alongside her. When she speaks, so will he; and when she's silent, he'll follow suit. I, an old man, won't do much good comforting her – I should have died first. Songs of the poets, philosophers' precepts – none of them will mitigate my daughter's grief or assuage her pain as much as her husband's voice, words that come from a mouth and a heart so closely joined to her own. I find solace in the fact that I've lived my life and death isn't far off. Whenever it comes, night or day, I'll greet the heavens as I depart this world, and I'll confess I have a clean conscience. In my long lifetime I've done nothing indecent, dishonorable, or illegal. In my whole life I've never acted out of greed or disloyalty. Instead I've performed many acts of generosity, loyalty, steadfastness, even at the risk of my own well-being. I have lived harmoniously with the best of brothers, and I'm so happy to see him acquire the highest achievements, thanks to your father's beneficence, and to have him safe and secure in friendship with you both. I've never pursued jealously, through treacherous means, the honors I've achieved. I have given myself over to nurturing my mind rather than my body. I have invested more in knowledge than in wealth. I chose poverty over outside support, preferring to be in need rather than to plead for help.

I've never been an over-spender, sometimes just getting by on my earnings. I have *spoken* the truth diligently and *listened* to it enthusiastically. I've believed it's better to be ignored than to brown-nose, to keep one's mouth closed rather than to lie, to be an inattentive friend rather than a constant flatterer. I have sought little, deserved much. I have accommodated everyone as much as I could within my resources. I have offered my ready help to those who deserved it; and to those who didn't I offered it anyway. And, even if I discovered someone less than grateful, I didn't hesitate offering my aid as much as I could. [. . .]

I have suffered ongoing serious illnesses, my dearest Marcus. Then, devastated by the most terrible misfortunes, I lost my wife, I lost my grandson in Germany. Ahhh, why me? I have lost my Decimanus. Even if I were made of iron, I couldn't write another single word right now. I've sent you this letter, which expresses it all.

Letters from Vindolanda

The following selections include letters recovered from the Roman fort of Vindolanda, located in modern-day northern England (the ancient Roman province of Britain). The fort was in use during the first century CE and through to the third. The letters were written in ink, on postcard-size wooden tablets; the collection includes both letters sent to the fort and copies or drafts of letters written by individuals and posted at Vindolanda. Many of them are in fragmentary state. Currently, approximately 1,200 tablets have been discovered at the fort, and around 752 have been transcribed; the latter include, in addition to letters, lists of supplies and foods, military reports, and other administrative documents. They give valuable insight into the function, organization, and communications of Roman garrison life in the northern reaches of the Roman Empire.

The epistolary tablets have various authors and cover a broad range of topics, including official business and the private affairs of leading army officials and their households. The largest number of letters by the same author is that of the letters written by Flavius Cerialis, a Roman prefect of equestrian rank of the 9th cohort of Batavians (stationed at Vindolanda around 100 CE); we also possess several letters of Cerialis' wife Sulpicia Lepidina, who lived at the fort too. Cerialis appears to have written regularly to Aelius Brocchus, a fellow equestrian officer presumably stationed at a nearby fort, whose wife, Claudia Severa, like Sulpicia, also seems to have accompanied her husband to his post. Judging by the extant correspondence, the two families seem to have maintained a close friendship. Cerialis' letters reveal that his household – like other well-to-do households in Italy – included not only his wife and children, but also a large number of slaves who helped manage it.

As archaeological remains, many of the letters are in a fragmentary state, exhibiting missing letters, phrases, and entire sections. The following selections comprise letters in varying degrees of completeness. In addition, many of the letters reveal different hands (as indicated), suggesting the involvement of scribes or secretaries. In many of the letters the closing hand is that of the address written on the outside.

195 *Draft of a letter from Flavius Cerialis to Crispinus* (Tab. Vindol. *II 225*)

The following three selections involve request/recommendation letters.

To his Crispinus.

Since Grattius Crispinus is going back [. . .] I'm very happy to take this opportunity to greet you, lord; you're my lord and I especially wish for your good health and the fulfillment of your every desire. For this is something you've always deserved from me, all the way up to this [. . .]. Relying on this [. . .] first of all greet Marcellus, an eminent man, my governor. He now extends the opportunity [. . .] of the gifts (?) of your friends which, with his presence, I know you have the most [. . .]. Now, in whatever way you want, carry out my hopes and set me up with enough friends so that, thanks to you, I can experience an enjoyable military post. I write to you from Vindolanda where I'm stationed for the winter.

196 *Copy of a letter from Brocchus to Flavius Cerialis, prefect* (Tab. Vindol. *II 233*)

Flavius Cerialis to his Brocchus, greetings.

If you love me, brother, I ask you to send me hunting nets. [. . .] Be sure to make these bits as strong as you can.

197 *Letter of recommendation from Karus to Flavius Cerialis (Tab. Vindol. II 250)*

FIRST HAND [. . .]ius Karus to his Cerialis, greetings.

Brigionus has asked me, lord, to recommend him to you. So I ask, lord, if he requests anything, please willingly help him out. Also, please recommend him to Annius Equester, the regional centurion stationed at Luguvalium. If you do this, I'll be indebted to you on behalf of us both. I hope you're in good health and enjoying great prosperity.

KARUS' HAND Goodbye, brother.
FIRST HAND To Cerialis, prefect.

198 *Birthday invitation from Claudia Severa to Sulpicia Lepidina (Tab. Vindol. II 291)*

FIRST HAND Claudia Severa to her Lepidina, greetings.

On the third day before the Ides of September, sister, I kindly invite you to come celebrate my birthday. Your presence will make the day more enjoyable for me. Say hello to your Cerialis. My Aelius and my little son also send their greetings.

CLAUDIA'S HAND I will await you, sister. Goodbye, sister, my dearest soul, and as I'm well, may you be well too.
FIRST HAND To Sulpicia Lepidina, wife of Cerialis, from Severa.

Figure 4.3 Tablet of Sulpicia from Vindolanda (modern-day Chesterholm, Northumberland), Roman Britain, ca. 100 CE. British Museum, London, Great Britain. © The Trustees of the British Museum / Art Resource, NY

199 Letter from Claudia Severa to Sulpicia Lepidina (Tab. Vindol. *II 292)*

FIRST HAND [. . .] greetings.

Just as I had promised, sister, I've asked Brocchus about coming to visit you; he answered that I should always feel free to visit you if I like, along with [. . .] to see you in whatever way I can. For there are certain crucial things which [. . .]. You'll receive my letter letting you know my plans. [. . .] I was and continue to be at Briga. Say hello to your Cerialis for me.

CLAUDIA'S HAND Goodbye, my sister, my dearest and most missed soul.
FIRST HAND To Sulpicia Lepidina, wife of Cerialis, from Severa, wife of Brocchus.

200 Letter from Chrauttius to Veldeius (Tab. Vindol. *II 310)*

Chrauttius to Veldeius, his brother and old tentmate, many greetings.

I ask you, brother Veldeius – I'm surprised you have written a word to me in so long – if you've heard anything from our superiors, or about [. . .] and what unit he's in. Give him and also Virilis the veterinarian my greetings, in my own words. Ask Virilis if you can send me, via one of our friends, the scissors he promised in exchange for money. And please, brother Virilis, say hello from me to sister Thuttena. Write back and tell us how Velbuteius is doing.

I hope you're as fortunate as can be. So long.

Deliver at London. To Veldedius, groom of the governor, from his brother Chrauttius.

201 Letter from Sollemnis to Paris (Tab. Vindol. *II 311)*

Sollemnis to Paris, his brother, many greetings.

I'm doing very well and I hope you are too. You're the most disloyal man: you haven't sent me even one single letter. In my opinion, I'm the one acting more kindly in writing you [. . .] to you, brother, my tentmate. Say hello to Diligens and Cogitatus and Corinthus for me, and please send me the names [. . .].

To Paris of the 3rd cohort of Batavians, from Sollemnis.

202 Anonymous letter about transporting stone (Tab. Vindol. *II 316)*

[. . .] You should decide, my lord, how many wagons you'll send for carrying the stone. For Vocontius' army unit [. . .] with wagons on one day [. . .]. If you don't ask Vocontius to get the stone in order he won't do it. Please write back what you want me to do. I hope you're in good health.

203 Letter from Masclus to Flavius Cerialis (Bowman and Thomas 1996: No. 3)

Masclus to Cerialis his patron, greetings.

I ask, lord, that you instruct us as to what you want us to have done tomorrow. Should we return all together with the standard or in turns? [. . .] [. . .] most fortunate and may you be agreeable toward me. [. . .] My fellow soldiers have no beer; please order some to be sent.

To Flavius Cerialis, prefect, from Masclus, decurion.

Papyri

The selections below represent letters written in Greek on papyrus. Many come from Oxyrhynchus, a city located in upper Egypt, where the dry climate facilitated the preservation of an enormous collection of papyri that contained official documents, military records, receipts, correspondence, and literary works – including the plays of the Greek comic poet Menander. The following selections are arranged in chronological order. Many, like the Vindolanda texts, are badly damaged. Often the letters display a conventional salutation expressing wishes for the recipient's favorable health. Months are given in the Egyptian dating system.

*204 Theon to Tyrranus (*P. Oxy.* 292) Around 25* CE

A letter of recommendation from Theon, to the financial administrator Tyrannus.

Many greetings from Theon to the most distinguished Tyrannus.

Heraclides, the courier delivering this letter, is my brother. I appeal to you as much as I can: take him as your friend and help him out. I've also written to your brother Hermias and asked him to tell you about Heraclides. You'll be doing me the biggest favor if he earns your approval. Above all, I pray that you have good health and prosperity in everything and remain free from harm. Goodbye.

ON THE REVERSE To Tyrannus the Dioecetes.

*205 Sarapion to Heraclides (*Sel. Pap.* 107) 41* CE

This letter deals with business matters, though the exact details remain somewhat obscure.

Sarapion sends greetings to our Heraclides.

I sent you two other letters, one through the courier Nedymus and the other through the swordsman Cronius. I received your letter from the Arab and it was distressing to read. Attend to Ptollarion at every moment; he might be able to relieve your debt. Tell him: "I'm different, I'm not like the rest. I'm a slave. I've sold you my goods at a discount. I don't know what my patron will do to me; we have many lenders. Please don't destroy us financially." Beg him each and every day, and maybe he'll take pity. If not, like everyone else, watch out for the Jews. The more attention you give him, the more you'll make him your friend. See if it's possible with the assistance of Diodorus to have the tablet signed through the prefect's wife. If you do your job, no one can fault you. Give my fond regards to Diodorus. Goodbye. Give my regards to Harpocration.

The first year of Tiberius Claudius Caesar Augustus Germanicus Imperator, the eleventh of the month of Mesore.

ON THE REVERSE Deliver to Alexandria in the Imperial Agora in [. . .] to Heraclides from Sarapion [. . .].

206 *Antonius to Dionyius* (P. Oxy. *2191) Second century* CE

Letter sent from Puteoli. Antonius informs Dionysius that he and his family have safely arrived in Italy.

Greetings from Antonius to his dearest Dionysius.

As soon as I stepped upon Italy's shores, I felt compelled to let you know that my family and I are in good health. The sailing was slow, but it wasn't a difficult trip, and my poor little body suffered none of the trouble one usually expects, especially with those sailing for the first time.

SECOND HAND [. . .]
THIRD HAND Written in Puteoli, Pauni 4.

ON REVERSE To Dionysius, steward, from Antonius, son of Ptolemaeus.

207 *Anonymous* (P. Oxy. *2192) Second century* CE

The first column is badly damaged and indecipherable. The second column consists of four different hands (the fourth is badly damaged and unintelligible). Hand 2 asks the recipient to send certain books and Hand 3, possibly representing a family member or friend, adds to the preceding request.

FIRST HAND Even if it were in my power, I cannot involve any of my relatives in such a matter, especially now that I know what I know about such things.

SECOND HAND I pray you're well, lord, my brother. Make me copies of Books 6 and 7 of Hypsicrates' *Comedic Characters* and send them to me. Harpocration says they're with Polion's books. But it's likely others possess them too. He also has prose abstracts of Thersagoras' work on tragic myths.

THIRD HAND Harpocration says that the bookseller Demetrius has them. I've charged Apollonides with sending me certain books from my own collection; you'll surely hear about this from Seleucus himself soon enough. If you discover any in addition to those I already have, make copies and send them to me. Diodorus and his buddies also have some that I don't possess.

208 Serenos to Isidora (P. Oxy. *528) Around second century* CE

Serenos writes to his wife Isidora expressing how much he misses her. It's not clear why she's away; some issue involving Kolobos is alluded to – the second half of the letter is rather obscure. The letter has several misspellings and grammatical mistakes, suggesting either carelessness or ignorance on the part of the writer (or scribe).

Serenos sends many greetings to his dear wife.

Above all, I pray you're well; every day and night on your behalf I bow before the goddess of pregnancies, Theoris, who holds you dear. I want you to know that since you left me I've been in mourning, weeping at night and grieving by day. Since I bathed with you on October 12, I haven't bathed or anointed myself again until now, November 12. The letters you've sent could move a stone – that's how much your words affected me. I wrote you back and gave the letter to a messenger to deliver, with your letters sealed inside. Contrary to what you've said and written in your letters, "But Kolobos made me a prostitute," he in fact said, "Your wife sent me a message saying, 'He sold off my necklace and himself loaded me into the boat.'" Are you saying this so I'll no longer be entrusted with the loading? Take note how many times I've sent for you. Let me know, are you coming or not? Take care.

ON THE REVERSE Deliver to Isidora from Serenus.

209 Apollinarius to his mom (Sel. Pap. *111) Second century* CE

Apollinarius, a soldier dispatched to Italy, writes to his mother, letting her know he has arrived safely.

Apollinarius sends many greetings to Taesis, his mother and lady.

Above all, I pray you're healthy. I'm doing well and I pray on your behalf to the gods here. I want you to know, Mom, I arrived in Rome safe and sound on the 25 of the month Pachon; I was assigned to the fleet at Misenum, but I don't know the ship's name. As I'm writing this letter I haven't yet left for Misenum. I beg you, Mom, take care of yourself and don't worry about me. For I've come to a great place. Please write and let me know how you're doing, along with my brothers and the rest of your family. I'll write you whenever I find a courier. I won't hesitate to write. Say hello to my brothers and Apollinarius and his kids, and to Karalas and his as well. I send greetings to Ptolemaeus and Ptolemaïs and her children and to

Heraclous and her kids. I greet everyone who adores you by name. I pray for your good health.

ON THE REVERSE Deliver to Taesis at Karanis, from her son Apollinarius at Misenum.

210 *Aprion to Epimachus* (Sel. Pap. *112) Second century* CE

Another soldier, this one named Apion, writes to his father Epimachus shortly after arriving at Misenum, where he's been stationed with the Roman fleet company Athenonica. Serapis is a Greco-Egyptian god. Because Apion wasn't a Roman citizen, he was assigned a Roman name for his military identity, to which he refers at the end of the letter.

Apion sends many greetings to Epimachus, his father and lord.

Above all, I pray you're healthy, doing well, and are prosperous – along with my sister and her daughter and my brother. Give thanks to Serapis for saving me during my dangerous sea voyage. When I arrived at Misenum, I received three gold coins from Caesar to cover traveling costs. So things are going well. I ask you, my lord and father, write me a letter, first, to tell me how you're doing, second, how my brother and sister are doing, and third, so I may respectfully welcome your handwriting since you educated me well and, thanks to this, I'm hoping I'll advance swiftly in my career, gods willing. I have sent you, via Euctemon, a portrait of myself. My Roman name is Antonius Maximus and my fleet is called the Athenonica. I pray for your good health. Send along my greetings to Capiton, my siblings, Serenilla, and my friends.

ON LEFT MARGIN P.S. Serenus, son of Agathaodaemon, says hello, and [. . .] and Tourbo, son of Gallonius, and [. . .]

To Epimachus at Philadelphia, from Apion his son.

ON REVERSE Deliver this letter from Apion to the First Cohort of the Apameni, to Julianus, assistant secretary, to be sent along to Epimachus his father.

211 *Taus to Apollonius* (Sel. Pap. *115) Second century* CE

Taus writes to her husband (?) Apollonius, who is serving as the district governor (*strategos*) of the Lesser Apollonopolite district (located in Upper Egypt). Her reference to Apollonius as "master" may refer to his position as master of the household, a common epithet. The wording of Taus indicates that some dispute may have been keeping her away from Apollonius.

Taus sends many greetings to Apollonius, her lord.

Above all I greet you, master, and I pray as always for your good health. I was very upset, my lord, when I heard you had been sick but, thank the gods, they protected you and kept you safe. I ask you, lord, if you like, please send for me to come; if not, I'll die since I can't lay my eyes upon you everyday. If only I were able to fly and come to you, falling at your knees. For, I'm distressed at not seeing you in person. So, be reconciled with me and send for me. Goodbye, my lord [. . .].

The 24 of Epeiph.

To Apollonius the *strategos*.

*212 Antonius to Nilous (*Sel. Pap. *120) Second century* CE

Antonius Longus writes to his mother Nilous, pleading for forgiveness. It's unclear what he's done to incur her wrath, but perhaps the conflict was financial in nature.

Antonius Longus sends many greetings to his mother Nilous. As always, I pray for your good health, and everyday I pray on your behalf to the god Serapis. I want you to know that I didn't expect you were going up to the metropolis at Arsinoe, and that's why I didn't come to the city. I was ashamed to come to your town Karanis, since I walk around like I'm rotten and decayed. I wrote to you that I'm naked. I beg you, mother, reconcile with me. Yes, I know what I've done to myself; I've learned a good lesson. I know I've made a mistake. I heard from [. . . .] who found you in the Arsinoite district, and everything he told you is correct. Don't you know that I'd prefer being mutilated than knowing I still owe an obol to a man [. . .] [eight subsequent lines are fragmentary]

ON REVERSE To Nilous his mother from Antonius Longus, her son.

*213 Sempronius to Saturnila (*Sel. Pap. *121) Second century* CE

Sempronius writes to his mother Saturnila and to Maximus, his brother. These were two letters written on the same sheet of papyrus. Possibly Saturnila couldn't read, so Maximus read the letter to her. If this is the case, it lends an additional dynamic to the pair of letters, especially considering the way in which Sempronius admonishes his brother.

Many greetings to Saturnila, his mother and lady, from Sempronius.

Above all, I pray for your good health and that of my brothers, free from all evil and harm. Everyday I pray to Serapis on your behalf. I've sent you so many letters, but I haven't received a single one from you in reply, even though there have been plenty of people sailing down this way. I'm asking you, my lady, please write back quickly about your well-being so I may stop worrying so much. For I pray for your good health daily. Say hello to Maximus and his wife, and Saturnilus and Gemellus, and Helena and her family. Let her know that I received a letter from Sempronius from Cappadocia. Give my personal greetings to Julius and his family, and also to Scythicus and Thermouthis and her kids. Gemellus says hi. Be well, my lady, as always.

Greetings to Maximus from his brother Sempronius.

Above all else, I pray that you're well. I've heard you've been reluctant to attend to our mother and lady. I implore you, sweetest brother, don't make her unhappy in any way. If our brothers give her any lip, go ahead and smack them. For you should be acting like their father. I know you're capable of pleasing her without my having to write you, but don't begrudge my letter chastising you. For we should revere our mother as if she were a goddess, especially a mom who's as good as ours. I've written to you, brother, knowing it's the sweetest gift to have such precious parents. Please send me a letter about how you're doing. Goodbye, brother.

ON THE REVERSE Deliver to Maximus from his brother Spempronius.

214 A mother to her son (Sel. Pap. *130) Second/third century* CE

A mother writes a note to her son about his schooling. The *paedagogus* was a slave who accompanied young boys to school.

[. . .] don't hesitate to write me if you need anything from here. I was saddened to hear from the daughter of our teacher Diogenes that he had sailed down the river; for I was content knowing he was going to keep an eye on you as much as possible. I felt it was important to send you a letter inquiring about your health and to hear about what you were reading. He said it was *Iliad Six*, and he testified to the conscientiousness of your *paedagogus*. So therefore, child, make sure you and your *paedagogus* make certain you're entrusted to a suitable teacher. Your sisters and Theonis' children (may evil stay away from them) send many greetings, as do all our friends. Give my hello to your distinguished *paedagogus* Eros.

ON THE REVERSE [. . .] to her son Ptolemaeus.

REFERENCES

Emperor Tiberius (14–37 CE)

Cancik, H., and Schneider, H. (2004) "Gytheumium." In *Brill's New Pauly*, vol. 5, p. 1070.

Lendon, J. E. (2001) *Empire of Honour: The Art of Government in the Roman World*. New York: Oxford University Press, pp. 160–75.

John the Elder

Muir, J. (2009) "Greek letters in the early Christian Church." In *Life and Letters in the Ancient Greek World*. New York: Routledge, pp. 148–76.

Rensberger, D. (2001) *The Epistles of John*. Louisville, KY: Westminster John Knox Press, pp. 117–27.

Fronto

Richlin, A. (2006) *Marcus Aurelius in Love.* Chicago, IL: University of Chicago Press.

Letters from Vindolanda

Bowman, A. K., and Thomas, J. D. (1996) "New writing tablets from Vindolanda." *Britannia, 27*, 299–328.

FURTHER READING

Emperor Tiberius (14–37 CE)

Gradel, I. (2002) *Emperor Worship and Roman Religion.* Oxford: Oxford University Press, pp. 1–26.
Levick, B. (2000) *The Government of the Roman Empire: A Sourcebook*, 2nd edn. New York: Routledge, pp. 133–4.

Emperor Claudius (41–54 CE)

Charlesworth, M. P. (1939) "The refusal of divine honours: An Augustan formula." *Papers of the British School at Rome, 15*, 1–10.
Hunt, A. S., and Edgar, C. C. (1934) *Non-Literary Papyri; Public Documents*, vol. 2. Cambridge, MA: Harvard University Press.
Levick, B. (1990) *Claudius.* New Haven, CT: Yale University Press.
Osgood, J. (2010) *Claudius Caesar: Image and Power in the Early Roman Empire.* Cambridge: Cambridge University Press.

Seneca the Younger

Bartsch, B., and Wray, D., eds. (2009) *Seneca and the Self*. Cambridge: Cambridge University Press.
Coleman, R. (1974) "The artful moralist: A study of Seneca's epistolary style." *Classical Quarterly, 24*(2), 276–89.
Edwards, C. (1997) "Self-scrutiny and self-transformation in Seneca's letters." *Greece & Rome, 44*(1), 23–38.
Inwood, B. (2007) "The importance of form in Seneca's philosophical letters." In R. Morello and A. D. Morrison, *Ancient Letters: Classical and Late Antique Epistolography.* Oxford: Oxford University Press, pp. 133–48.
Inwood, B. (2008) *Reading Seneca: Stoic Philosophy at Rome.* Oxford: Oxford University Press.
Lee, M. (1925) "The ethical teaching of Seneca in his *Epistulae ad Lucilium.*" *The Classical Weekly, 19*(5), 35–8.
Veyne, P. (2002) *Seneca: The Life of a Stoic.* New York: Routledge.
Wilcox, A. (2012) *The Gift of Correspondence in Classical Rome.* Madison: University of Wisconsin Press.

Paul the Apostle

Church, F. F. (1978) "Rhetorical structure and design in Paul's letter to Philemon." *The Harvard Theological Review, 71*(1–2), 17–33.

Freed, E. (2005) *The Apostle Paul and His Letters*. London: Equinox.
Frilingos, C. (2000) "For my child, Onesimus: Paul and domestic power in Philemon." *Journal of Biblical Literature*, *119*, 91–104.
Horsley, R., ed. (1997) *Paul and Empire: Religion and Power in Roman Imperial Society*. Harrisburg, PE: Trinity Press International.
Meeks, W. (1983) *The First Urban Christians: The Social World of the Apostle Paul*. New Haven, CT: Yale University Press.
Segal, A. (1990) *Paul, the Convert*. New Haven, CT: Yale University Press.
White, J. (1984) "New Testament epistolary literature in the framework of ancient epistolography." In H. Temporini and W. Haase, eds., *Aufstieg und Niedergang der römischen Welt*, 2.25.2, pp. 1730–56.

Jude

Charles, J. D. (2005) *Literary Strategy in the Epistle of Jude*. Scranton, PA: University of Scranton Press.
Green, M. (1968) *The Second Epistle General of Peter, and the General Epistle of Jude: An Introduction and Commentary*. Grand Rapids, MI: Eerdmans.
Lyle, K. (1998) *Ethical Admonition in the Epistle of Jude* (Studies in Biblical Literature 4). New York: Peter Lang.

Martial

Fitzgerald, W. (2007) *Martial: The World of the Epigram*. Cambridge: Cambridge University Press.
Rimell, V. (2009) *Martial's Rome: Empire and the Ideology of Epigram*. Cambridge: Cambridge University Press.
Sullivan, J. P. (2005) *Martial: An Unexpected Classic*. Cambridge: Cambridge University Press.

Statius

Boyle, A., and Dominik, W., eds. (2003) *Flavian Rome: Culture, Image, Text*. Leiden: Brill.
Janson, T. (1964) *Latin Prose Prefaces: Studies in Literary Conventions*. Stokholm: Almquit & Wiksell.
Newlands, C. (2002) *Statius' Silvae and the Poetics of Empire*. Cambridge: Cambridge University Press.
Pavlovskis, Z. (1967) "From Statius to Ennodius: A brief history of prose prefaces." *Rendiconti dell'Istituto Lombardo, Classe di Lettere, Scienze morale*, *101*, 535–67.
Zeiner, N. K. (2005) *Nothing Ordinary Here: Statius as Creator of Distinction in the* Silvae. New York: Routledge.

Pliny the Younger

Carlon, J. (2009) *Pliny's Women*. Cambridge: Cambridge University Press.
De Blois, L. (2001) "The political significance of friendship in the *Letters* of Pliny the Younger." In M. Peachin, ed., *Aspects of Friendship in the Graeco-Roman World* (Journal

of Roman Archaeology Supplement 43). Portsmouth, RI: Journal of Roman Archaeology, pp. 129–34.
Gibson, R., and Morello, R. (2012) *Reading the Letters of the Younger Pliny*. Cambridge: Cambridge University Press.
Hoffer, S. (1999) *The Anxieties of Pliny the Younger*. Atlanta, GA: Scholars Press.
Leach, E. (2003) "*Otium* as *luxuria*: Economy of status in the Younger Pliny's Letters." *Arethusa*, *36*, 147–65.
Morello, R. (2003) "Pliny and the art of saying nothing." *Arethusa*, *36*, 187–209.
Riggsby, A. (1995) "Pliny on Cicero and oratory self-fashioning in the public eye." *American Journal of Philology*, *116*, 123–35.

John the Elder

Aune, D. (1987) *The New Testament in its Literary Environment*. Philadelphia, PA: Westminster Press.
Meeks, W., ed. (1989) *The Harper Collins Study Bible*. New York: Harper Collins.

Fronto

Champlin, E. (1980) *Fronto and Antonine Rome*. Cambridge, MA: Harvard University Press.
Freisenbruch, A. (2007) "Back to Fronto: Doctor and patient in his correspondence with an emperor." In R. Morello and A. D. Morrison, eds., *Ancient Letters: Classical and Late Antique Epistolography*. Oxford: Oxford University Press, pp. 235–56.
Grant, M. (1994) *The Antonines: The Roman Empire in Transition*. London: Routledge.
Haines, C. R. (1928) *Fronto: Correspondence*. Cambridge, MA: Harvard University Press, pp. ix–xlii.
Van den Hout, M. (1999) *A Commentary on the Letters of M. Cornelius Fronto*. Leiden: Brill.
Whitehorne, J. E. G. (1977) "Was Marcus Aurelius a hypochondriac?" *Latomus*, *36*, 413–21.

Letters from Vindolanda

Birley, A. R. (1979) *The People of Roman Britain*. London: B. T. Batsford.
Bowman, A. K. (1994) *Life and Letters on the Roman Frontier*. New York: Routledge.
Bowman, A. K., and Thomas, J. D. (2003) *The Vindolanda Writing Tablets*, vol. 3. London: British Museum Press.
Bowman, A. K., and Woolf, G. (1994) *Literacy and Power in the Ancient World*. Cambridge: Cambridge University Press.
Salway, P. (2001) *A History of Roman Britain*. Oxford: Oxford Paperbacks.
Terras, M. (2006) *Image to Interpretation: An Intelligent System to Aid Historians in Reading the Vindolanda Texts*. Oxford: Oxford University Press.

Papyri

Bagnall, R., and Cribiore, R. (with contributions by E. Ahtaridis) (2006) *Women's Letters from Ancient Egypt, 300* BC–AD *800*. Ann Arbor: University of Michigan Press.

Bowman A. K., Coles, R. A., Gonis, N., and Obbink, D., eds. (2007) *Oxyrhynchus: A City and Its Texts* (Egypt Exploration Series). London: Egypt Exploration Society.
Grenfell, B. P., and Hunt, A. S. (1898) *Oxyrhynchus Papyri*. London: Egypt Exploration Fund.
Johnson, W. (2004) *Bookrolls and Scribes in Oxyrhynchus*. Toronto: University of Toronto Press.
Maclennan, H. (1935) *Oxyrhynchus: An Economic and Social Study*. Princeton, NJ: Princeton University Press.
Parsons, P. (1975) "Oxyrhynchus and Rome." *Harvard Studies in Classical Philology*, *79*, 1–24.
Parsons, P. (2007) *City of the Sharp-Nosed Fish: Greek Lives in Roman Egypt*. London: Weidenfeld & Nicolson.

CHAPTER FIVE

Epistolary Theorists

Many ancient authors wrote about letter-writing; several of these were rhetoricians who discussed the epistolary genre in rather theoretical terms; these theorists dealt with letters as part of larger discussions on writing and style, or as part of didactic handbooks for students and professional letter-writing scribes.

215 (Pseudo-)Demetrius (On Style, *223–35)*

The following selection is attributed to the Peripatetic philosopher Demetrius of Phalerum, although some scholars believe this attribution to be spurious. Given questions surrounding the author's identification, the date of composition is also debated, ranging anywhere from the third century BCE to the first century CE. This excerpt, originally composed in Greek, comes from a larger work *On Style.* In this section (Pseudo-)Demetrius discusses the epistolary genre as a type of writing requiring a plain, straightforward style.

Since letter-writing also requires a plain style, we'll consider it, too. Artemon, who in fact edited Aristotle's letters, says one should write letters in the manner of a dialogue, since the epistle is like one half of a conversation. What he says is somewhat correct, but not completely. For a letter deserves a little more care and attention than a conversation: the latter mirrors someone speaking extemporaneously, whereas the former is written down and sent, almost as if it were a gift.

Who would converse with a friend as Aristotle does when, in writing to Antipater about the old exiled man, he says: "If he should be condemned to wander throughout each and every land with no hope of ever returning home, surely we cannot blame people like him when they want to return to their eternal

Roman Letters, First Edition. Noelle K. Zeiner-Carmichael.

home: Hades." A man conversing sounds more like an orator than someone just chatting with a friend. Frequent sentence breaks are also unsuitable for letters, for a break can cause confusion; imitating conversation belongs not so much to writing as it does to a forensic speech, as in the opening lines of Plato's dialogue the *Euthydemus*: "Who were you conversing with yesterday in the Lyceum, Socrates? There was quite a large crowd surrounding you." And then, further on in the dialogue, he adds, "No, he seemed to be some stranger, the guy you were talking to. Who was it?" All types of conversational imitation like this are more appropriate for an actor, not for a letter-writer.

Like a dialogue, a letter should exhibit plenty of character. For each of us writes a letter that's almost like an image of our own soul. It's possible to see the writer's character in every form of composition, but none so much as in a letter.

A letter's length, just like its style, requires moderation. Letters too long and written in a rather inflated style would better be labeled not "letters," but "treatises," with "Dear So-and-So" tacked onto them. We see this in Plato's and in Thucydides' writings. When it comes to structure, a letter should have some freedom. For it's ridiculous to employ long, periodic sentences as if you were writing a formal forensic speech. And not only is it ridiculous; it's not conducive to friendship either – which, as the saying goes, demands you to "call a spade a spade" and not to speak in a roundabout manner.

We should keep in mind not only the style, but also the particular topics suitable for letters. Aristotle, who's considered the master of perfect letter-writing, says: "I'm not writing about this since it's not suitable for a letter." For, if anyone includes topics dealing with logic or natural history in his letter, then undoubtedly he writes – but it's not a *letter* he's writing.

The letter's beauty involves friendly advice and a few proverbs; these alone should be a letter's only piece of philosophy, since a proverb is relevant to people and thus universally true; but if someone offers pithy statements or exhortations, he no longer appears as if he's talking conversationally, but artificially. Aristotle, however, sometimes employed proofs suitable for letters; for example, when he was trying to show that one should offer equal benefactions to both large and small cities, he wrote: "The gods are the same in each – since the Graces are gods, you'll store up equal gratitude no matter what size either city is." So the point he's making is suitable for a letter, and hence so is the proof, too.

Since we sometimes write for cities and kings, letters like these should be a touch more elaborate. For one should adjust the letter to its recipient accordingly; however, the style shouldn't be so elaborate that the epistle becomes a treatise, as we find with Aristotle's letters to Alexander, or Plato's to Dion's friends.

In short, when it comes to style, the letter should comprise two characteristics: it should be elegant and unembellished.

216 *Pseudo-Libanius (*Epistolary Styles, *1–4; 46–51)*

The following selection comes from a larger work *Epistolary Styles*, written by an unknown author and incorrectly attributed to Libanius. The work serves as a handbook for letter-writing; in addition to defining the letter, "Libanius" outlines various letter types by making instructions on their proper style, and he concludes with representative sample letters. The work, written in Greek, was likely composed between the fourth and sixth centuries CE.

The epistolary style is varied and comprises many types. So, when it comes to anyone wanting to write a letter, they should do so not haplessly or casually, but with great art and precision. The best letter comes from knowing what a letter is – that is, generally speaking, from knowing what the proper conventions are and all the different epistolary categories.

A letter is a sort of written conversation between two people absent from each other; it thus fulfills a particular need. Further, the letter-writer composes as if speaking to the recipient in person. The letter is classified according to numerous types; just because a letter has only one name, and just because something is called a letter, it doesn't follow that there's only one type or one category; in fact there are many different types, as I mentioned before.

The following is a categorical list enumerating the different types of letter. There are letters of: (1) advice; (2) blame; (3) request; (4) recommendation; (5) irony; (6) thanks; (7) friendship; (8) entreaty; (9) threat; (10) denial; (11) command; (12) apology; (13) reproach; (14) sympathy; (15) conciliation; (16) congratulations; (17) contempt; (18) counter-argument; (19) reply; (20) provocation; (21) consolation; (22) insult; (23) news; (24) indignation; (25) representation; (26) praise; (27) instruction; (28) refutation; (29) slander; (30) reproof; (31) enquiry; (32) encouragement; (33) consultation; (34) declaration; (35) mockery; (36) jesting; (37) secret code; (38) suggestion; (39) grief; (40) mixed types. So there you have the various epistolary divisions.

If someone wants to write a letter carefully, s/he should not only employ the appropriate methodology, but should adorn the letter with elegant speech and Attic style – though only a moderate amount or s/he risks over-embellishment. Grandiloquence beyond what's necessary, verbosity, and over-Atticism turns a letter into something other than a letter, as all the ancient writers attest, especially Philostratus of Lemnos. He says: "A letter should be in a style that's more Attic than casual everyday speech and more casual than Attic; it should be neither too elevated nor too plain, but somewhere in between."

In adorning a letter, the writer should focus on clarity, maintain moderate brevity, and include some archaic words. Clarity is the best guide in every literary genre, but especially when it comes to the epistolary one. Nonetheless, one should neither sacrifice clarity for the sake of brevity nor go on and on, trying to be clear, but one should aim for the middle road, imitating the most accurate and gifted archer: that's neither the one who overreaches the target set up nearby nor the one who aims at the area in front of the target and thus falls short, but the one who aims for the middle and hits his target. In the same way, the eloquent person isn't someone who chatters on and on, beyond what's necessary, or someone who tries to be too concise because of his ignorance of speaking properly, and thus obscures the letter's point; the eloquent person is the one who aims at the length that is perfect for expressing eloquently exactly what he needs to say.

A letter's length should be guided by its content; a long letter is not completely a mistake, since sometimes it's appropriate to elaborate for a particular purpose. Charming stories, allusions to myths and ancient literary works, the use of fitting proverbs along with philosophical doctrines, are all ways to fill out a letter – but the last should only be employed casually, not in formal arguments.

Now that I've said all this about a letter's form and what's sufficient for intelligent readers, I'll also attach some examples of letters, arranging them by title according to type. Before embarking upon writing a letter, one should avoid flattery and tackiness: one shouldn't babble on and on or address the recipient with formal titles; rather one should begin like this: "So-and-So sends greetings to So-and-So." All our ancient authors who are celebrated for their wisdom and eloquence clearly wrote in this manner, and whoever wants to emulate them should follow in their footsteps.

FURTHER READING

Grube, G. M. A. (1961) *A Greek Critic: Demetrius on Style*. Toronto: University of Toronto Press.

Malherbe, A. (1988) *Ancient Epistolary Theorists*. Atlanta, GA: Scholars Press, pp. 1–11.

Poster, C. (2007) "A conversation halved: Epistolary theory in Greco-Roman Antiquity." In C. Poster and L. Mitchell, eds., *Letter-Writing Manuals and Instruction from Antiquity to the Present*. Columbia: University of South Carolina Press, pp. 21–51.

Schenkeveld, D. M. (1964) *Studies in Demetrius* On Style. Amsterdam: A. M. Hakkert.

Schenkeveld, D. M. (2000) "The intended public of Demetrius *On Style*: The place of the treatise in the Hellenistic educational system." *Rhetorica, 18*(1), 29–48.

Sullivan, R., (2007) "Classical epistolary theory and the letters of Isocrates." In C. Poster and L. Mitchell, eds., *Letter-Writing Manuals and Instruction from Antiquity to the Present*. Columbia: University of South Carolina Press, pp. 7–20.

General Index

Roman Letters, First Edition. Noelle K. Zeiner-Carmichael.

Concordance of Texts

Author/Work	Selection No.
Catullus	
13	51
35	52
68	53
Cicero	
Ad Brut.	
1.3	49
Att.	
1.1	2
1.2	3
1.5	1
1.13	7
1.14	8
2.14	9
3.3	10
3.13	13
4.1	14
7.6	27
8.3	29
9.6A	31
9.7C	30
9.11A	32
9.18	33

Roman Letters, First Edition. Noelle K. Zeiner-Carmichael.

Author/Work	Selection No.
Cicero	
Att. (continued)	
12.15	41
13.15	44
13.44	45
16.9	48
Fam.	
2.11	22
4.5	42
4.6	43
5.1	4
5.2	5
5.7	6
5.12	15
7.1	16
7.5	17
7.7	18
7.8	19
7.23	38
7.26	39
8.14	25
9.1	34
9.21	36
9.26	37
12.3	46
12.4	47
14.4	11
14.2	12
14.14	28
14.20	35
15.5	23
15.6	24
15.17	40
16.4	26
16.16	21
Quint.	
2.6	20
(Pseudo-)Demetrius	
On Style, 223–35	215

Author/Work	Selection No.
Fronto	
Ad amicos	
1.12	192
Ad Ant.	
1.3	188
1.4	189
2.4	190
2.5	191
Ad Caes.	
1.2	174
3.2	169
3.3	170
3.4	171
3.5	172
3.6	173
3.11	167
3.12	168
3.13	180
4.6	175
4.7	176
4.9	177
5.18	181
5.19	182
5.22	178
5.23	179
5.36	184
5.37	185
5.50	183
5.52	186
5.53	187
Nep. am.	
1	193
2	194
Horace	
Epist.	
1.3	59
1.5	60
1.6	61
1.8	62
1.9	63
1.10	64

Author/Work	Selection No.
Horace	
Epist. (continued)	
1.11	65
1.13	66
1.16	67
1.18	68
1.20	69
John	
2	165
3	166
Jude	97
Martial	
Epig.	
1.70	98
2.1	99
8, preface, 1	100
9, preface	101
Ovid	
Her. 1	72
Pont.	
1.9	79
1.10	80
3.3	81
3.8	82
4.13	83
Tr.	
1.1	73
1.6	74
1.11	75
4.7	76
5.7	77
5.8	78
P. Oxy.	
292	204
528	208
2191	206
2192	207
Paul	
Philem.	96

Author/Work	Selection No.
Pliny	
Ep.	
1.1	106
1.2	107
1.6	108
1.9	109
1.11	110
1.12	111
1.13	112
1.14	113
1.15	114
1.16	115
1.20	116
2.2	117
2.6	118
3.6	119
3.10	120
3.14	121
3.21	122
4.1	123
4.2	124
4.7	125
4.14	126
4.19	127
4.22	128
5.6	129
5.8	130
5.16	131
6.1	132
6.6	133
6.7	134
6.20	135
6.32	136
6.34	137
7.9	138
7.33	139
8.10	140
8.11	141
8.16	142
9.2	143
9.3	144

Author/Work	Selection No.
Seneca	
Ep.	
1.2	86
1.4	87
1.7	88
1.8	89
1.12	90
2.18	91
2.21	92
3.27	93
4.40	94
5.47	95
Statius	
Silv.	
1, preface	102
3, preface	103
4.4	104
5, preface	105
Suetonius	
Aug. 71.2	54, 55
Claud.	
4.1–3	56
4.4–5	57
4.6	58
Tab. Vindol.	
II 225	195
II 233	196
II 250	197
II 291	198
II 292	199
II 310	200
II 311	201
II 316	202
1996: No. 3	203